IMAGES
of America

GILLESPIE COUNTY

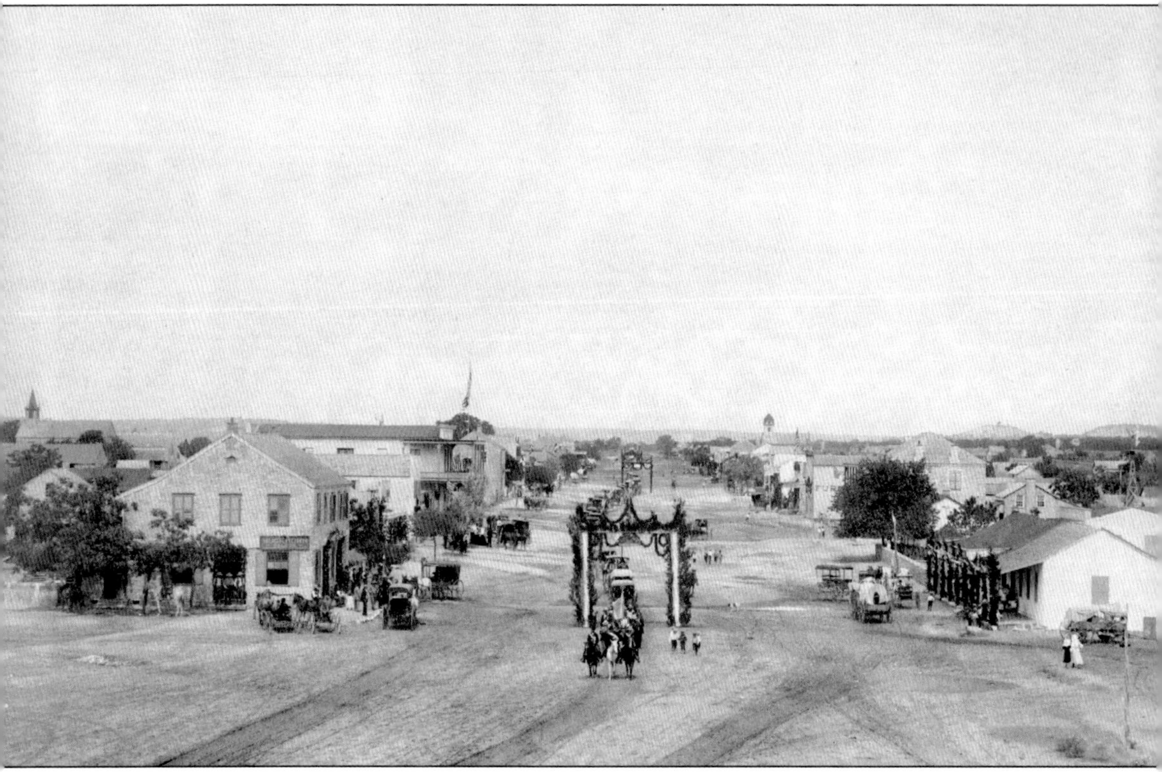

This is a view looking from the top of the Vereins Kirche, west on Hauptstrasse (Main Street), and a panorama of the 1890s parade celebrating the 50th anniversary of the Saengerfest. (Courtesy of GCHS.)

ON THE COVER: The 50th-anniversary parade celebrating the founding of Fredericksburg was the last public event to take place while the original Vereins Kirche stood in the middle of Hauptstrasse (Main Street). (Courtesy of Lee and Betty Ethel.)

IMAGES
of America

GILLESPIE COUNTY

Gillespie County Historical Society

ARCADIA
PUBLISHING

ISBN 978-0-7385-9649-5

Published by Arcadia Publishing
Charleston, South Carolina

Printed in the United States of America

Library of Congress Control Number: 2012949909

For all general information, please contact Arcadia Publishing:
Telephone 843-853-2070
Fax 843-853-0044
E-mail sales@arcadiapublishing.com
For customer service and orders:
Toll-Free 1-888-313-2665

Visit us on the Internet at www.arcadiapublishing.com

Contents

ACKNOWLEDGMENTS

The Gillespie County Historical Society (GCHS) is appreciative to the individuals, families, organizations, and businesses that donated photographs depicting Gillespie County and Fredericksburg's history. We are grateful to the following for sharing photographs selected for this publication: Albert Community Club, Arion Men's Choir, Paula Babb, Hattie Bierschwale, Clara Ahrens, Tyrus Cox, Crabapple Community Club, Helen Crouch, Doris Eckert, the John D. Eckert family, Betty and Lee Ethel, Ehrhard Fischer, Fredericksburg High School *Mesa*, The Friends of Gillespie County Country Schools, German Texas Heritage Society (GTHS), Gillespie County Court House, Bertha and Arthur Grobe, Elbert Hahne, Dorthy Hannemann, Emil Jentsch, Erwin and Helen Kammlah, Richard Klein, John H. Kothmann, Raymond Kuenemann, Gertrude and Harvey Land, Victor Meier, Nora Moellendorf, Gilbert and Alta Nagel, Nimitz Homecoming, Verdie Pezarro, Dr. Paul Phillips Jr., Elmond J. Roeder, Saengerfest, Rudolph Schnappauf, Otto Schneider, the Schumann family, Roy Stroeher, Billy Teague, Opal Treibs, Judy Vordenbaum, Herbert Wahl, Lorine Novian Wallendorf, Douglas and Joreen Wehmeyer, Wehmeyer/Johnson Collection (Louise C. Johnson), Marcella Weiershausen and Sam Whitten. Special thanks go to the Dietel family, expressly Fred, Norman, and Erna for their contribution of the large *The Radio Post* collection.

Recognition also goes to the volunteers of the Photograph Identification Project at GCHS: Joan Bonn, Walter Fuhrmann, Debbie Klinksiek, Myra Klinksiek, Jimmie Lee Rolston, Elaine Thomas, Helen Usener, and Laura Wilson. Special thanks go to the many individuals who assisted the committee in the identification of the photographs.

For more than a year prior to publication, the committee worked to identify photographs that would best depict the story of Gillespie County and Fredericksburg and to write captions for each photograph. The following are recognized for their tireless efforts in the compilation: Jeanette Beckmann, Curtis Cameron, Kenneth Crenwelge, Myra Klinksiek, Linda Langerhans, Billy Teague, and Evelyn Weinheimer. The committee is grateful to Laura Bruns, our Arcadia acquisitions editor, for guidance.

Finally, this book would not have been possible without the support of the GCHS Board of Directors and the employees of the Pioneer Museum.

INTRODUCTION

The story of Fredericksburg and Gillespie County began to unfold much earlier than its founding on May 8, 1846. In 1836, the Republic of Texas, having won its independence from Mexico, owned millions of acres of undeveloped land available for settlement. At the same time, the German and Prussian principalities were experiencing political, economic, and social unrest offering limited prospects. In Texas, land grants had become available, and many people from throughout the German provinces—such as Hannover, Saxony, Prussia, Niederland, Schleswig, Holstein, Mecklenburg, Nassau, Rhineland, Anhalt, Hamburg, and Hessen—were enticed to "come to Texas." United by a common language, composed of several regional dialects, emigrants chose to seek a new life in a land that permitted greater freedom of thought and expression, economic opportunity, and religious freedom. With faith and a belief in creating a better life for themselves and posterity, the early pioneers of Fredericksburg and Gillespie County took the bold step to realize their dreams.

In the early 1840s, a small group, all titled German aristocrats, organized the Society for the Protection of German Immigrants in Texas, or Adelsverein. Without a good understanding of the territory that was to be settled, the early pioneers faced many problems that resulted from the Adelsverein's lack of planning. Land grants were not surveyed in advance, nor had a viable plan to meet the cost of such an undertaking been developed. Only two colonization contracts had bearing on this stage of German colonization in Texas: the Burgeois-Ducois and the Fisher-Miller contracts. The first was nullified before any colonization took place; the second was based on a poorly executed survey. The Fisher-Miller Grant had been ill-advisedly purchased; it was hardly accessible and was home to Comanche Indians.

People of all occupations and educational backgrounds willingly signed on to forge a new life in Texas. Leaving behind family, home, and most possessions, they bade farewell and endured a long, difficult ocean passage lasting two months or more. The first group of immigrants, recruited by Henry Fisher, arrived in Galveston in July 1844. Adelsverein colonists, under the administration of Prince Solms of Solms-Braunfels, Germany, began arriving in March 1845, landing in Galveston and then transferring by coastal craft to Port Lavaca. Thousands more landed at Galveston, Carlshaven, and Indianola in the latter part of 1845. The continued war between Texas and Mexico, and its need for horses and wagons, left these immigrants without transport inland. Weeks and months on the Texas coast without sufficient food, water, and shelter, followed by the difficult journey of another three months by oxcart or walking to reach New Braunfels left many immigrants behind in shallow graves.

Following Prince Solm's departure, a new commissioner, Gen. Freiherr Otfried von Meusebach, was appointed to represent the society's interests. Upon arrival, he adopted the name John O.

Meusebach. It was he who chose the site of Fredericksburg rather than continuing on to the 3.878 million acres in the Fisher-Miller Grant in the heart of Comanche territory. The site he chose was well timbered, near the Pedernales River, with two creeks known as Bene or Town (Stadt) Creek and Baron's Creek flowing through the area. The name Friedrichsburg (Fredericksburg) was chosen in honor of Prince Frederick of Prussia.

The immigrant group arriving in Fredericksburg on May 8, 1846, numbered 120 men, women, and children. A month later, a second group of immigrants joined them; others followed later in 1846. Upon arrival, in lieu of the 320 acres in the Fisher-Miller Grant for which they had contracted, each family received a town lot measuring 100 by 200 feet and, by 1847, each had received a 10-acre out lot. Soon, most families were able to build cabins of *fachwerk* (half-timbered) or native limestone homes.

Within a few years, some immigrants chose to move to acreage in the outlying areas of Fredericksburg, where they established the communities of Liveoak, Klein-Frankreich, Pecan Creek, Meusebach Creek, Palo Alto, Crabapple, Rheingold, Cave Creek, Grapetown, Cherry Spring, Rocky Hill, Luckenbach, Mecklenburg (Pilot Knob), Grape Creek, Squaw Creek, Cherry Mountain, Doss, Willow City, Nebo (Eckert), Tivydale, Albert, Stonewall, Harper, Morris Ranch, and Cain City. Others ventured into the Fisher-Miller Grant to lay claim to their 320 acres; some sold their acreage and returned to Gillespie County to purchase additional land there.

Religion and education were a priority to the first German settlers. Within a year (by 1847) and with limited funds, these pioneers donated their labor to build the Vereins Kirche, where Catholics, Lutherans, and Methodists worshipped and where during the week children attended school in the mornings. The Vereins Kirche was demolished in 1897; in 1935, a replica was constructed in the center of Marktplatz dedicated to Fredericksburg's founders.

In the spring of 1847, Meusebach and a small group of men went to meet the Comanche warriors and their chiefs on the San Saba River, near where Fort Colorado was later established, to make a treaty between the settlers and the Comanche Nation. This treaty remains as the only one in American history that was never broken by either party.

Also, in 1847, the region encompassing Fredericksburg became a precinct of Bexar County. That December, 150 settlers of the area petitioned the Texas Legislature to create Gillespie County; the petition was granted in 1848, naming the county after Capt. Robert A. Gillespie, who died in the Battle of Monterrey in 1846 during the Mexican War. Fredericksburg is the county seat. The 1848 state census credits Gillespie County with 966 inhabitants; the US Census of 1850 counted 1,235 Gillespie County inhabitants plus 754 residents of Fredericksburg.

Disease took many lives in the summer of 1846 and again in 1849, when a cholera epidemic took its toll; the struggle for survival continued for many years. The Mormon colony of Zodiac, led by Elder Lyman Wight, was established on the Pedernales River just east of Fredericksburg in 1847. Settlers were supplied with ground meal and lumber from the Mormon mills and learned how best to cultivate their lands, thereby receiving significant assistance from the Mormons.

In 1848, the United States government established Fort Martin Scott, about one mile east of Fredericksburg as one of a series of forts providing a barrier between Comanche territory and early Texas settlements. The sale of surplus agricultural products to the fort and increased business to merchants as well as employment opportunities brought added income to settlers. Trade increased in 1849 when adventurers heading for the California Gold Rush found Fredericksburg the last place to purchase supplies before reaching El Paso.

Gillespie County residents had no direct interest in the Civil War; however, many immigrants recalled the suffering brought through the German Prussian wars; most Germans were sympathetic to the Union. In 1862, a group of men sympathetic to the Union decided to flee the Confederacy and the *Haengerbund* (hanging mob) by hiding in Mexico. While camped on the upper Nueces River, renegade Confederate soldiers attacked and after a hard-fought battle, known as the Nueces Massacre, only a few escaped to Mexico. Others remained in Gillespie County, volunteered either for the Union army or the Confederacy and served until the end of the war. Yet, others remained quiet from the onset, and were not required to enlist except perhaps to be hired by the government to drive provisions and ammunitions wagons. These men were listed on the muster rolls of Captain Braubach and are now remembered as former Texas Rangers.

The 25th anniversary of Fredericksburg's founding in 1871 came as the tensions following the Civil War were easing. In 1896, the 50th anniversary was one of the first opportunities for the citizens of Gillespie County to engage in a countywide celebration. The 75th and 100th anniversaries came at the end of World War I and World War II, respectively. Young men and women of Gillespie County readily served in both conflicts and numerous county casualties were of German descent.

Gillespie County prospered through the tenacity and integrity of its settlers. Today, Gillespie County continues to be recognized for its cultural identity and observance of a lifestyle based in long-established traditions. Today, the population of 24,837 in Gillespie County is a combination of people whose heritage is traced to the pioneer families and families who have chosen to make their homes here. All recognize a combination of factors that have contributed to an environment widely noted for its quality of life. The county seat of Fredericksburg, with its population of 10,530, is at a junction where mercantile enterprise has long provided services to those crossing the state. As a major crossroads for more than 150 years, it continues to serve everyone with its noted hospitality.

Throughout the county, there are excellent schools, health care facilities, and a wide variety of family-owned businesses. Many of the county's residents continue to work independently in the fields of ranching and agriculture. Gillespie County continues to be a destination for hunting and horse racing and more recently birding, cycling, and motorcycling.

Gillespie County's citizens are cognizant of the value of preserving its early architecture, which sets it apart from so many urban Texas communities. Much of the cultural heritage is based in its strong sense of community and family. Music remains a major component in nearly every public celebration: parades celebrate the county fair, Fourth of July, and Christmas. The annual county fair has been held for over 120 years. Marktplatz, Fredericksburg's Market Square, is host to numerous festivals including Oktoberfest, Night in Old Fredericksburg, and the Food and Wine Festival. Travelers from far and near take delight in the diversity of local cuisine, which incorporates not only the Texas German and Mexican traditions, but a wide offering of many cuisines, reflecting current trends in cooking by prize-winning chefs. The area is nationally recognized as an up-and-coming wine region, and wineries and vineyards offer visitors numerous on-site wine-tasting opportunities. Numerous parks provide indoor and outdoor activities for residents and visitors—including Enchanted Rock State Natural Area, Lady Bird Johnson Park and Golf Course, Lyndon B. Johnson National Historical Park and the Lyndon B. Johnson State Park & Historic Site, National Museum of the Pacific War, and Pioneer Museum.

One

Hub of the County

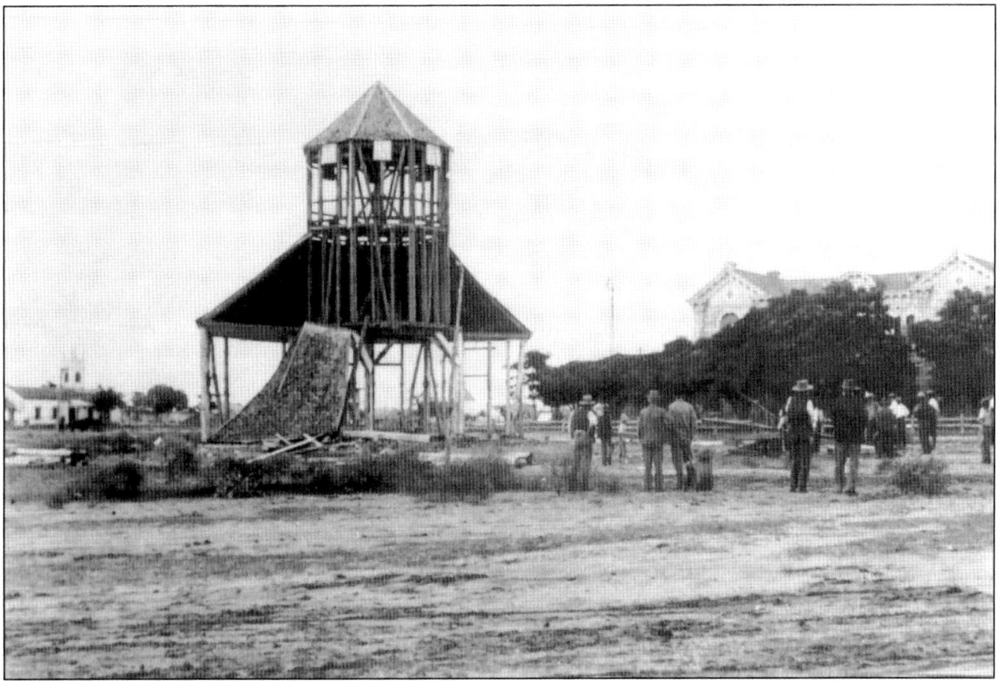

In his book *Fredericksburg, Texas . . . The First Fifty Years*, Robert Penniger writes of the Vereins Kirche: "The building has been converted into an open pavilion for the 50th anniversary jubilee. The stonewalls have been removed and decorations have been added. But its days are numbered and soon this memorial of earlier days and bitter struggles will have to yield to the breath of the new era and will continue to live only in pictures and in the memories of the people.". (Courtesy of *Fredericksburg Standard*.)

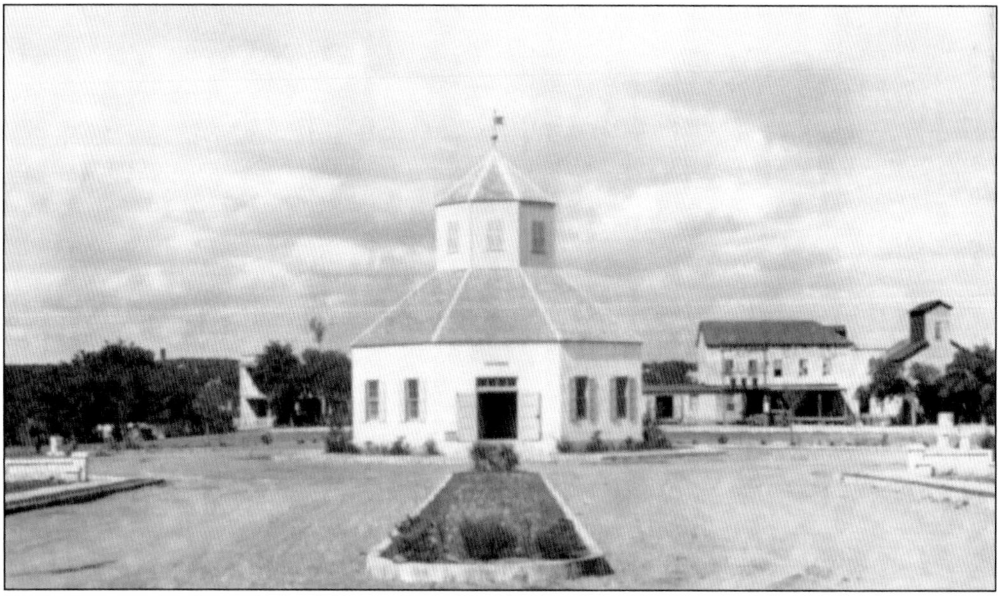

The replica of the first Vereins Kirche was built and dedicated to Fredericksburg's founders in 1935. Roosevelt's Public Works Administration provided the funds for construction, the city furnished the materials, the public school donated the land, the Civil Works Administration provided the labor, and Lee Kiehne drew up the blueprints. Serving as a museum and library until 1967, the building has been the chamber of commerce office and now museum for historical society memorabilia. (Courtesy of Nora Moellendorf.)

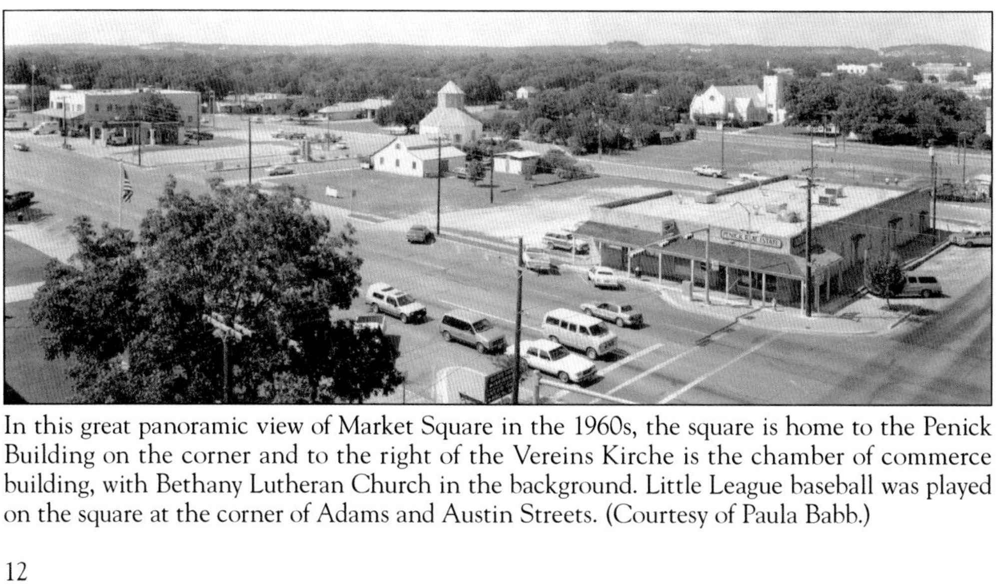

In this great panoramic view of Market Square in the 1960s, the square is home to the Penick Building on the corner and to the right of the Vereins Kirche is the chamber of commerce building, with Bethany Lutheran Church in the background. Little League baseball was played on the square at the corner of Adams and Austin Streets. (Courtesy of Paula Babb.)

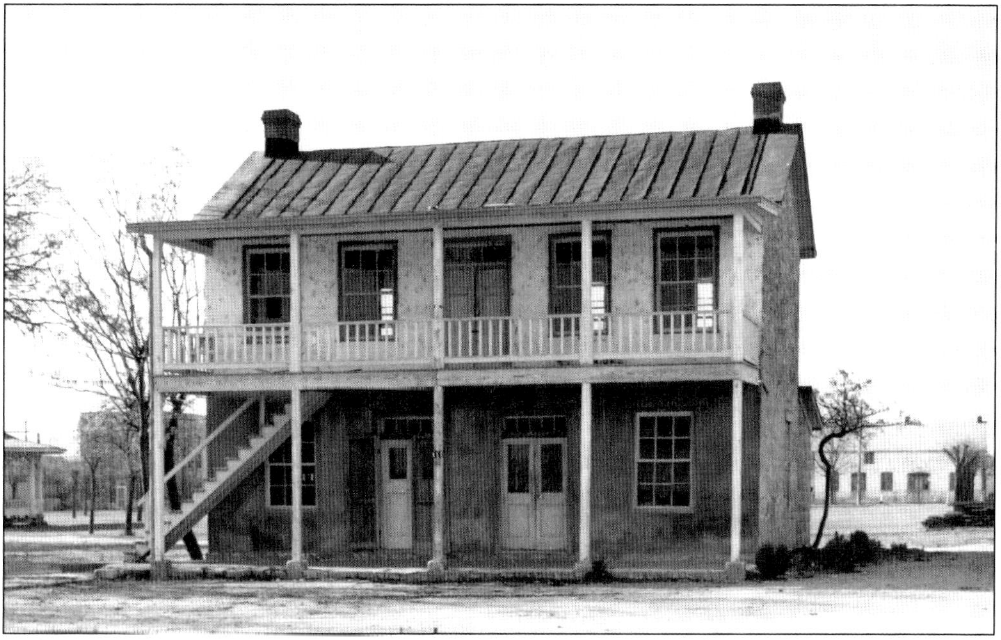

Gillespie County's first courthouse, built in 1852, was located on the corner of San Saba (now West Main) Street and Seventh (now South Crockett) Street. A two-story construction of stone and plaster, it measured 30 feet 10 inches by 36 feet, with a gabled roof and a two-story front porch. The downstairs was a single room for county offices; the courtroom on the second floor was reached by the exterior stairs. It was razed in 1940. (Courtesy of Tyrus Cox.)

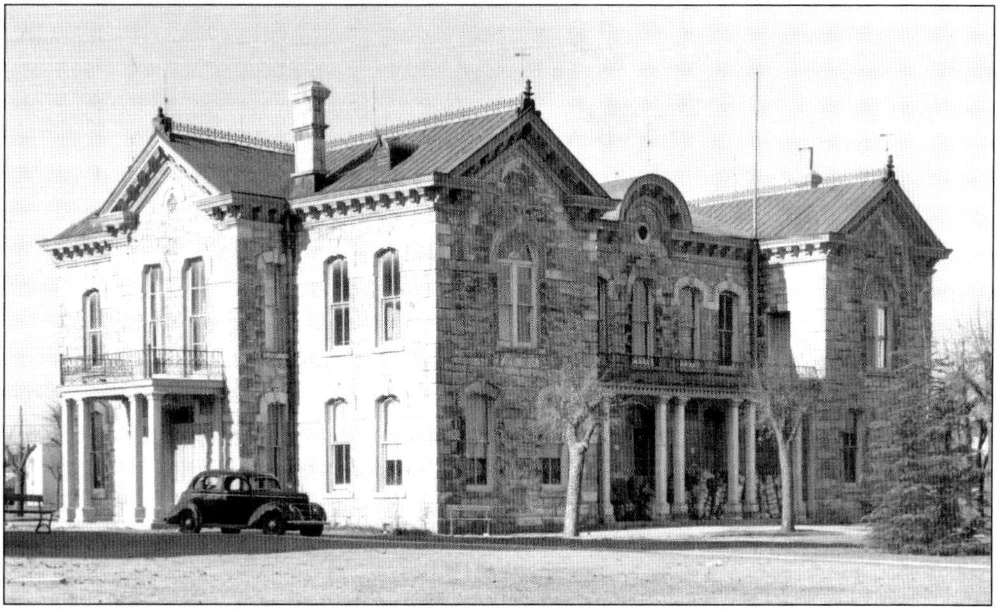

The second Gillespie County Courthouse was completed in November 1882, at a total cost of approximately $27,000, including furniture. The architect was Alfred Giles, also a prominent stonemason. On May 7, 1967, the refurbished courthouse was dedicated as the McDermott Building and houses the Pioneer Memorial Library. The project was made possible through the generosity of Eugene and Margaret McDermott of Dallas. (Courtesy of Gillespie of County Courthouse.)

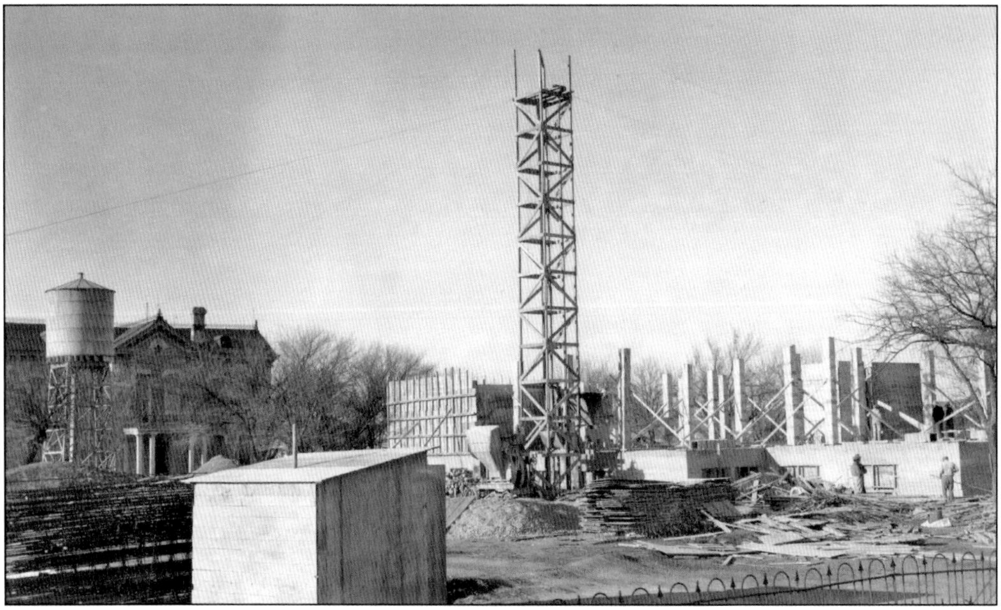

In 1935, citizens of Gillespie County began talking about building a third county courthouse with United States government aid in the form of a WPA grant. Voters rejected a $150,000 bond in May 1938. In June of that same year, the federal government offered a $65,450 grant amounting to 45 percent of the projected total cost, prompting the passage of the next bond election and allowing construction to begin. (Courtesy of Dietel Collection.)

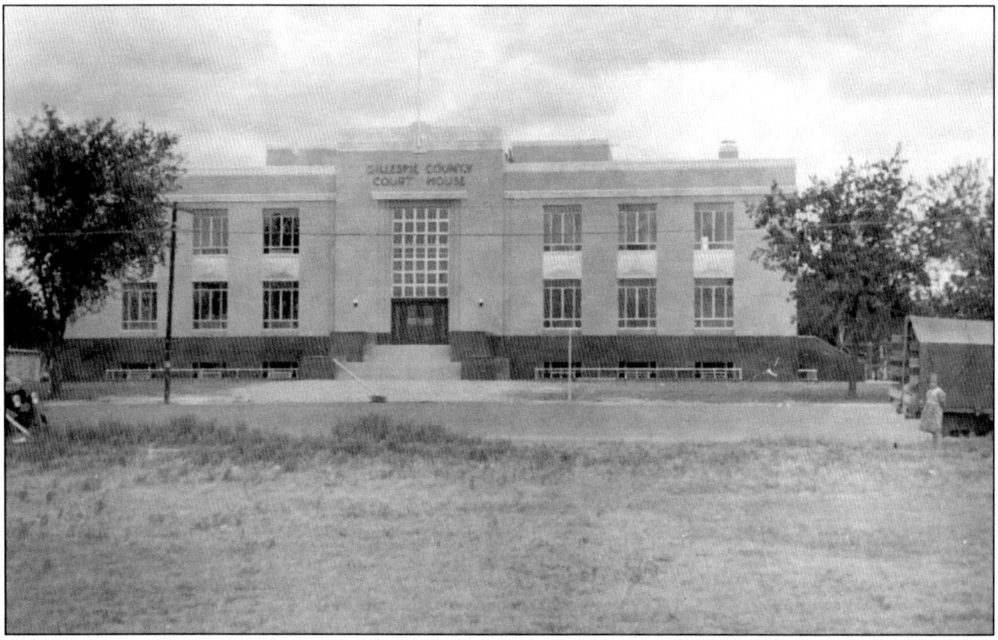

Following an earlier defeat, a new bond election for construction of the third Gillespie County Courthouse was passed in August 1938. Construction began immediately, and the courthouse was completed in July 1939—and still houses the county records and courtroom. Market Square across the street at that time was open space, with the exception of a gas station at the corner of Main and Adams Streets. (Courtesy of Dietel Collection.)

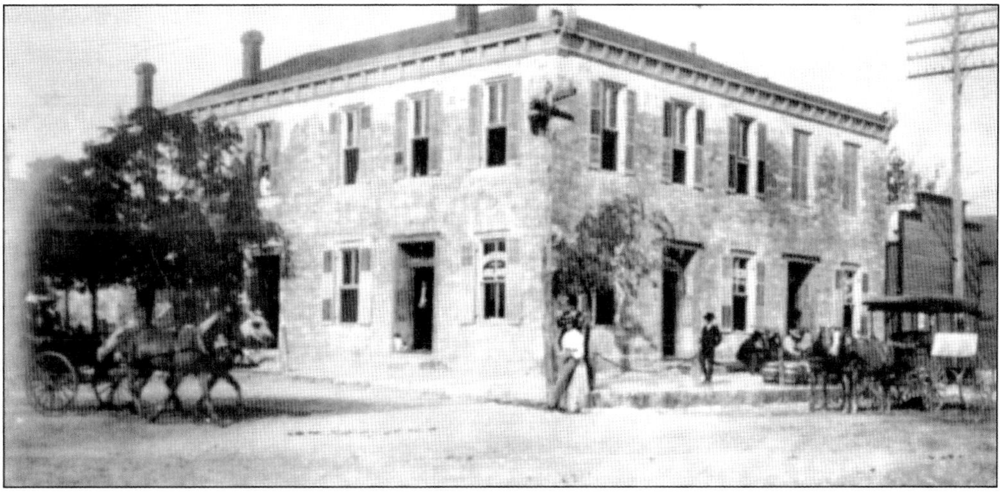

Lot 242 was purchased by Johann Leyendecker, who established Fredericksburg's first school in 1853. Heinrich Ochs, county clerk and schoolteacher, purchased the property in 1868 and built what was long known as the Buckhorn Saloon (later the Plaza Hotel). Three generations of the Ochs family made their homes upstairs, while Heinrich's son, Herman, operated the saloon downstairs until about 1908. The building became home to Security State Bank in 1941. (Courtesy of Bill Teague.)

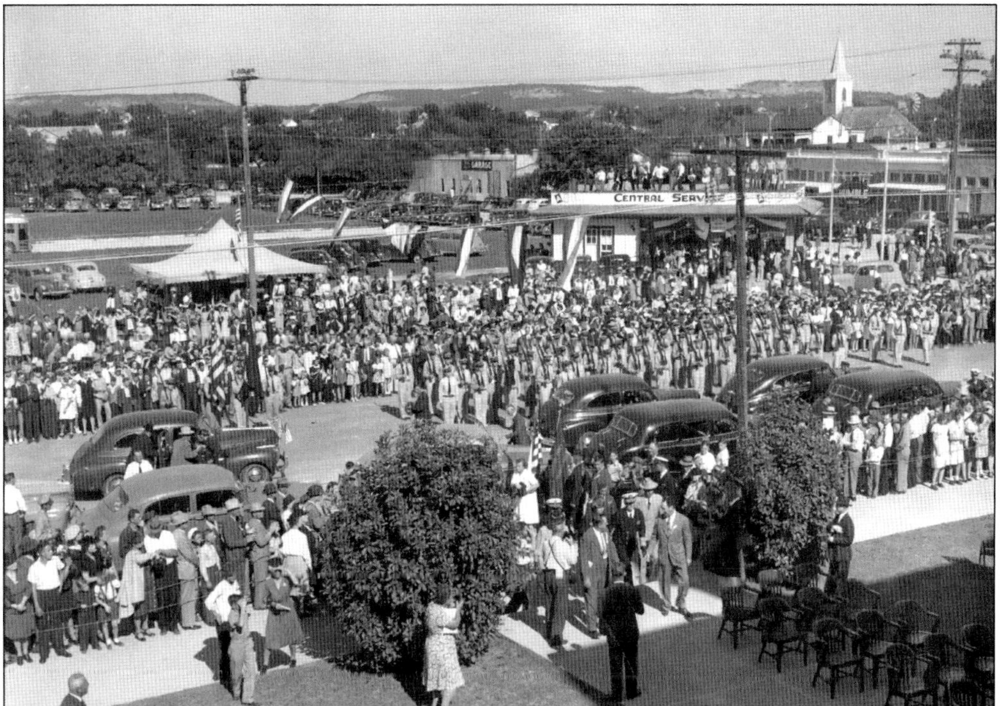

On October 13, 1945, Fredericksburg welcomed its native son, Fleet Admiral Chester W. Nimitz, with a parade, public program in front of the courthouse, and a dinner in Hotel Nimitz. He was escorted by state and city dignitaries on his way to the rostrum at the county courthouse. Gov. Coke R. Stevenson was among the distinguished guests. (Courtesy of Nimitz Museum.)

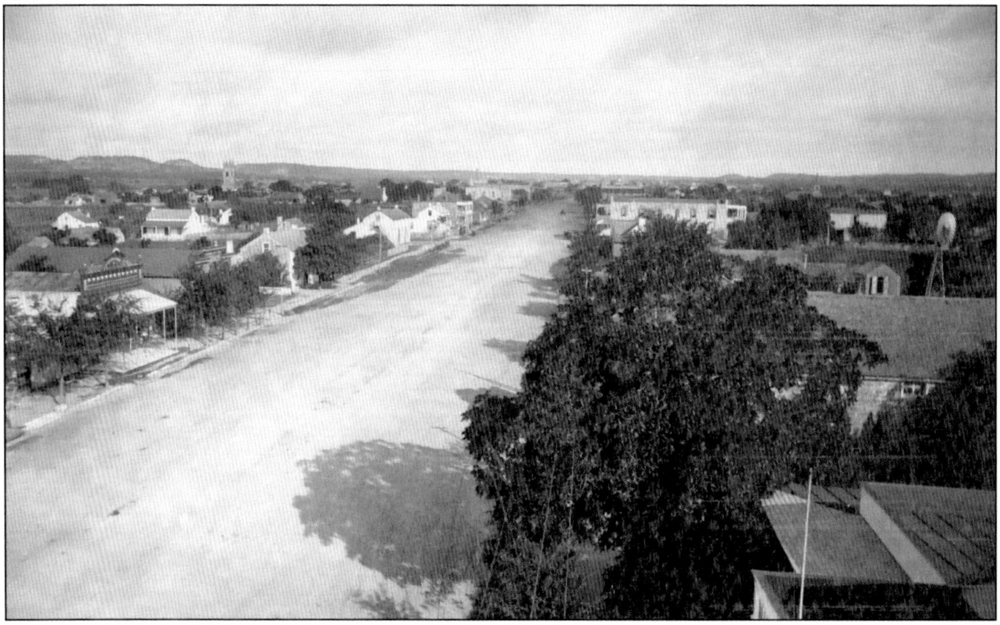

Looking toward the west end of Main Street (Hauptstrasse) in 1903 from the top of the Nimitz Hotel at the intersection of Main and Washington Streets, traffic is limited to two vehicles, possibly buggies, at the west end of Main Street. The original Holy Ghost Church steeple dots the far distant left sky, and windmills are prominently scattered throughout the town. (Courtesy of Tyrus Cox.)

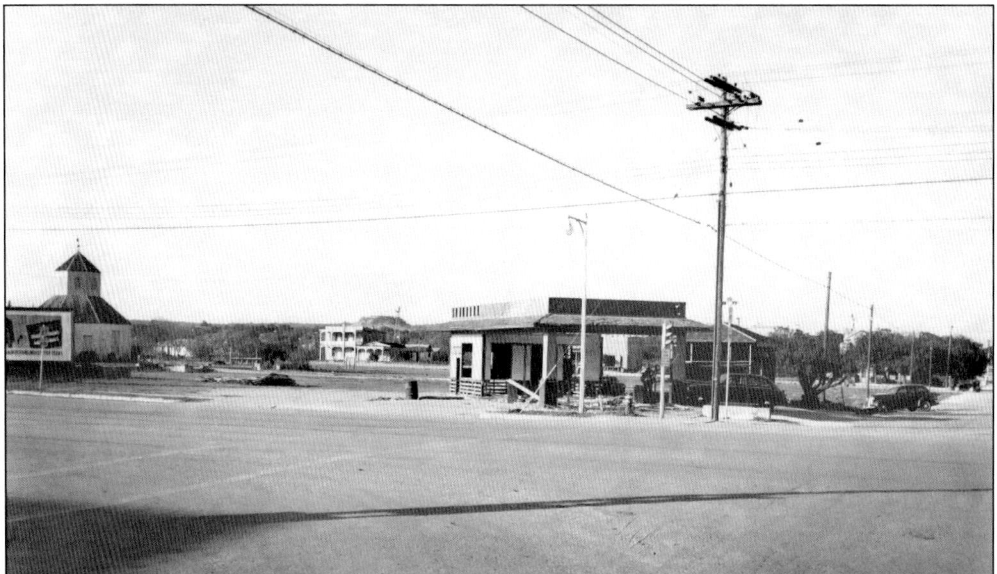

The Central Service Station built by E.H. Riley in 1923 and first operated by Alfred Riley was torn down in 1950 to be replaced by Fredericksburg's newest and most modern business structure, built by William Schroeder. The Pioneer Memorial, a replica of the historic and pioneer Vereins Kirche, is seen at left. The Hennig family home on Austin Street is seen in the background. (Courtesy of Dietel Collection.)

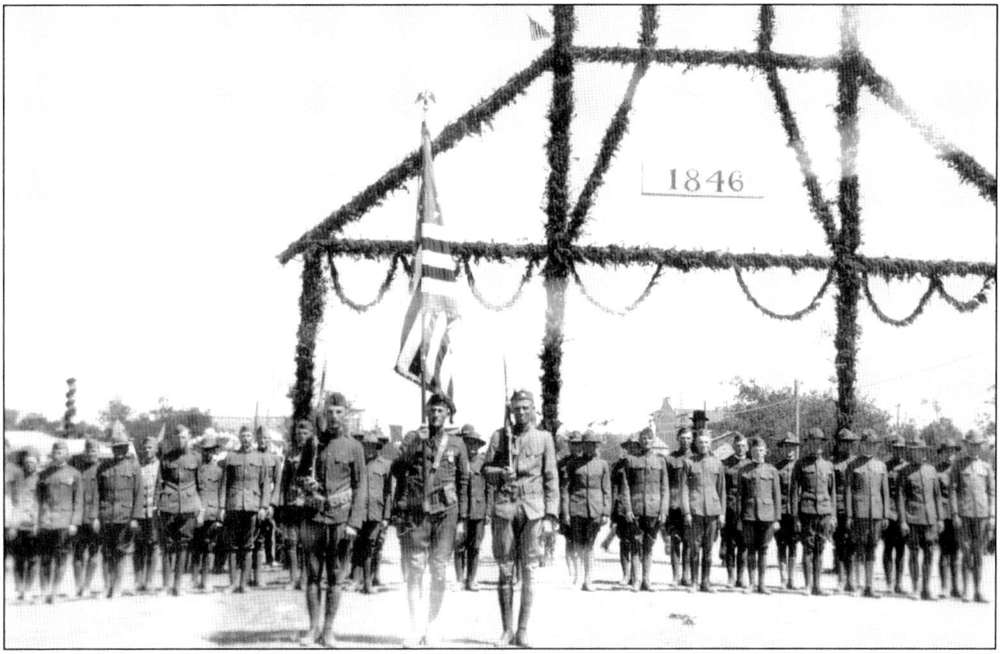

An extra, special parade was held during the 75th anniversary festivities on May 9, 1921. World War I was just over. Celebrants came by automobile to honor the military veterans passing through the Vereins Kirche Frame. The frame replica was erected in the middle of Main Street where the original Vereins Kirche had stood from 1847 to 1897, the year the original was demolished. (Courtesy of Schoenewolf/Gold.)

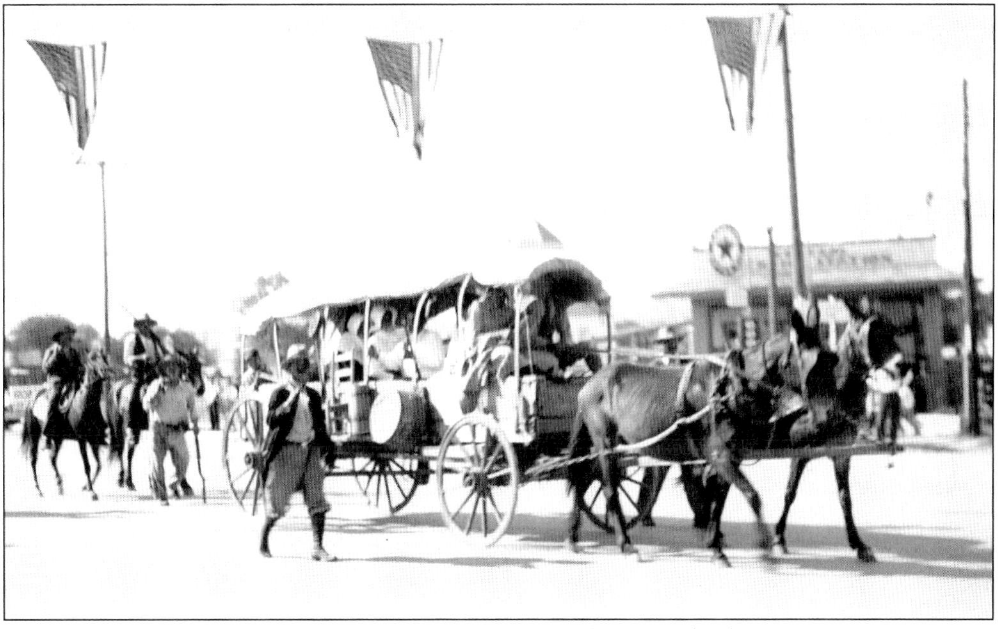

This postcard photograph was taken at the intersection of Main and Adams Streets. A gas station is on the corner, with the Vereins Kirche in the background. The covered wagon is a part of the 1935 parade to celebrate the dedication of the Vereins Kirche replica. The roof of that building is barely visible behind the covered wagon. (Courtesy of Wahl Collection.)

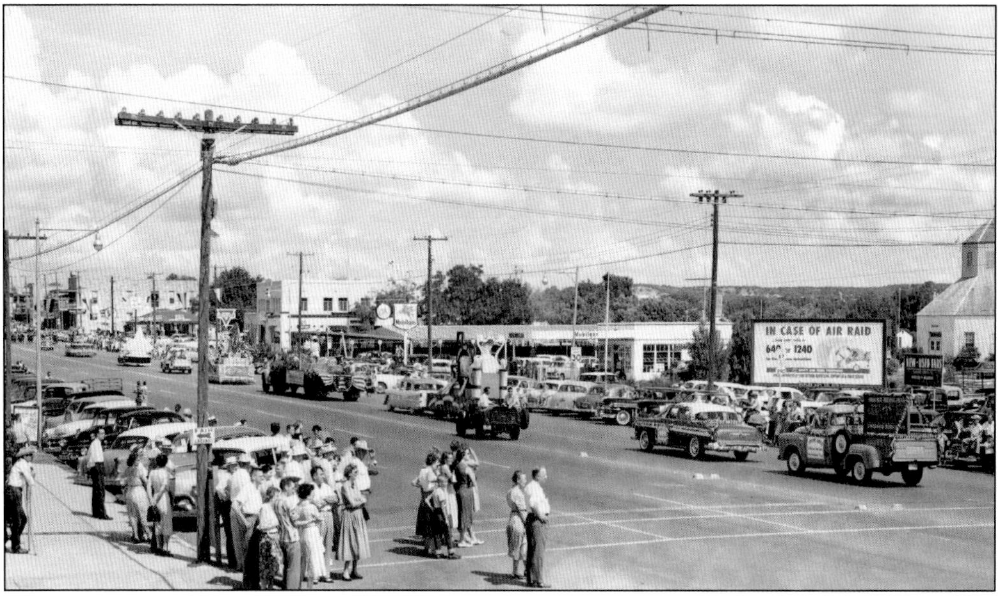

Crowds gather on both sides of Main Street at the corners of Adams and Main Streets to watch a parade in May 1956. The Vereins Kirche can be seen at the right of the photograph. Gas stations were still plentiful on Market Square at that time, and billboards were common along Main Street. (Courtesy of GTHS.)

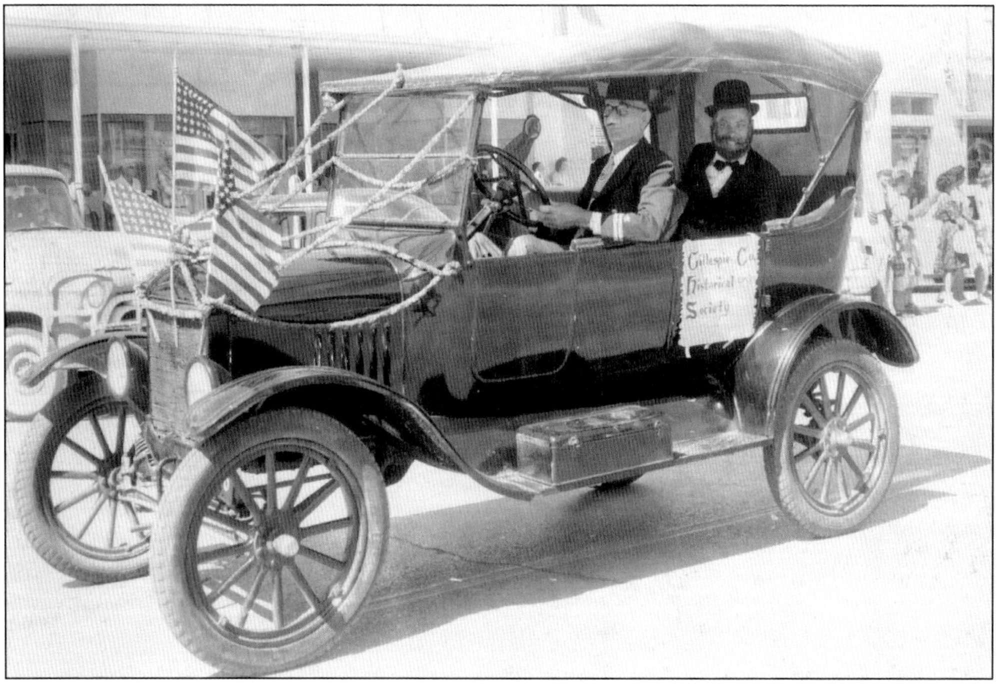

Parades travel east and west on Main Street. The Gillespie County Historical Society officials have often dressed in period costumes and been chauffeured in this touring car by drivers like Randolph "Dolphie" Jung to participate in the Gillespie County Fair Parade. In the 2011 parade, the society officials were the parade marshals and rode on a flatbed truck to commemorate the 75th anniversary of the society. (Courtesy of GCHS.)

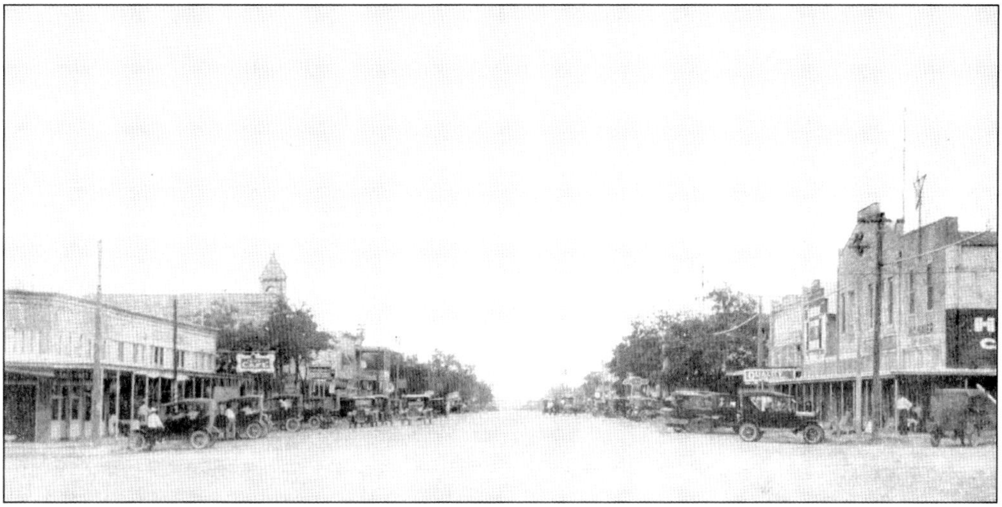

Souvenir postcards of Fredericksburg depict Main Street in the early 1920s. This postcard sold by Central Drug Store is dated August 2, 1929. That drugstore in the center of this, the 100 block of East Main on the north side of the street, was one of three Fredericksburg drugstores. (Courtesy of German Texas.)

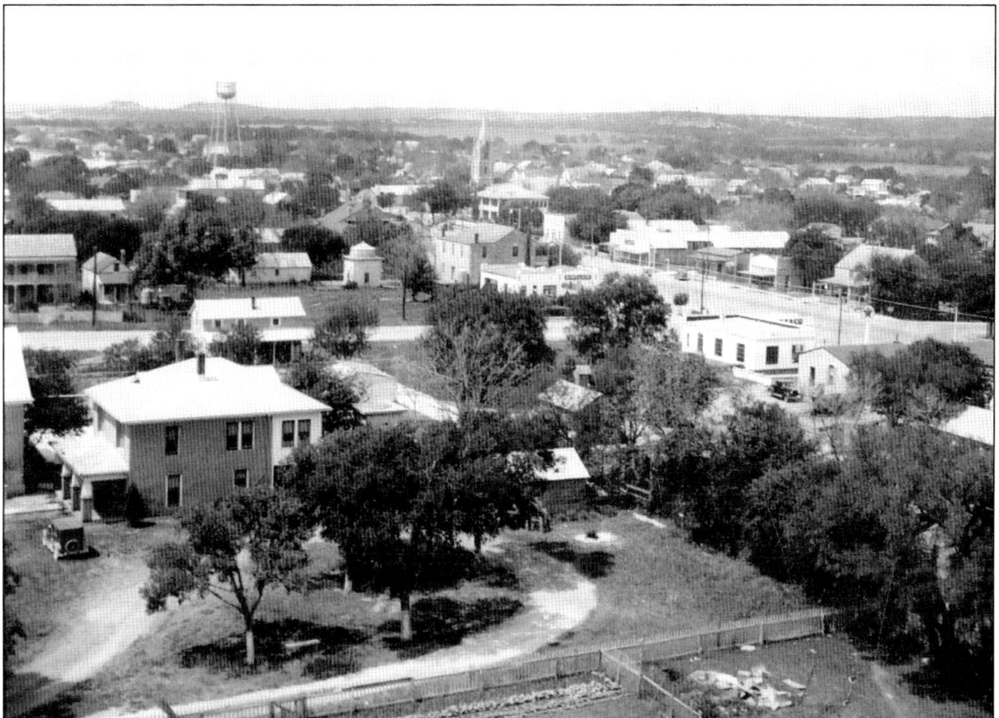

A photographer in the steeple of St. Mary's Catholic Church took this overview photograph of the west end of Fredericksburg around 1925. The businesses and homes visible are in the 400 block of West Main Street. Zion Lutheran Church steeple is at the west end of the block, and the city water tower is visible further west. (Courtesy of Dietel Collection.)

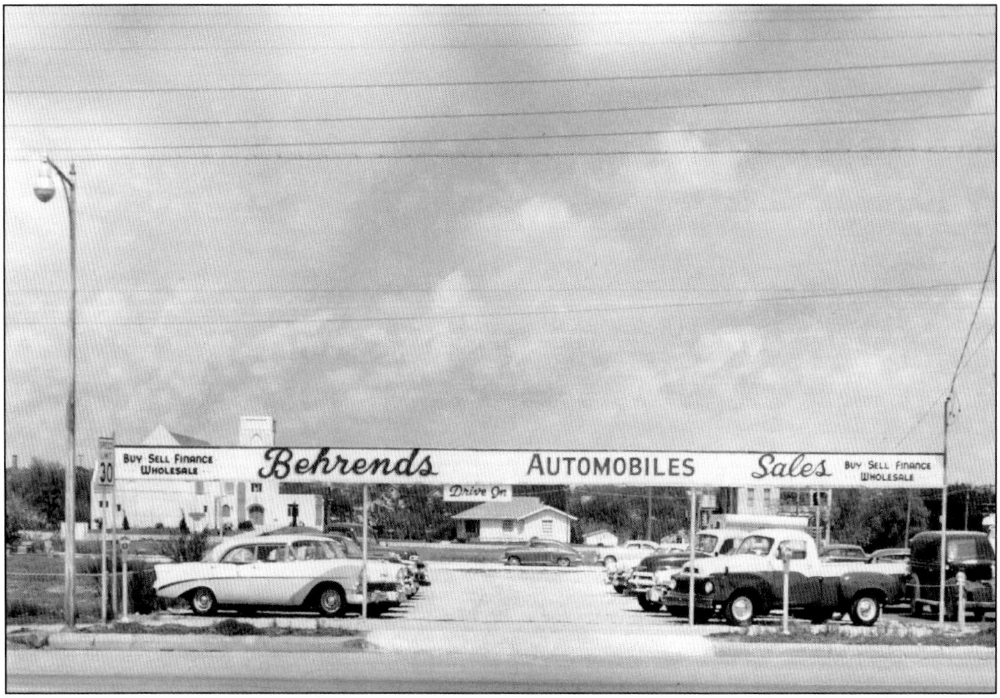

Automobile sales were conducted on the vacant lots of Market Square in the mid-1900s. Market Square was divided into four sections by the street that was directly in front of and to the sides and back of the Vereins Kirche. Two car dealerships—Heins and Behrend—had lots for selling their automobiles in the center of town. (Courtesy of Dietel Collection.)

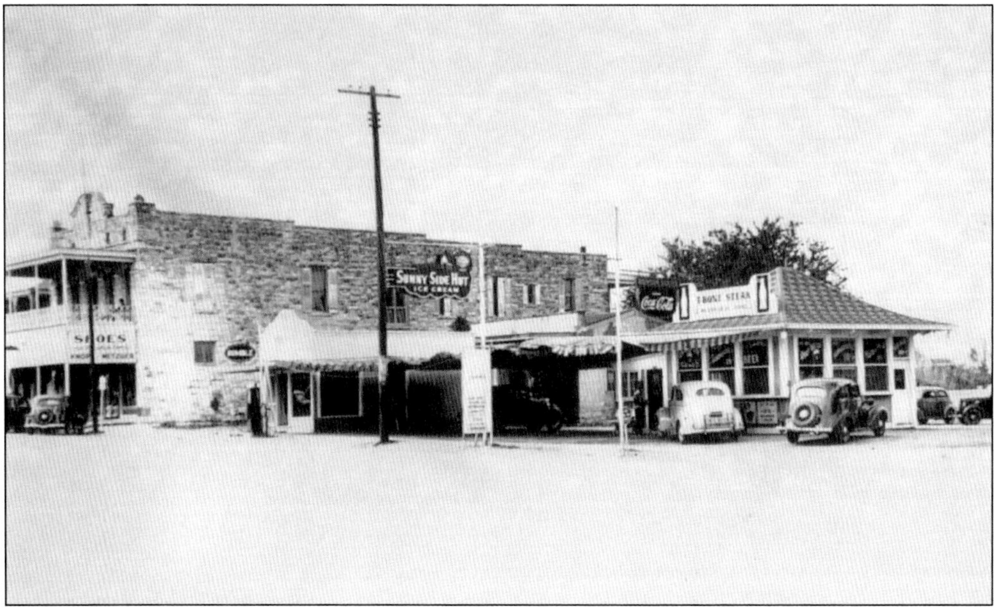

Sunny Side Hut, located in the 200 block of West Main Street on the north side, was the spot to find a hamburger and malt or shake in the mid-1900s in Fredericksburg. Many young boys took their dates to get a drink at the popular drive-in. Slim and Mary Hollmig were the proprietors. Next door was the Schwarz Building, where Knopp and Metzger sold shoes. (Courtesy of Bill Teague.)

The sounds of "let's play ball" used to ring out on Market Square during the 1950s. Market Square underwent a great change in the 1990s when the Marktplatz was redesigned to look as it is today. The AdelsVerein Halle stands now on the former site of the Little League baseball field along with two other pavilions and the garden behind the Vereins Kirche. (Courtesy of Dietel Collection.)

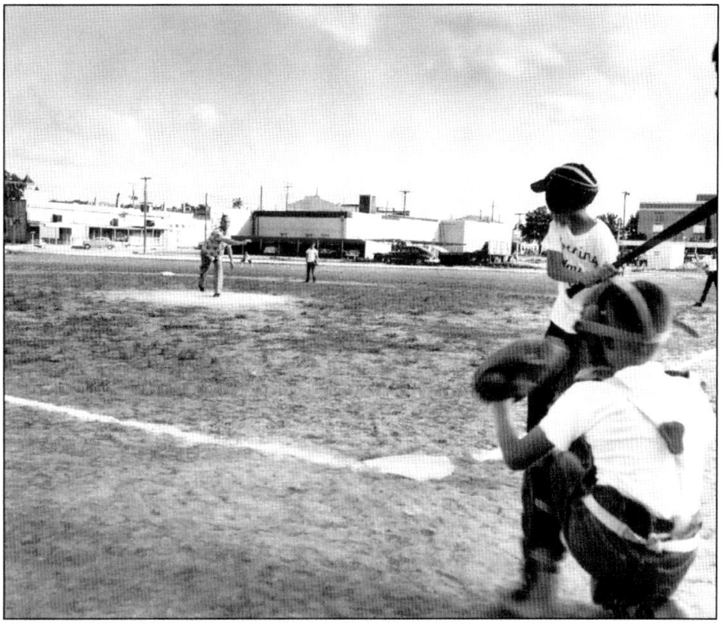

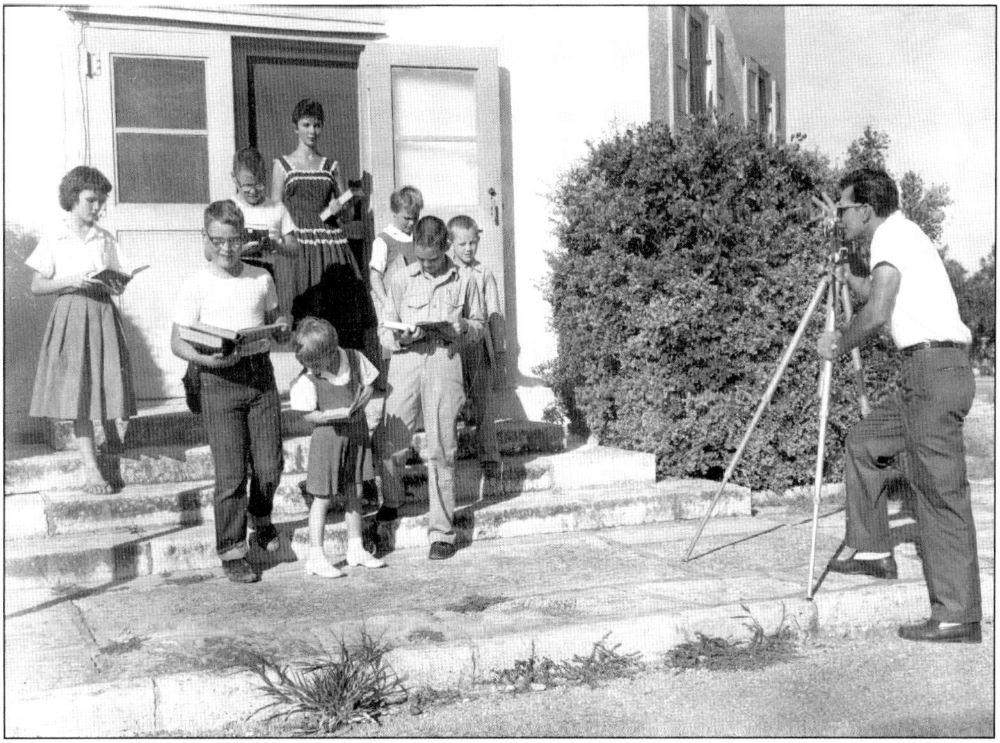

Young students check out the library after school for independent reading and assignments. The avid "bookworms" are, from left to right (first row) Frosty Rees, Elsa Rees, and Chuck Van Bibber; (second row) Cathy Van Bibber, Buddy Rees, Mary Helen Rees, and Chris Van Bibber; (at the door) Carol Ann Arhelger. The photographer is Tom Nebbia, a *National Geographic* photographer gathering material for a feature article on Texas in September 1959. (Courtesy of Dietel Collection.)

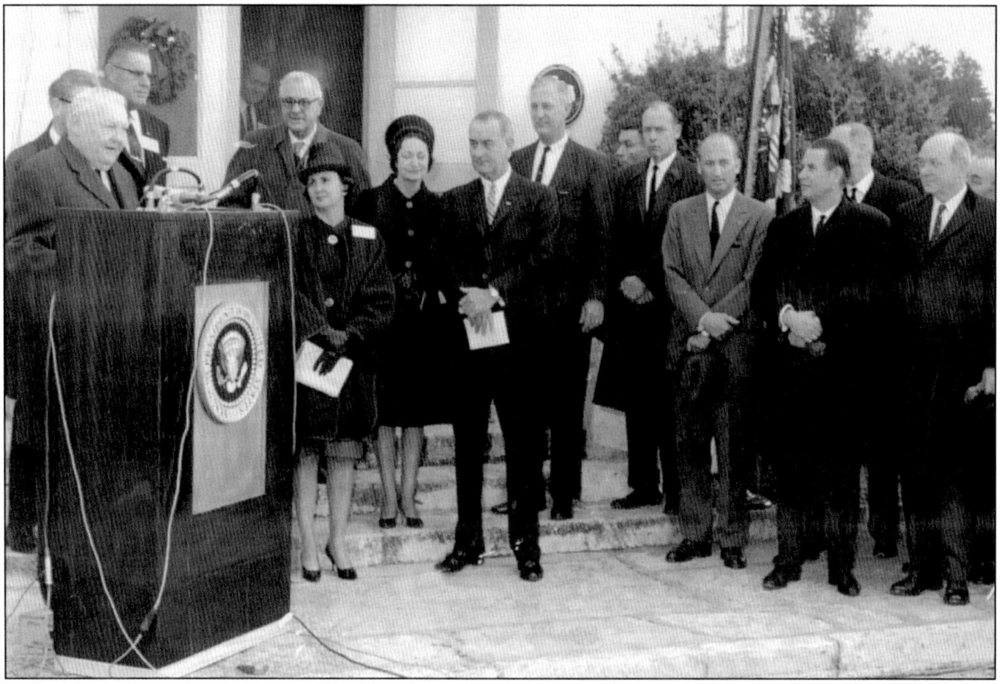

Foreign visitors like to come to Fredericksburg. This 1963 photograph shows German chancellor Ludwig Erhard, who accompanied Pres. Lyndon Johnson and his wife. The chancellor is at the podium in front of the Vereins Kirche. To his left in the back are, from left to right, FISD superintendent Fred Thompson, Mayor Sidney Henke, and civic leaders Hans Hannemann and Arthur Stehling. In front are, from left to right, Emily Keidel, Lady Bird Johnson, President Johnson, Russ Warner, and six unidentified men. (Courtesy of GCHS.)

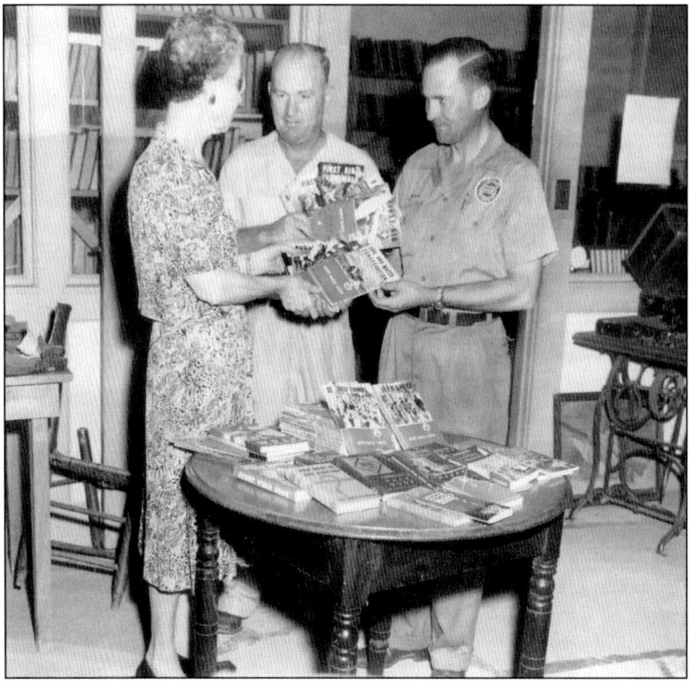

Ada Peden, the Pioneer Memorial librarian, accepts books from civic leaders Tyrus Cox (left) and Hans Hannemann to add to the shelves of the library in the Vereins Kirche. At one time, the building housed the library books along with historical artifacts— like tools, saddles, and treadle sewing machines— for the Gillespie County Historical Society. (Courtesy of Dietel Collection.)

Two

Building the Future

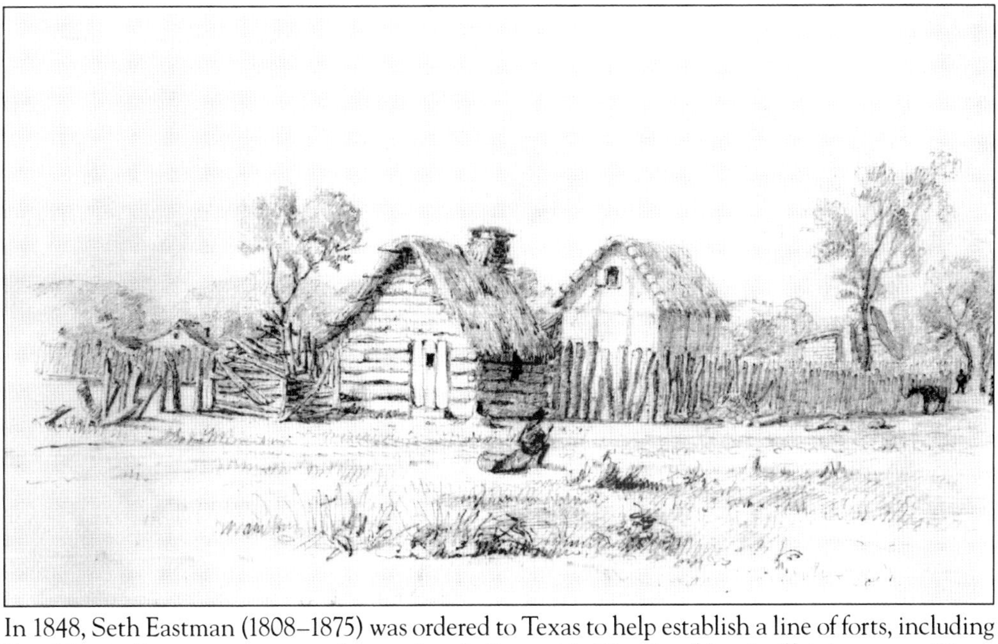

In 1848, Seth Eastman (1808–1875) was ordered to Texas to help establish a line of forts, including Fort Martin Scott, to protect settlers against Indian raids. The sketchbook of his journey to Texas and his tour of duty consists of nearly 150 drawings, including 65 Texas scenes. Eastman was intrigued by the Texas Hill Country, and his sketchbook provides 15 historically significant views of the two-year-old settlement of Fredericksburg. (Courtesy of GCHS.)

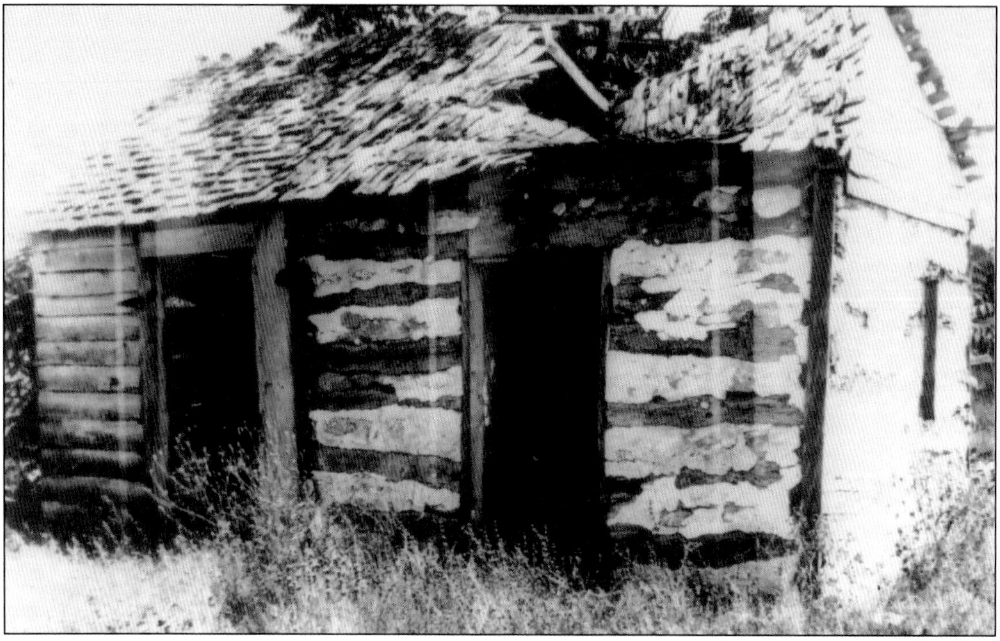

In January 1846, thirty-six men, including three surveyors, arrived at the station chosen by Meusebach, which was to become Fredericksburg; they built a temporary shelter, then, this log house. After completing their survey, they buried their tools, building a fire on top of the disturbed earth to erase evidence of the location. The log house, located in the southeast quadrant of Main and Washington Streets, was torn down in the 1950s. (Courtesy of Bill Teague.)

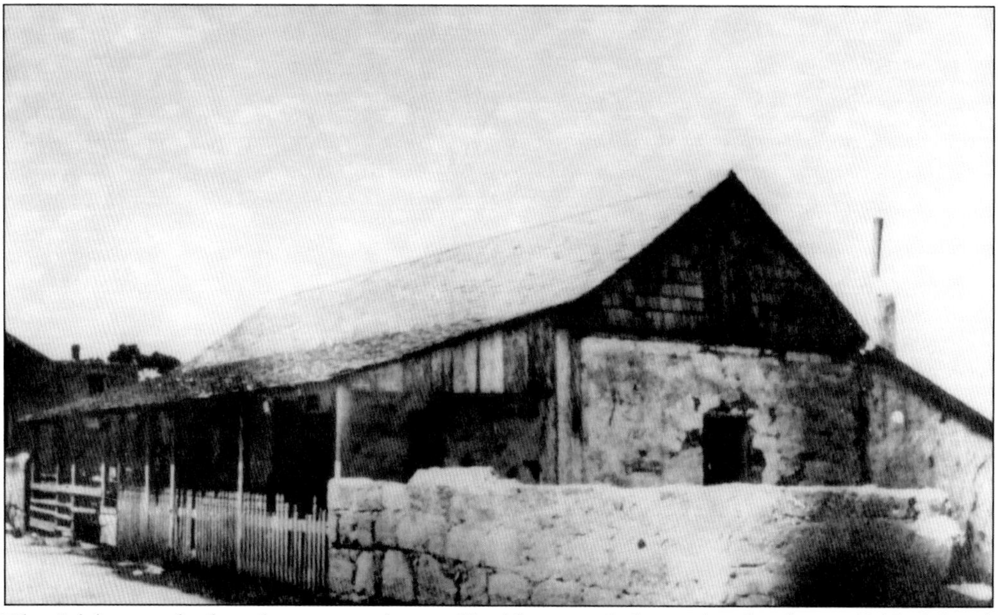

The Adelsverein built and maintained several buildings, including a slaughterhouse (*Schlachthaus*) and meat distribution house (*Fleischhalle*). A warehouse for provisions was constructed in July 1846; a stable was added later. The official map of the Verein locates these at the southern end of the town where Baron and Bene (Town) Creeks converge, in the first block into the town, on the right of San Saba Strasse (Main Street). (Courtesy of Bill Teague.)

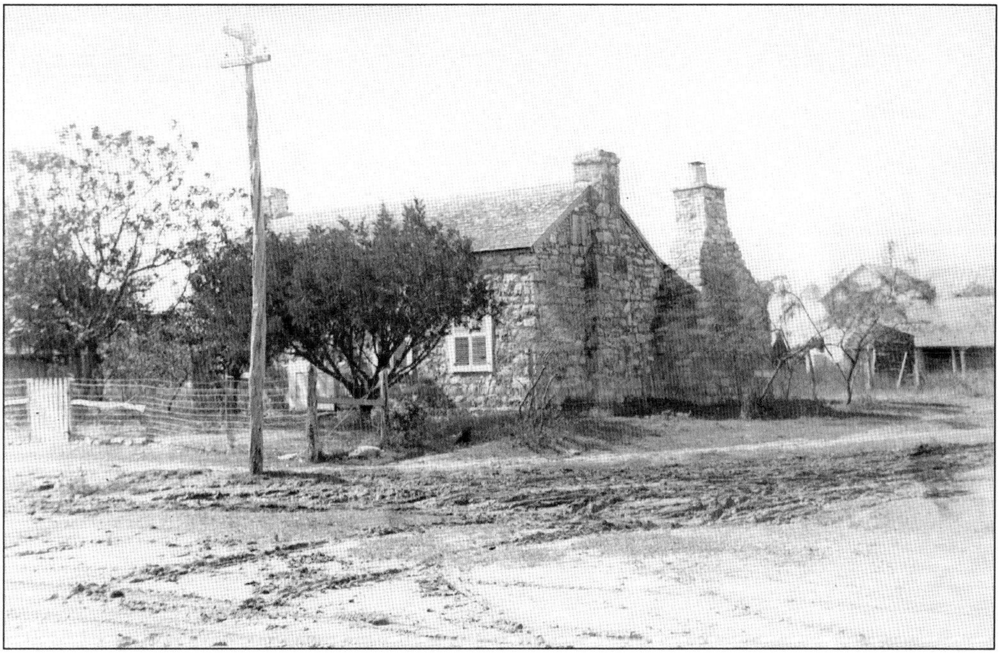

Johann Peter and Maria Elizabeth Tatsch arrived in Fredericksburg in 1852; in 1856, they built a large log barn and set up a workshop. John then designed and built a small two-room limestone home; a later addition included a 12-foot-long-by-18-inches-wide kitchen fireplace. John finished the woodwork for the home, including doors, stairways, and solid, well-designed furniture. The home is located at North Bowie and West Schubert Streets. (Courtesy of GCHS.)

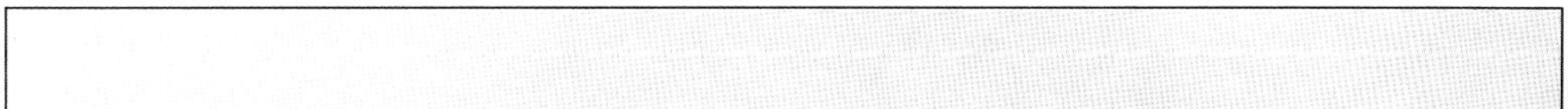

In 1857, Heinrich Cordes purchased eight town lots located on the banks of Town Creek, now the corner of North Crockett and Mistletoe Streets. There, he built this one-room log house, chinked with rocks and mortar, soon adding a kitchen constructed of native limestone with a stone floor and cooking fireplace. Henry and Minna Henke Cordes raised five children in this home—Sophie, Charles, Heinrich Jr., Minna, and Augusta. (Courtesy of Wehmeyer/Johnson Collection.)

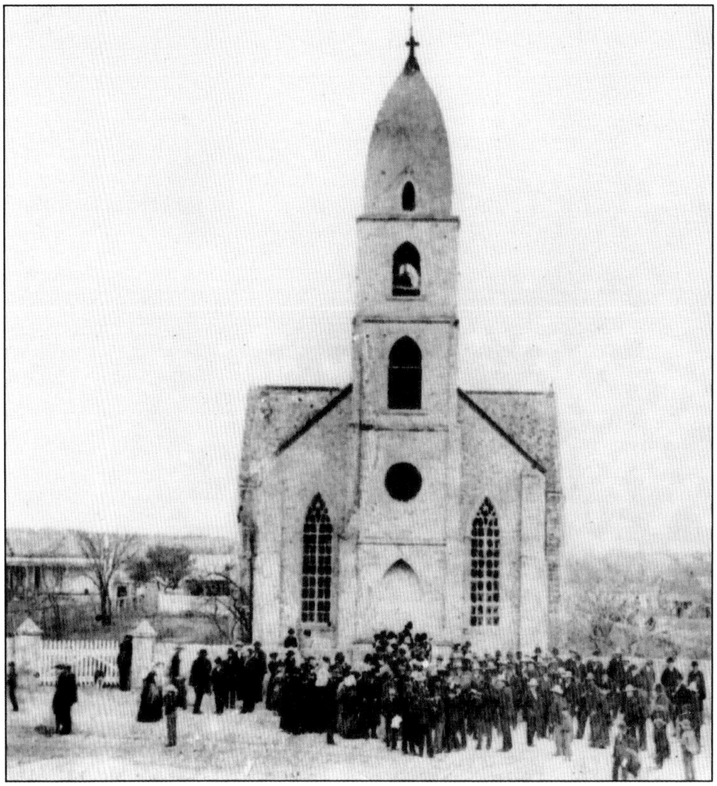

Plans for the Marienkirche were drawn in 1860 by a Father Gallus; under the supervision of Fr. Peter Baunach, construction began on February 26, 1861. Parishioners staked out the site, hauled stone and sand, burned lime, procured wood, and provided the vast majority of the labor. Work was done for free, and money was paid only for that which had to be bought. The church was consecrated November 22, 1863. (Courtesy of Lee and Betty Ethel.)

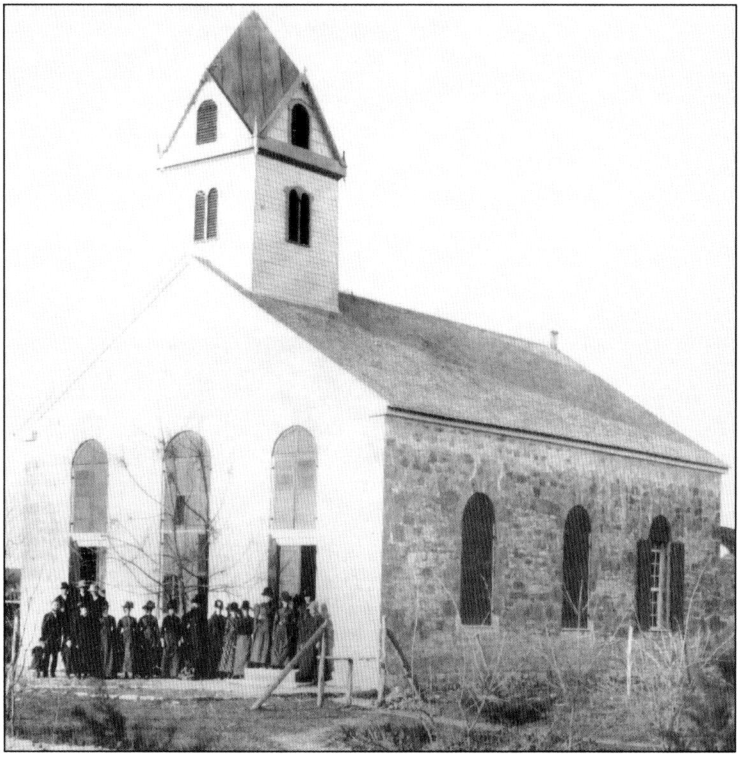

In 1852, the Zion Lutheran congregation was formed by six families who withdrew from the Vereins Kirche. Philipp F. Zizelmann arrived in Galveston on September 2, 1851, with five other 1851 graduates of the Pilger Mission von St. Chrischona in Basel, Switzerland, and became the congregation's first pastor. A permanent organization was established in 1853; and on March 7, 1854, the cornerstone for their church was laid. (Courtesy of GCHS.)

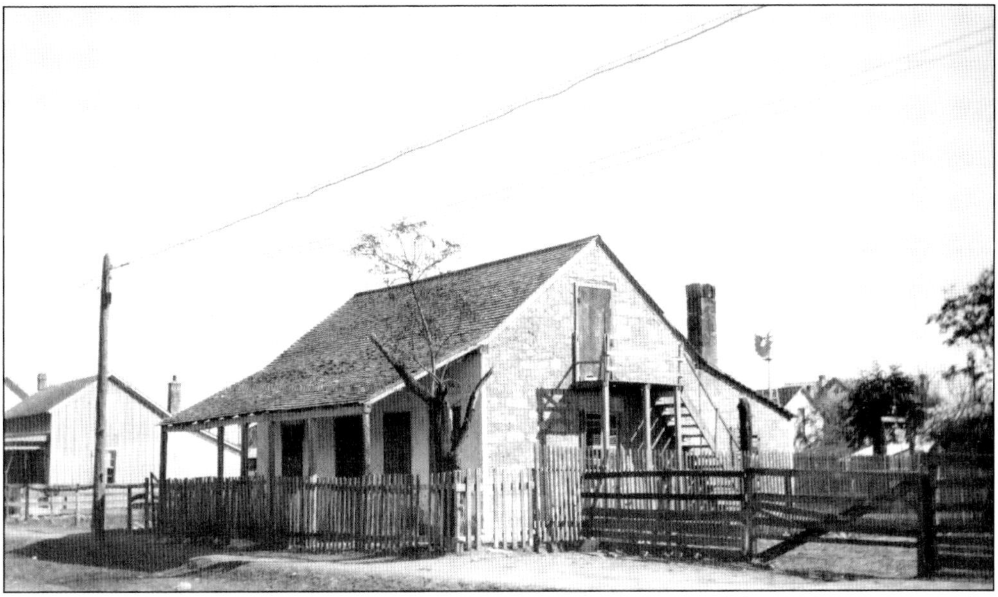

In 1855, Johann and Katherine Knopp Fritz built their limestone rock home facing west in the present-day 100 block of North Milam Street. In his blacksmith shop, during the construction of the Marienkirche (1861–1863), Johann made hundreds of nails for the church roof and benches. His untimely death in 1864 left Katherine with eight children to rear: Peter (21), William (19), Maria, John, Fred, Franz, and Christian (all school-age), and Anton (3). (Courtesy of Wehmeyer/Johnson Collection.)

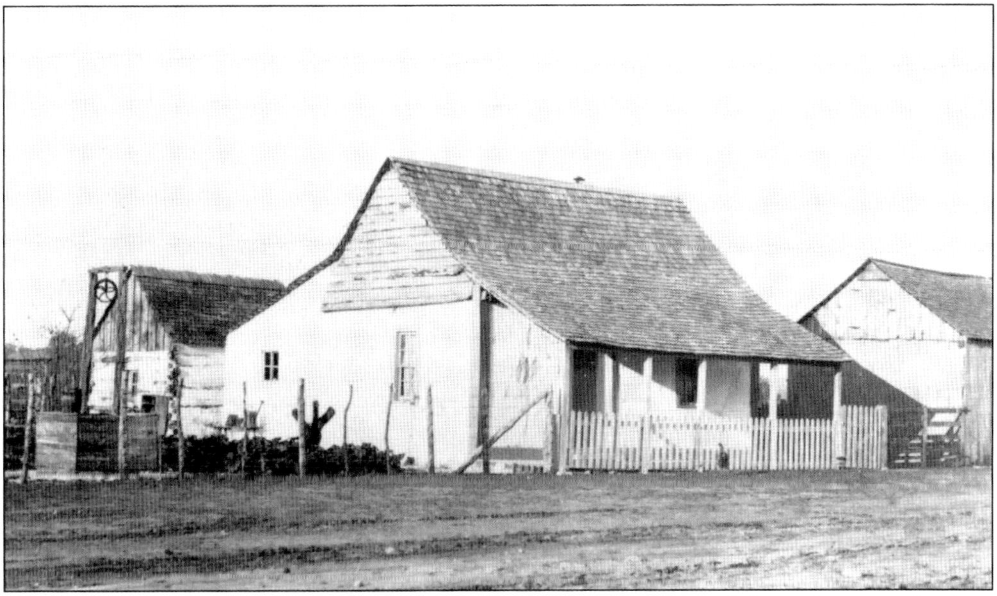

Peter Walter, his wife Margarethe, and their four children emigrated from Germany, landing on the Texas coast in November 1846. They, like hundreds of German immigrants, traveled by oxcart and on foot to New Braunfels. Arriving in Fredericksburg in 1847, Peter was granted town lot No. 464 by the German Emigration Company; a log cabin was constructed and later the *fachwerk* structure, which serves today as a chapel for St. Barnabas Episcopal Church. (Courtesy of Wehmeyer/Johnson Collection.)

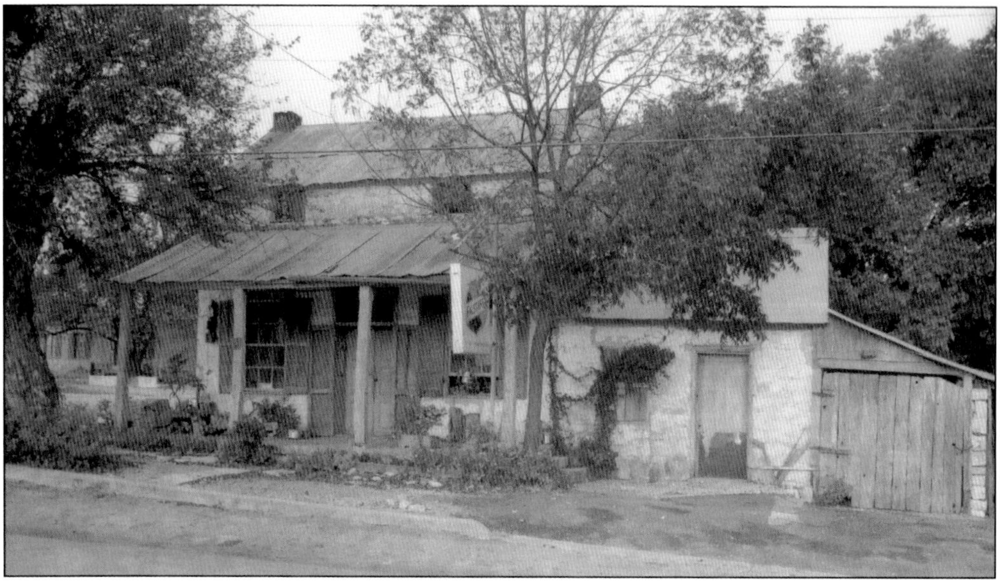

The oldest section of the two structures located at 112 North Crocket Street, of *fachwerk* construction, was built in about 1862 by Franz Wilhelm Krueger, who operated an apothecary business there until his death in 1865. In 1867, the property was purchased by Friedrich Weihmiller for $410. Here, he, his wife, Caroline Steffensen (the widow Kirchner), and her three children made their home and operated a blacksmith shop until 1881. (Courtesy of Tyrus Cox.)

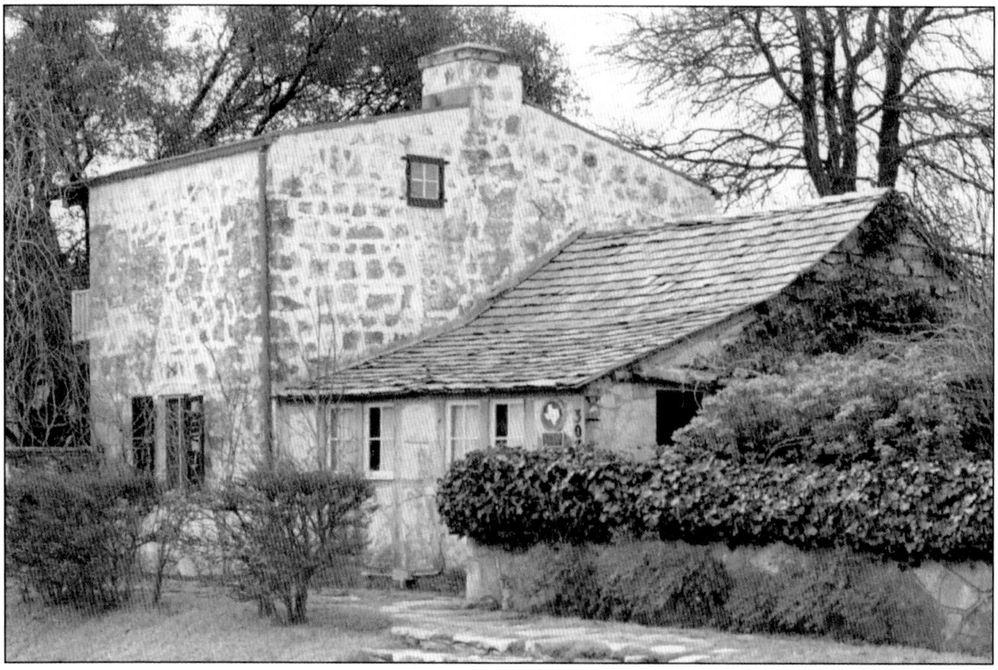

The Christian and Elisabeth Margaretha Mohr Crenwelge home, at 307 West Schubert Street, was built overlooking the banks of Town Creek in about 1856. To what began as a one-story log house, a *fachwerk* kitchen was soon added, subsequently followed by a two-story solid rock addition. Christian farmed a 10-acre lot near Cross Mountain, operated a molasses press and limekiln, and is listed as a cabinetmaker in the 1860 census. (Courtesy of GCHS.)

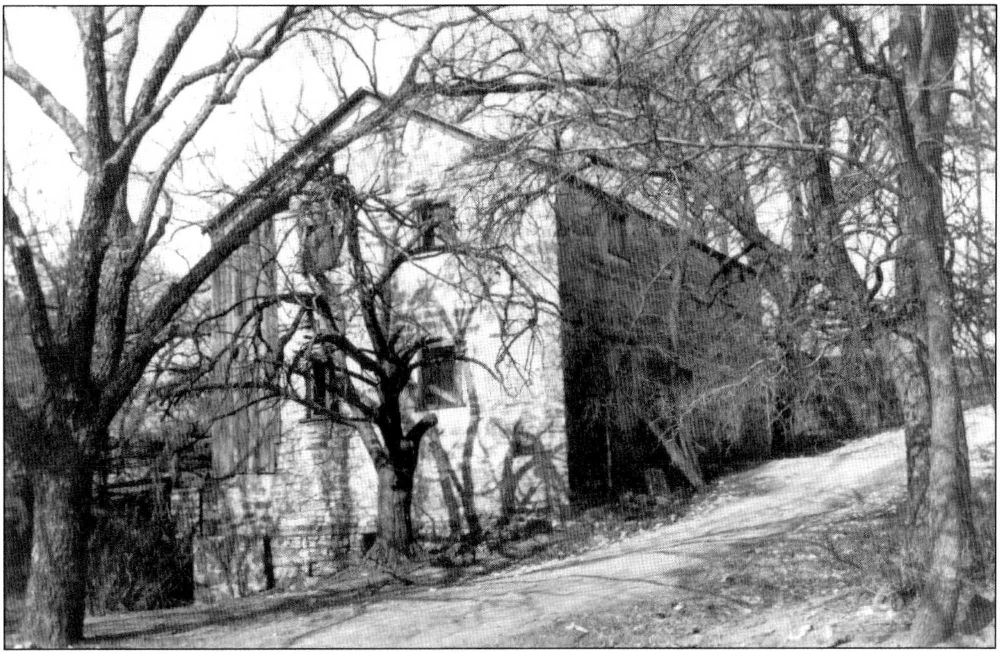

Established in 1849 by brothers John and Thomas Doss, Lange's Mill is one of the last and best-preserved burr mills in Texas. Named for Wilhelm F. Lange, who ran it from 1859 to 1878, the mill used a large burrstone for grinding as opposed to traditional sandstone or limestone; its products were famed throughout the region. Lange's descendants continue to own the property located in northwest Gillespie County. (Courtesy of Wehmeyer/Johnson Collection.)

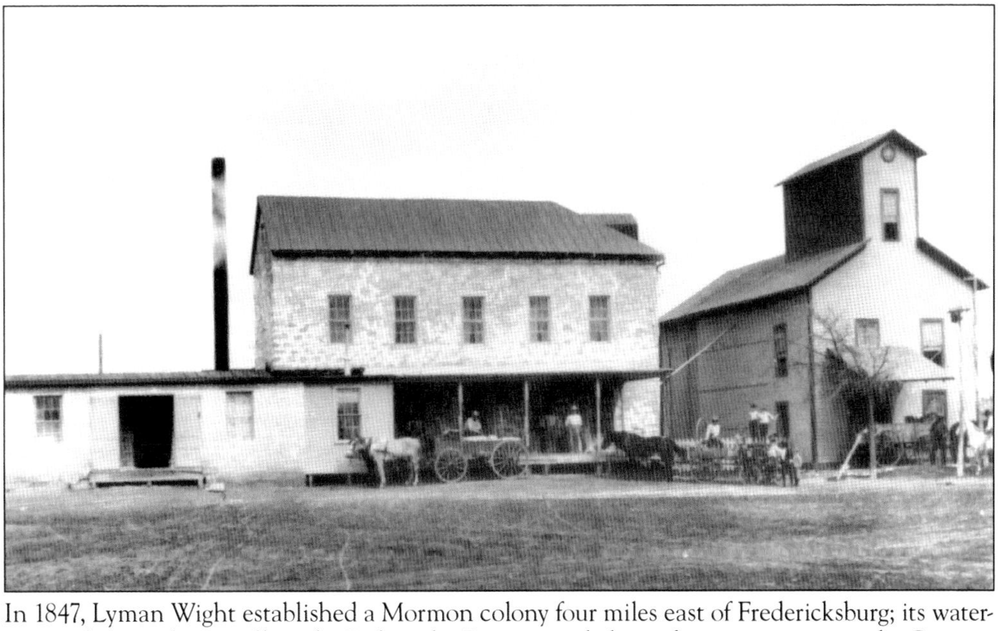

In 1847, Lyman Wight established a Mormon colony four miles east of Fredericksburg; its water-powered saw and gristmill on the Pedernales River provided significant assistance to the German colonists. When their colony left the area in 1853, two of Elder Wight's sons remained in Texas; one son returned in 1856 to build the Fredericksburg Steam Mill, owned by Frank van der Stucken, William Wahrmund, and Frederick Wrede. (Courtesy of GCHS.)

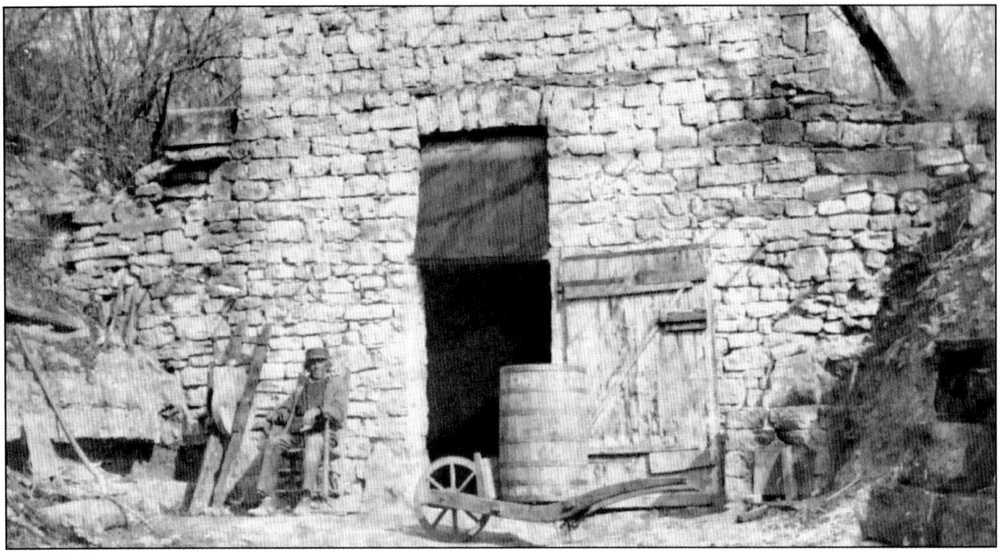

Peter "Hermit" Berg emigrated from Germany in 1857; he withdrew from society following the refusal of his German fiancé to follow him to Texas. A skilled stonemason and craftsman, Peter inhabited a hand-dug cave for many years, building his own furniture, Dutch windmill to pump water and grind corn, and whiskey still. He constructed a functioning pipe organ, built of brass and wood scraps with pipes of paper producing distinct musical tones. (Courtesy of Victor Meier.)

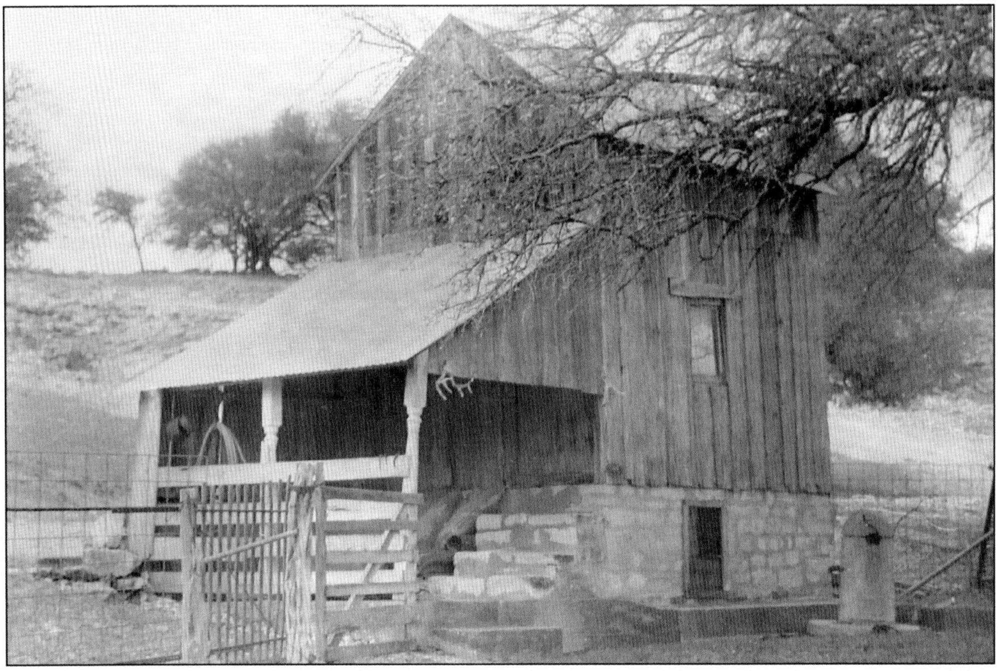

Jacob and Johanna Warnecke Land were among early pioneers of the Crabapple community. This small frame-and-stone structure was home to Jacob, Johanna, and their eight children—Peter (married Louise Burrer), Mary (married August Grosenbacher), Auguste (married Ferdinand Jenkins), Katie (married Brooker), Sophia (married William Burrer), Wilhelm (married Ida Burrer), Henry (married Louise Grobe), and Johanna (married William Hohmann). The home and land are still owned by Jacob's descendants. (Courtesy of Gertrude and Harvey Land.)

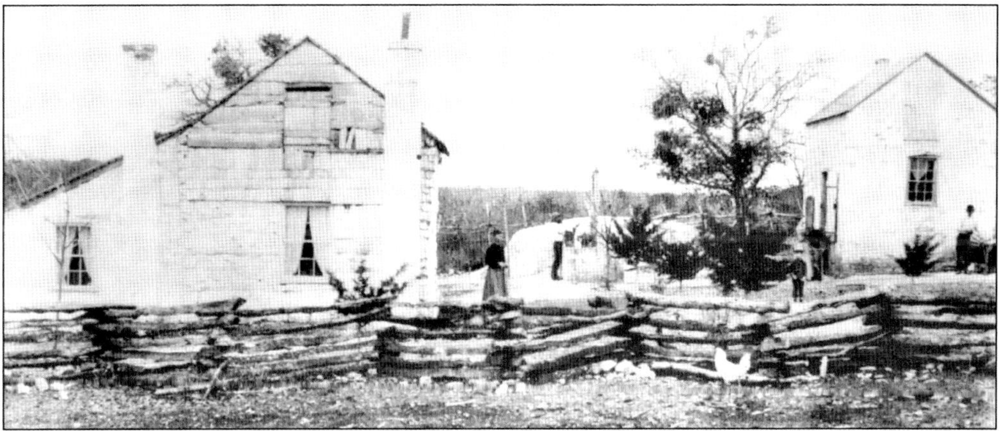

The Friedrich Karl Ludwig and Ilse Conradine Henriette Hotopp Kiehne homestead is located in the Rheingold community. The original log home was enlarged with a stone lean-to kitchen and in later years, a larger two-story home was built. The area is enclosed with a split rail fence, the rails stacked in an interlocking zigzag fashion that is self-supporting and easy to construct, repair, and disassemble. (Courtesy of Bill Teague.)

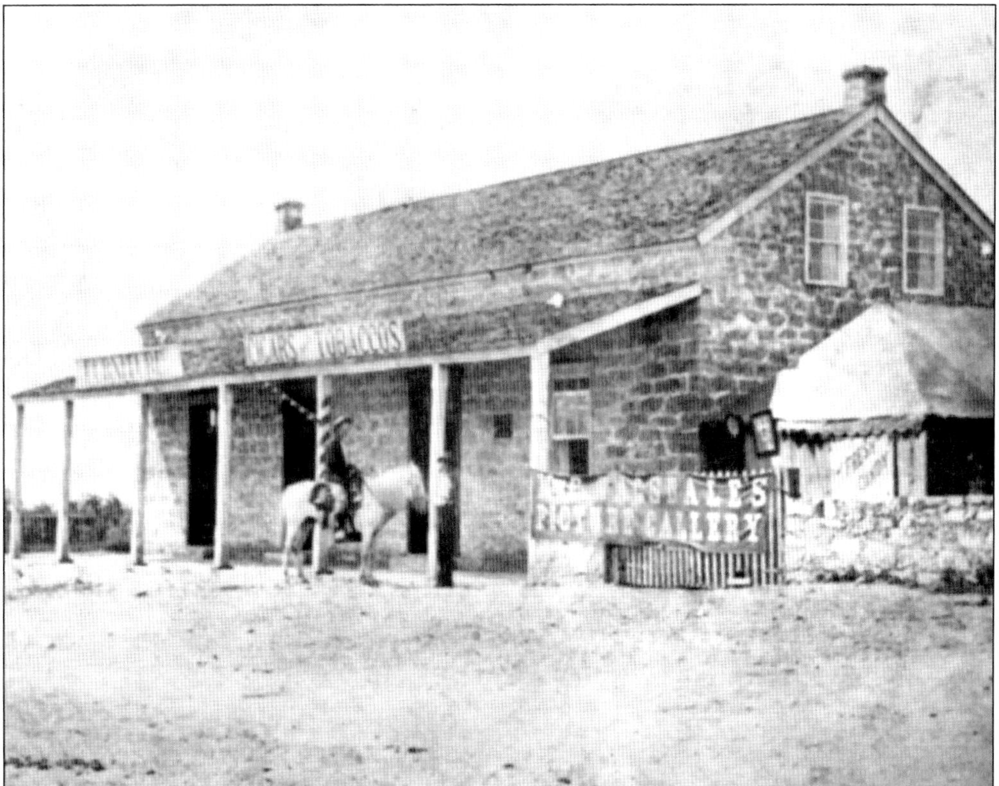

Located on the southwest corner of Main and Llano Streets, this structure was operated for many years by numerous owners as a general merchandise store; it typically also served as a residence for the owner. A fabric sign advertises McArthur C Ragsdale's picture gallery, which has been set up beneath a tent. Earning a meager living, Ragsdale worked "the circuit," traveling from town to town during the 1870s and 1880s. (Courtesy of GCHS.)

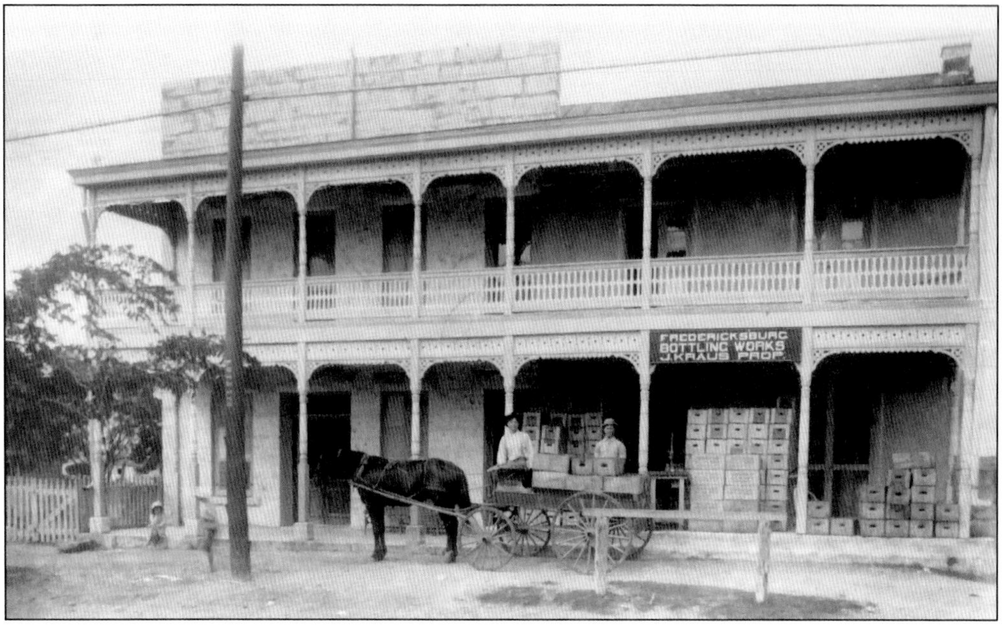

The original (west half) of the Kraus Building was constructed by Wilhelm Luckenbach around 1870. Purchased by Jacob Kraus in 1898, it soon became home and family business Kraus Bottling Co. for Jacob and Theresia Segner Kraus. The building was enlarged (east half) in 1906. Originally selling only one red soda water and one white soda water, Kraus later bottled Iron Brew, which quickly became a local favorite. (Courtesy of GCHS.)

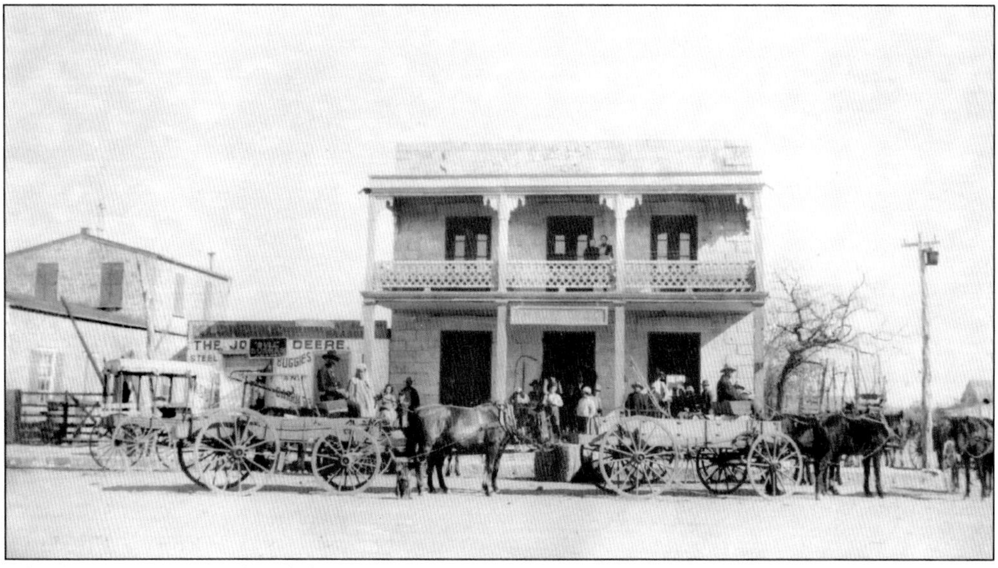

Charles F. Priess completed this two-story limestone building as a home and business in 1883 at the corner of San Saba (East Main) and Garten (North Lincoln) Streets. He operated a general merchandise and hardware store; the large cellar served as storage for his Lone Star Beer distributorship. Later, businesses at this location included R.M. Burrier & Co., Burrier and Maier, Rossenwasser and Levy, and beginning in 1938, Keidel Hospital. (Courtesy of GCHS.)

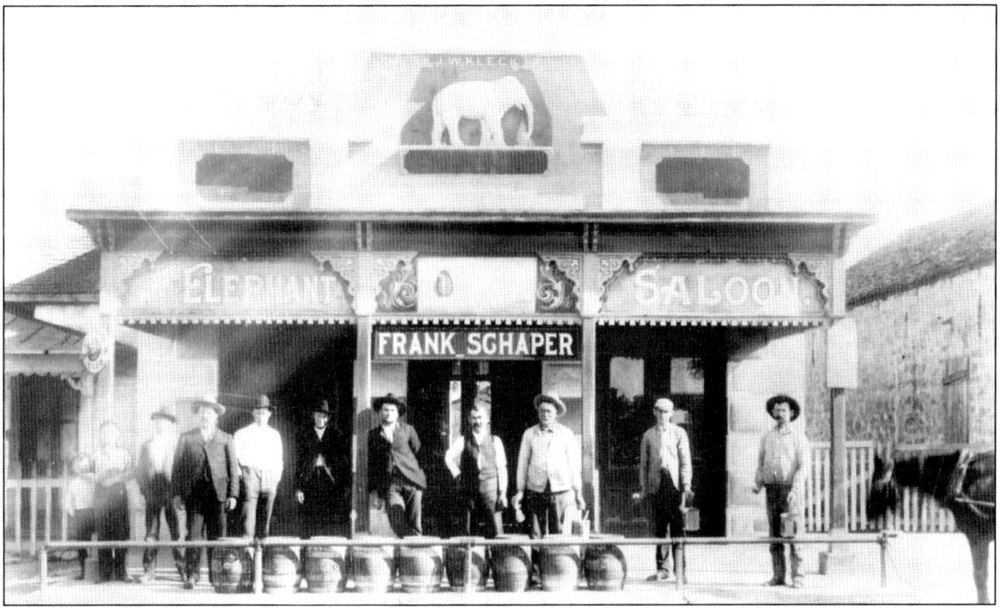

Built in 1888 by John Kleck, the White Elephant was operated by numerous saloonkeepers until Prohibition went into effect in 1919. At the turn of the century, when the Sunday laws were enacted, Frank Schaper was the proprietor; although it was unlawful to be open for business on Sunday, it was soon common knowledge that while the front doors would be locked, the back doors would be open for customers. (Courtesy of GCHS.)

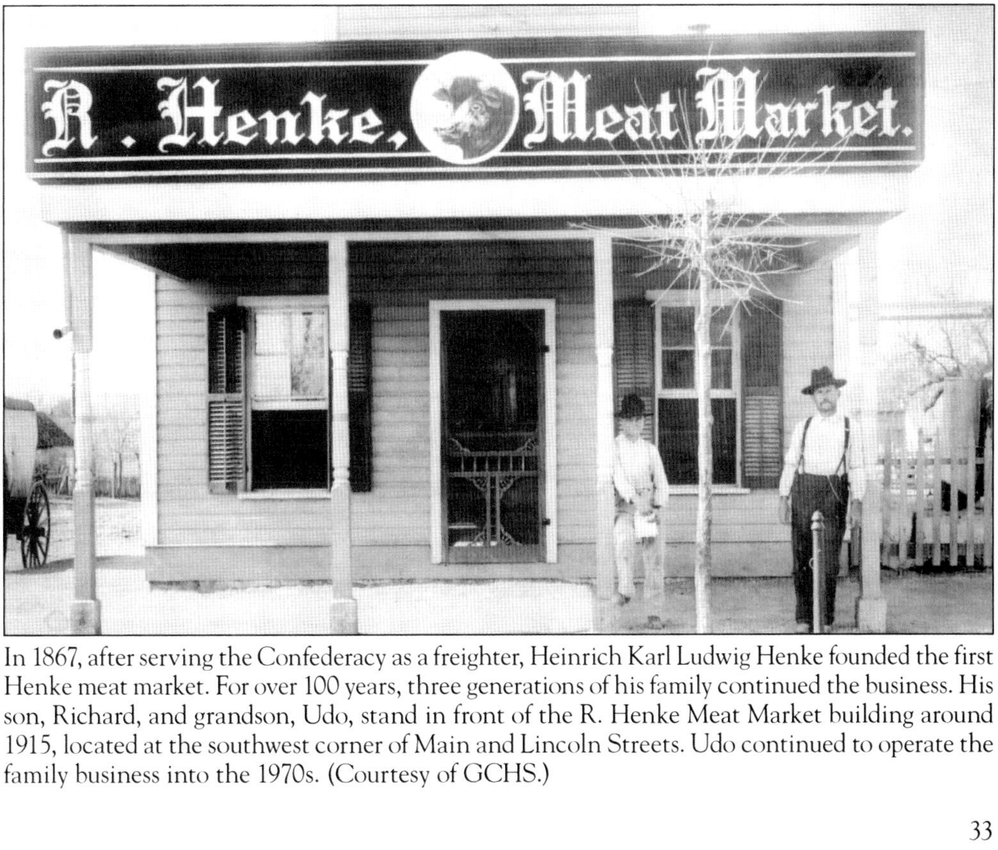

In 1867, after serving the Confederacy as a freighter, Heinrich Karl Ludwig Henke founded the first Henke meat market. For over 100 years, three generations of his family continued the business. His son, Richard, and grandson, Udo, stand in front of the R. Henke Meat Market building around 1915, located at the southwest corner of Main and Lincoln Streets. Udo continued to operate the family business into the 1970s. (Courtesy of GCHS.)

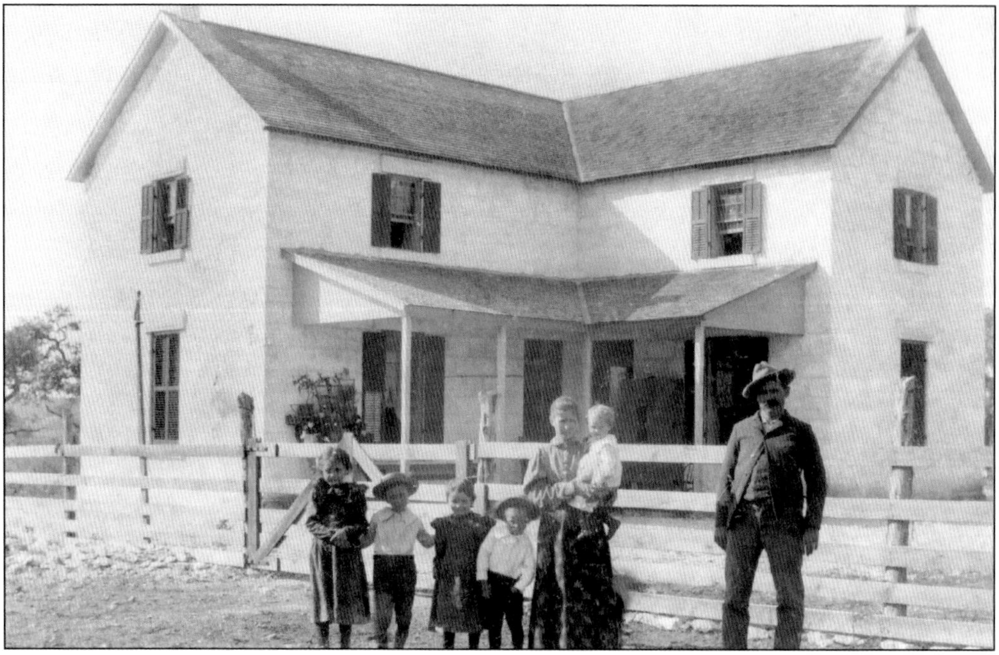

By the 1870s, many families had prospered and substantial homes had been built. Much of their history was preserved for future generations by the traveling photographers of that era. Standing in front of their home in the Wolf Creek community around 1895 are Otto and Emilie Koennecke Henke with their children Olga (later married to Felix Fuhrmann), Edward (later married to Emma Real), Lina, Guenther (later married to Else Jordan), and Gertrude (later married to Eddie Krauskopf). (Courtesy of GCHS.)

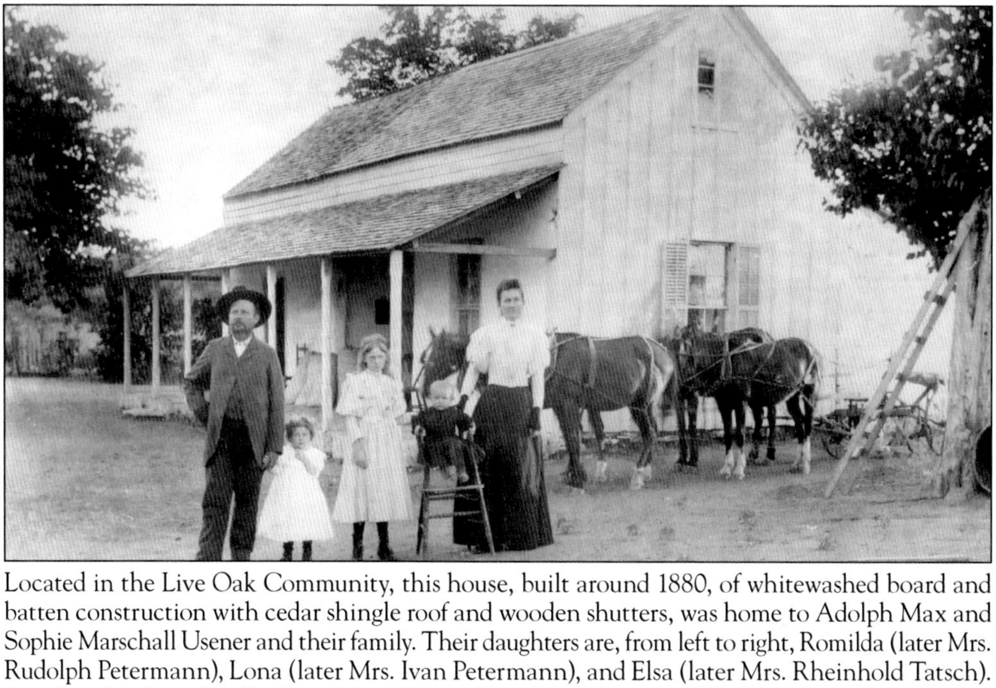

Located in the Live Oak Community, this house, built around 1880, of whitewashed board and batten construction with cedar shingle roof and wooden shutters, was home to Adolph Max and Sophie Marschall Usener and their family. Their daughters are, from left to right, Romilda (later Mrs. Rudolph Petermann), Lona (later Mrs. Ivan Petermann), and Elsa (later Mrs. Rheinhold Tatsch). Another daughter, Estella (later Mrs. Alonzo Lewis), was born in 1898. (Courtesy of GCHS.)

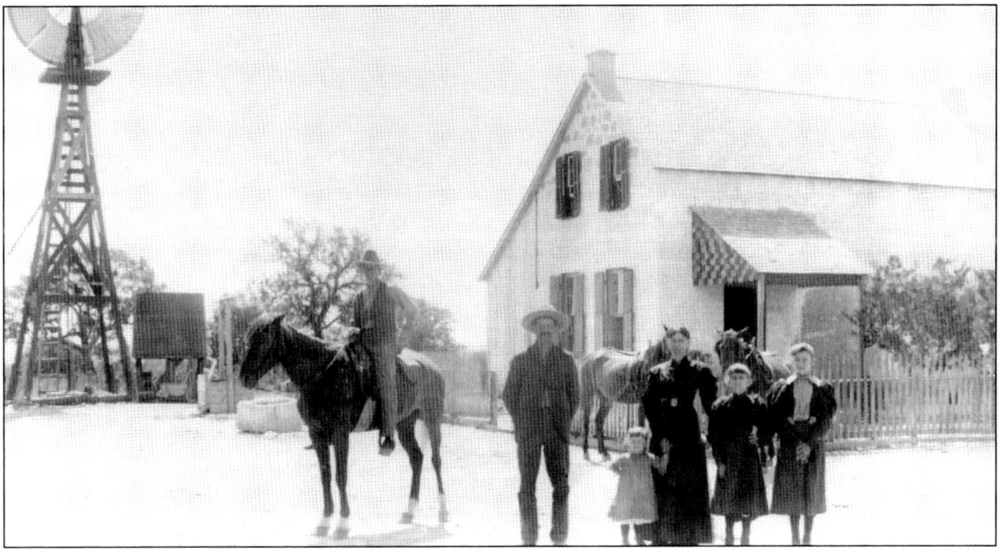

The Ferdinand August and Mathilde Dannenberg Marschall home is located in the Live Oak Community. While the hand-dug well and encasement remains, a c. 1900 modern four-leg wooden tower windmill, its wheel a circle of wood slats, stands nearby; the cypress water tank made the water readily available to the home and livestock. Standing with their parents are, from left to right, Elma (later Mrs. Eddie Jordan), Olga (later Mrs. Otto Zenner), and Bertha (later Mrs. Ernest Zenner). (Courtesy of GCHS.)

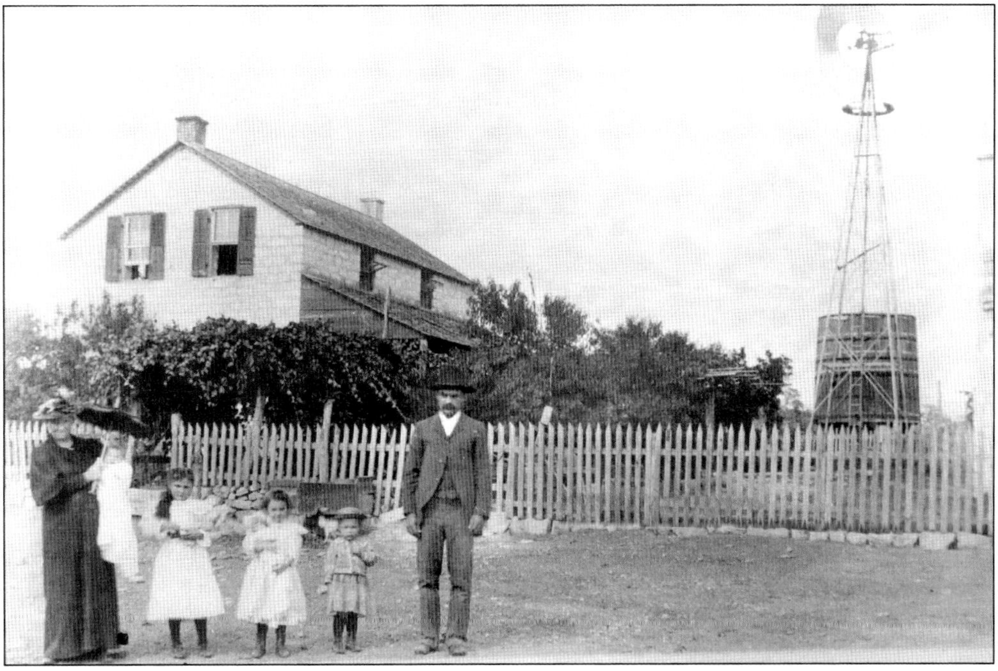

In 1852, Amandus Stehling was deeded land just west of Fredericksburg, built his log home, and was married to Barbara Vogel. In the late 1800s, Amandus worked alongside his son, John, to build a large limestone home that has been occupied by John's family for five generations. Shown in this 1897 photograph are, from left to right, Mary Lewis Stehling holding Richard, Christina, Cecelia, Paul, and John. Born later were Adela and Arthur. (Courtesy of GCHS.)

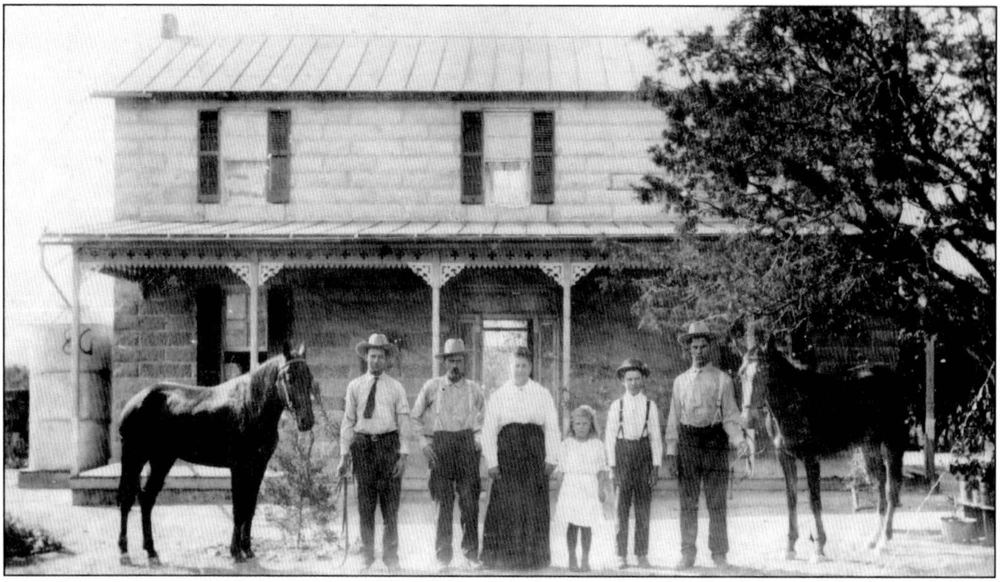

In this c. 1905 photograph, Ernst and Anna Leyendecker Grona stand with their children Henry, Emma, Robert, and Alfred in front of their home, located four miles from Fredericksburg on the Kerrville Highway. The impressive home is built of cut limestone with a standing seam tin roof and is trimmed with intricately cut gingerbread. Census records from 1900 indicate that Ernst was a farmer. (Courtesy of GCHS.)

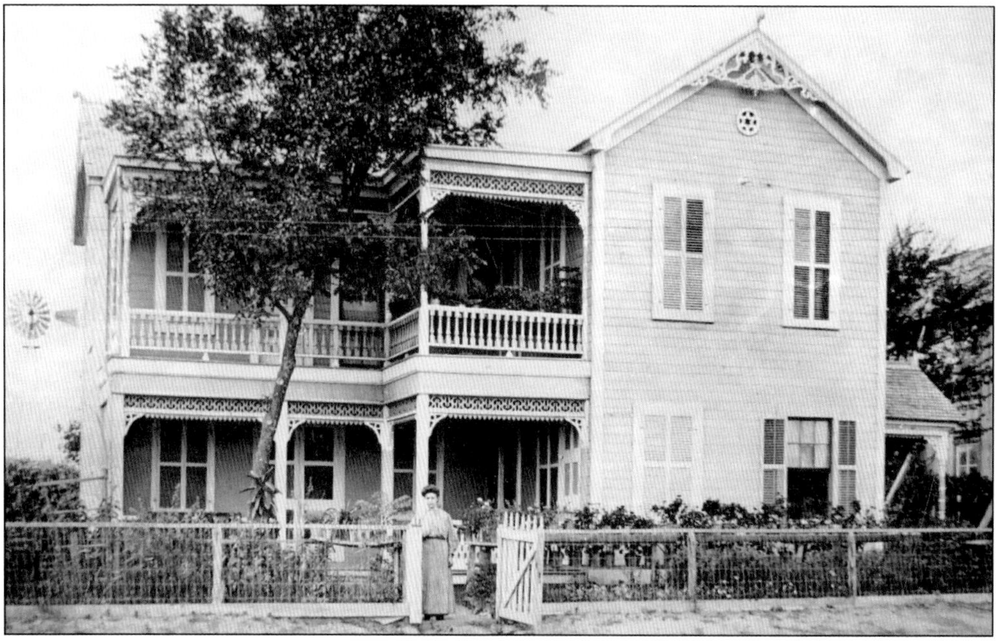

Located at 413 West Creek Street, the Frederick Kuenemann home of original *fachwerk* (half-timbered) design from 1847, with later Victorian additions with embellishments from around 1880, reflects both the meager circumstances endured and the growth to an affluent, socially vigorous life the family achieved by the turn of the century. Frederick's son, Heinrich, organized the Kuenemann Lumber Company in 1883, building the lumber mill, furniture shops, and offices adjacent to and across the street from the home. (Courtesy of GCHS.)

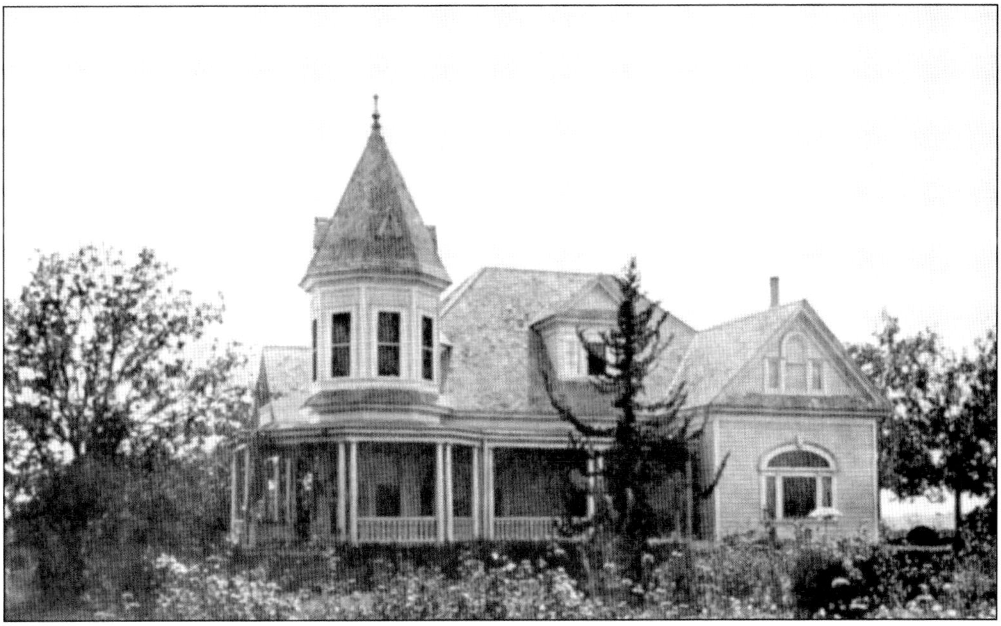

August and Hulda Meckel Zincke's home stood at the far west end of Main Street. The lovely Queen Anne Victorian home, with its turret, curved porches, and expansive gardens, was famed for its elegance. However, following the post–World War II trend of modernization and business expansion, the home was demolished in 1962; many historic Fredericksburg buildings were lost during the 1950s and 1960s. (Courtesy of GCHS.)

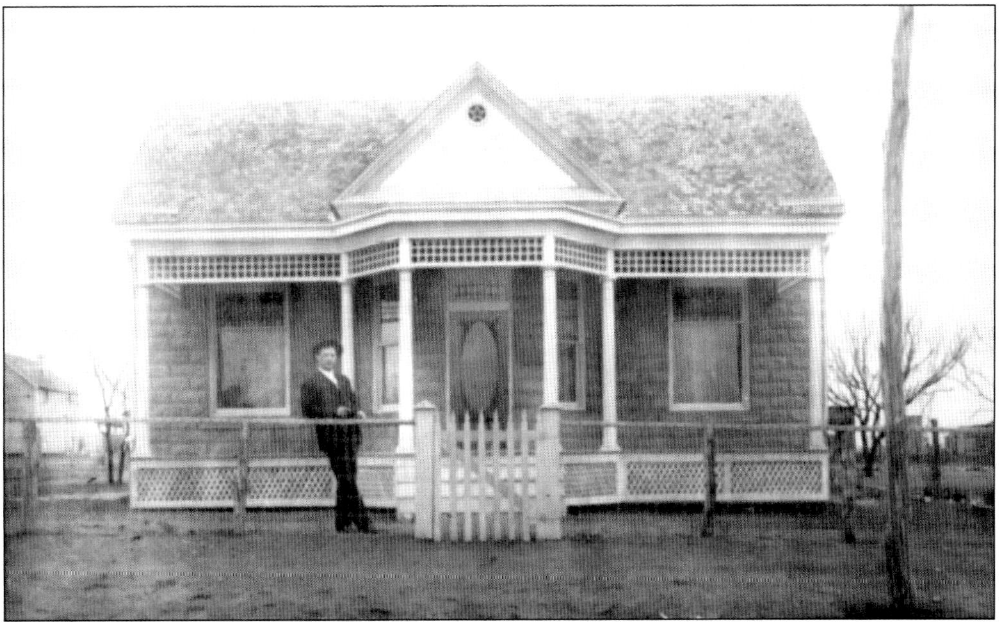

At 21 years of age, Otto Richard Stoffers completed this four-room Roos block home in early 1910 in preparation for his marriage to Minna Pfiester. This prefabricated cement block, developed in Fredericksburg by the Basse brothers to mimic stone, was manufactured locally from the late 1800s to the early 1920s. Blocks produced by the Roos brothers bear a raised mark that resembles a *7* or an *L*, which distinguishes it from Basse block. (Courtesy of Kuenemann Collection.)

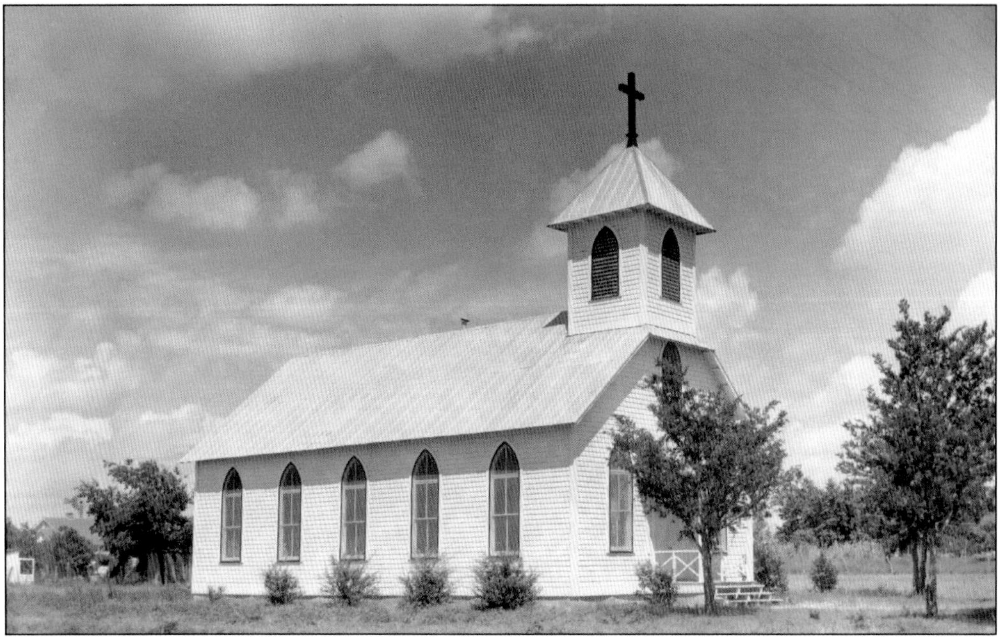

Built in 1919, through the labors and donations of its congregation, Our Lady of Guadalupe Catholic Church continues to serve Spanish-speaking Catholics in the Fredericksburg area. While the early painted windows have been replaced with stained glass and an event hall for meetings and celebrations has been added, the small wooden church continues as a symbol of the community's Spanish heritage. (Courtesy of Dietel Collection.)

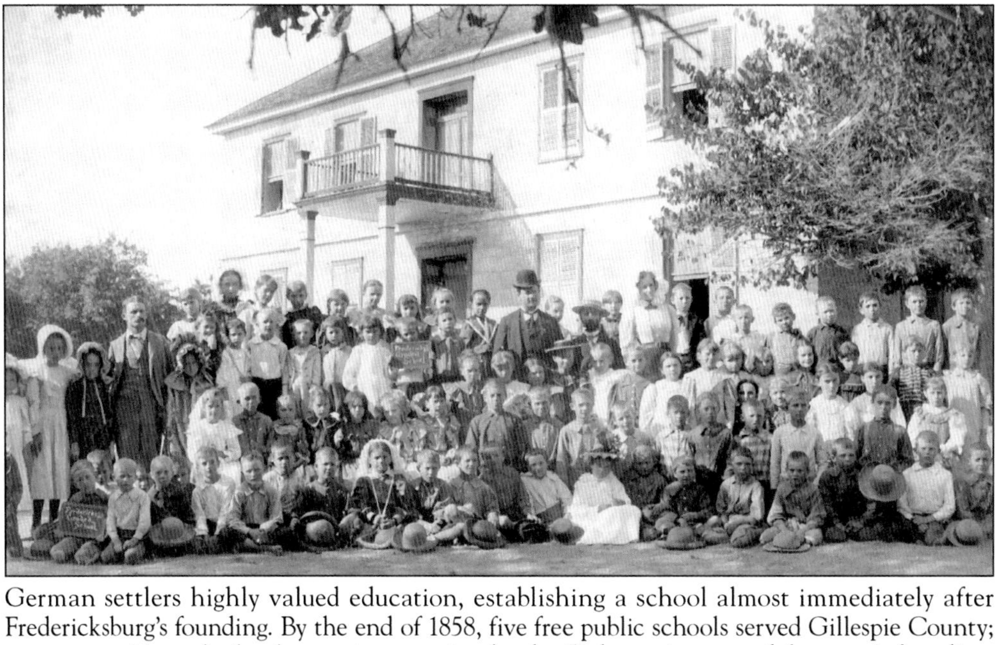

German settlers highly valued education, establishing a school almost immediately after Fredericksburg's founding. By the end of 1858, five free public schools served Gillespie County; as many as 44 rural schools were in operation by the 50th anniversary of the town's founding. Fredericksburg College (building seen here) was founded in 1876 and discontinued in 1884; the building and property were sold to Fredericksburg ISD and remains in use today. (Courtesy of Fisher Collection.)

Three

Horses to Wings

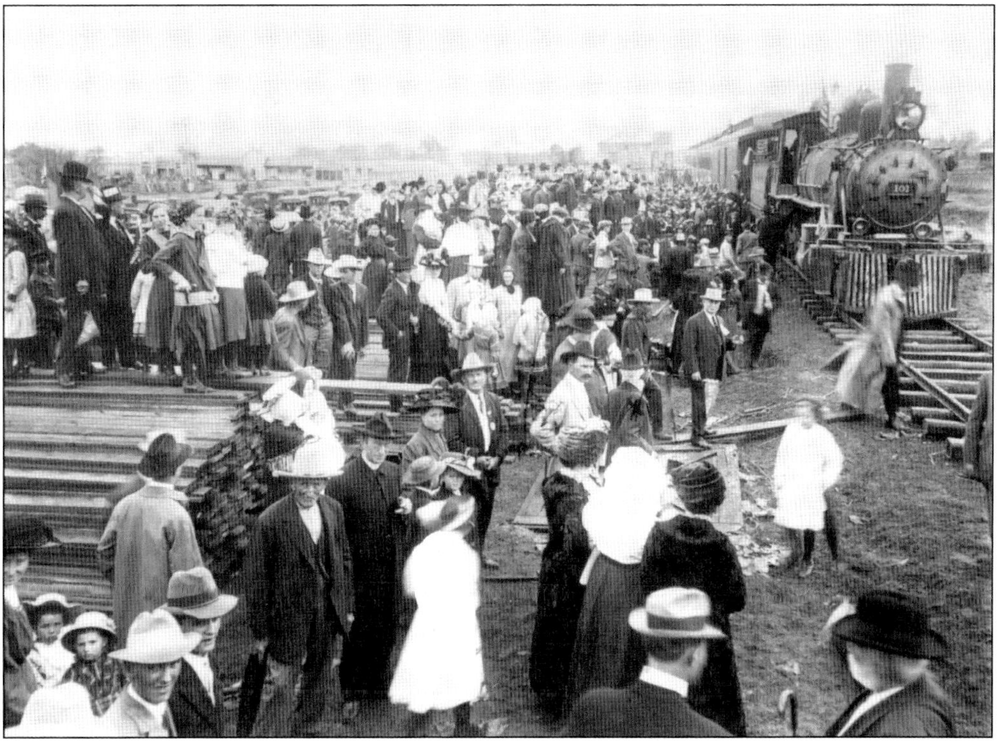

A major factor in Fredericksburg's progress was the construction of the San Antonio, Fredericksburg & Northern Railway. The first train arrived on November 17, 1913, and was welcomed with a three-day celebration that was much diminished by several days of heavy rain. The railroad reorganized as the Fredericksburg and Northern in 1917 and remained in operation until July 25, 1942, when it ceased operations, a victim of improved roads and automobiles. (Courtesy of Bill Teague.)

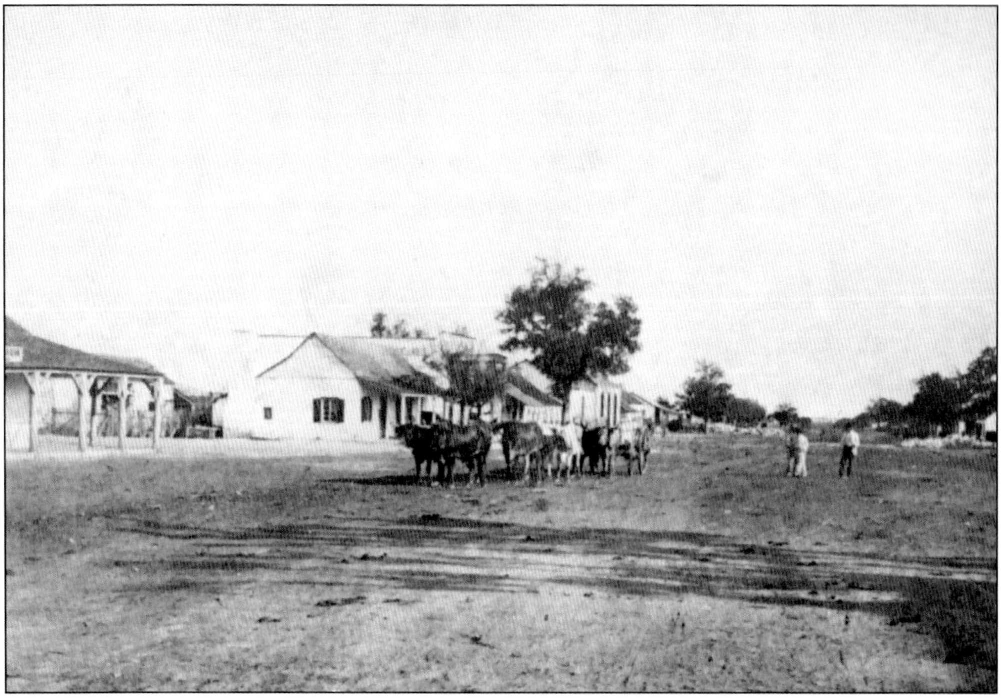

In 1846, surveyor Hermann Wilke laid out the town of Friedrichsburg between Bene Creek (Town Creek) and Baron's Creek. Patterned after German villages, with one long main street paralleling the two creeks, lots were laid out for the immigrants. Hauptstrasse (Main Street) was strategically planned extraordinarily wide to accommodate a team of eight oxen, pulling a wagon of supplies, to make a turnabout (180-degree turn) in the street. (Courtesy of GCHS.)

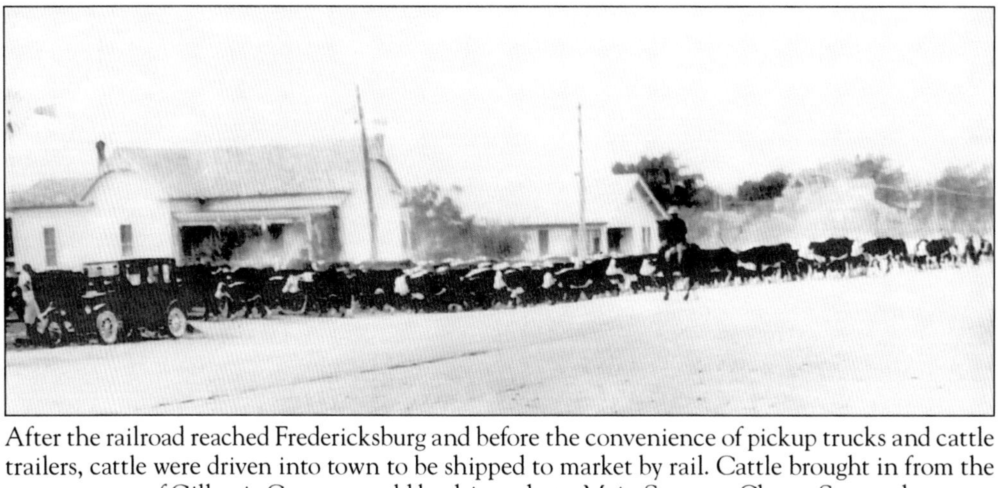

After the railroad reached Fredericksburg and before the convenience of pickup trucks and cattle trailers, cattle were driven into town to be shipped to market by rail. Cattle brought in from the western parts of Gillespie County would be driven down Main Street to Cherry Street, then onto Creek Street to the livestock yards, where they would be loaded onto railroad cars for shipment to market. (Courtesy of Bill Teague.)

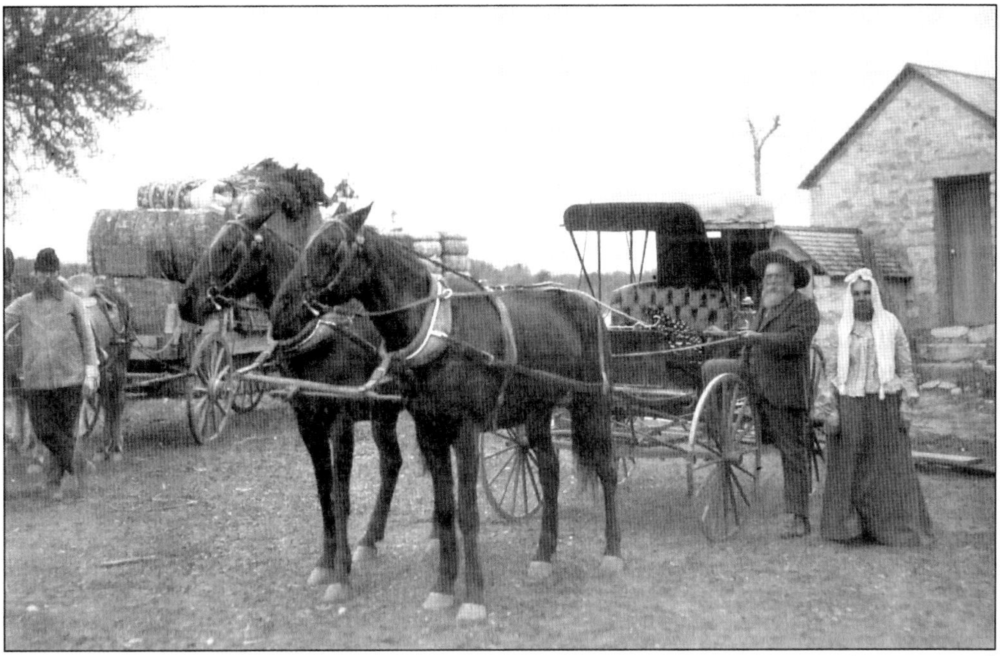

Johann Adam and Katharina Koehler Hahn have prepared for a trip to town from their Stonewall farm around 1904 with a wagon loaded with cotton bales that will be sold in town or freighted to San Antonio markets. Leaving early Saturday morning will allow time to shop for staples and farm supplies, visiting with friends and family, and attending church services on Sunday morning prior to returning home. (Courtesy of Lorine Novian Wallendorf.)

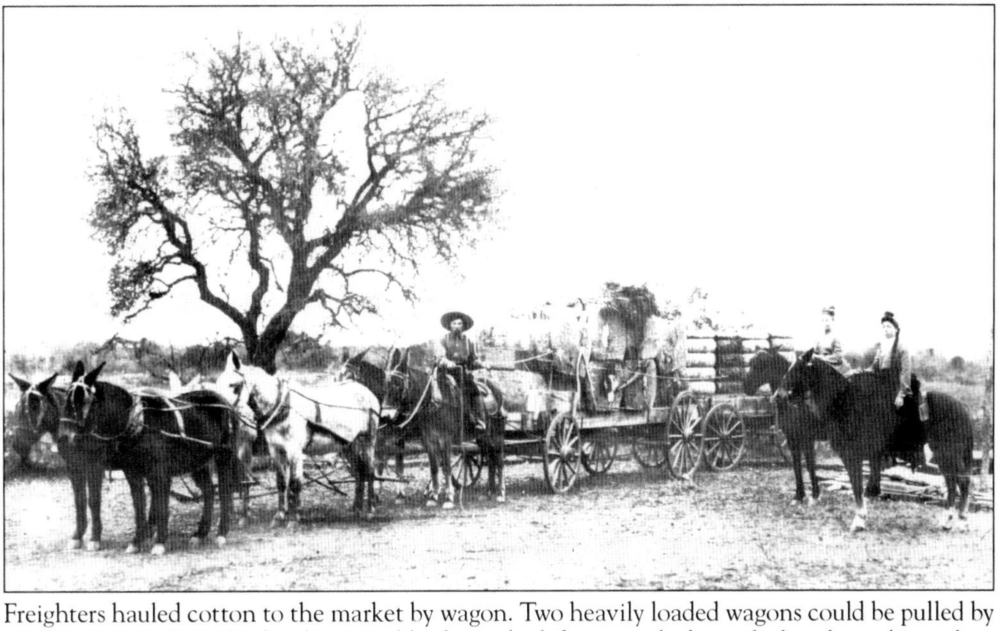

Freighters hauled cotton to the market by wagon. Two heavily loaded wagons could be pulled by a team of six mules. The freighter would ride on the left rear mule, his right hand on a long whip, to guide each mule, his left hand on a rope tied to a brake pole on the wagon. After delivering the cotton, wagons would be loaded with supplies for delivery to local merchants. (Courtesy of Dietel Collection.)

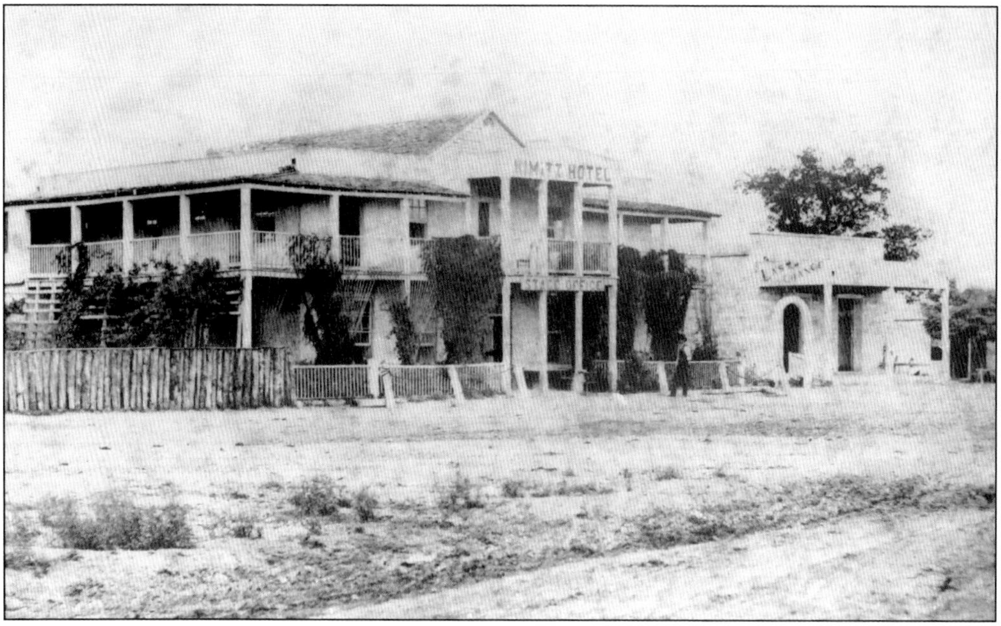

Among the first settlers arriving in Fredericksburg was Charles Henry Nimitz, who soon married Sophia Mueller, and for a period of time they were cooks at Fort Martin Scott. He established the Nimitz Hotel (about 1855); the hotel's original structure was a six-room adobe house. The "superstructure" was added to the hotel in about 1888, modeled after a "Mississippi Dampfer," and became a landmark along the route traveled to El Paso and California. (Courtesy of GCHS.)

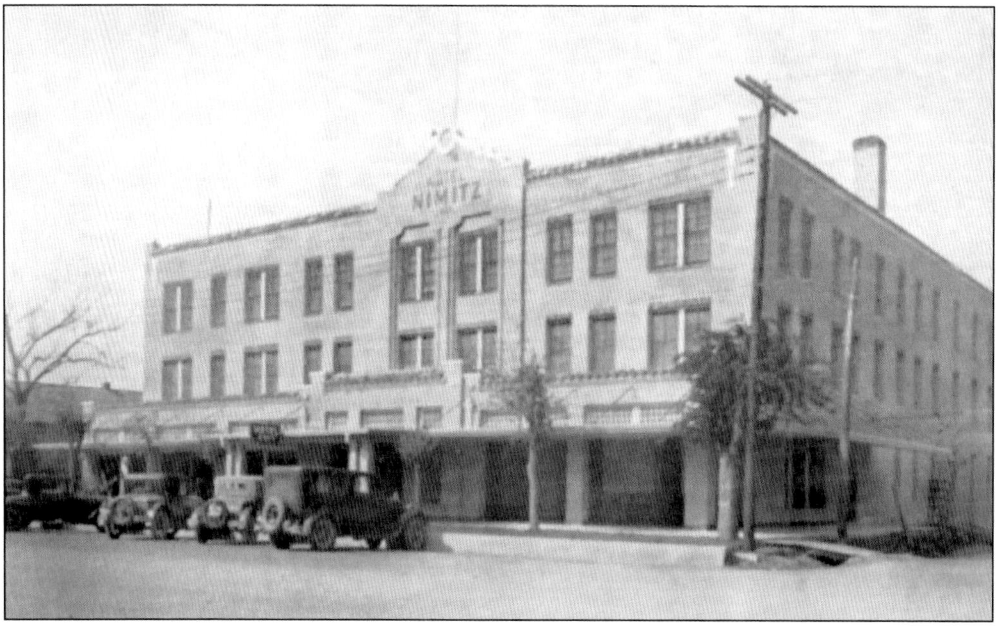

In 1926, the Nimitz Hotel was purchased by 15 local investors and renovated to a more modern architectural style; the hotel continued operation until 1963. In subsequent years, under various state commissions, with funding obtained by the Nimitz Foundation, the museum underwent several renovations including a return to the original steamboat facade. Ownership was transferred to the Texas Historical Commission in 2005. (Courtesy of Rudolph Schnappauf.)

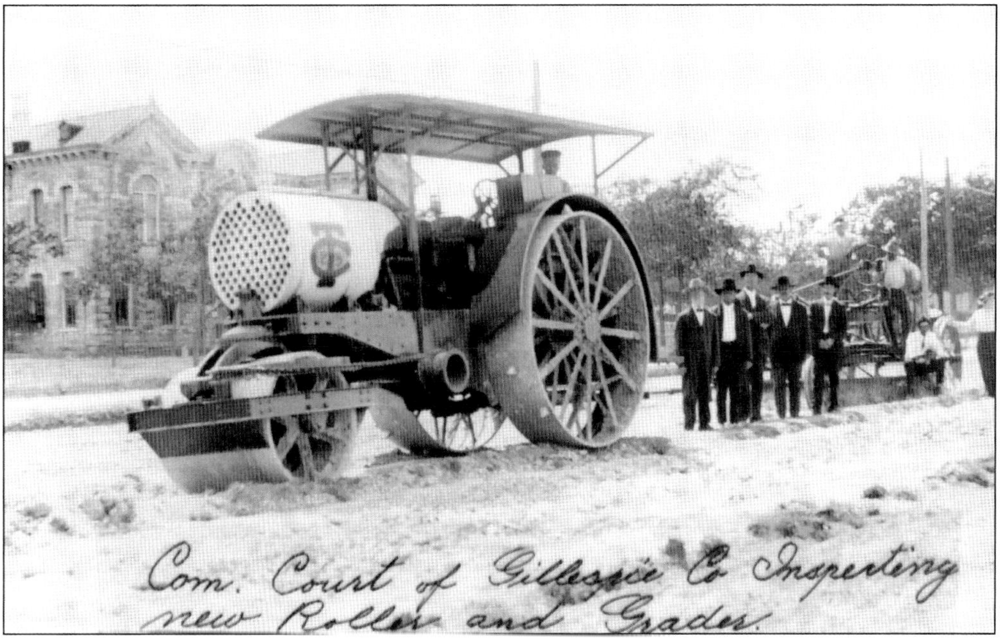

Members of the 1918–1919 Gillespie County Commissioner's Court inspect a new roller and grader that would be used initially to pave Main Street. The roller-packer wheel, attached to the front of the steam-operated tractor, could be filled with water for additional weight. The tractor would pull the grader; the grader operator steered from a standing position as the grader was not equipped with a seat. (Courtesy of GCHS.)

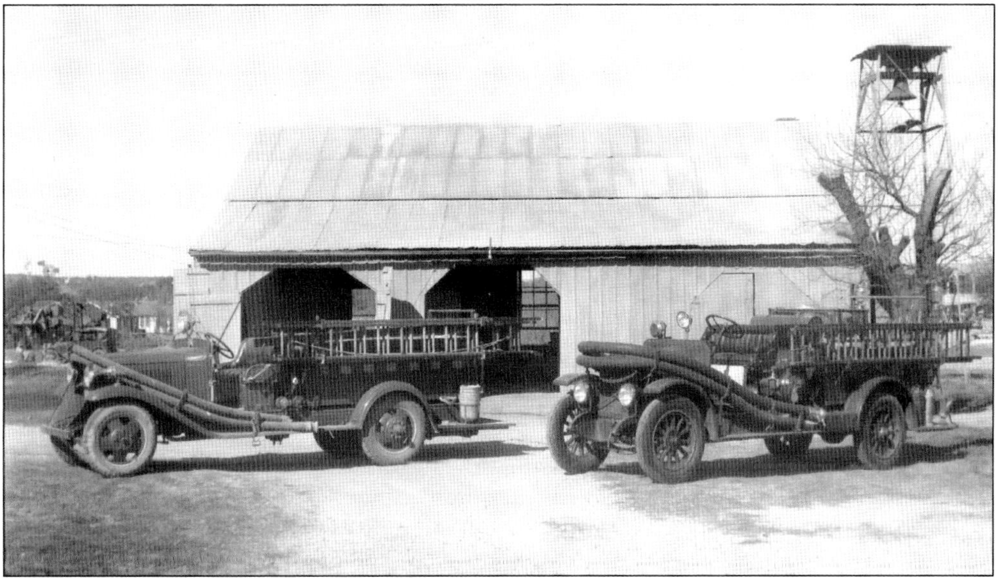

Established in 1883, the Fredericksburg Volunteer Fire Department, along with five rural volunteer fire departments, serves all of Gillespie County. Prior to its current location, the department was located between the county courthouse (now Pioneer Memorial Library) and the old county jail. A bell tower, located behind the building, alerted volunteers to fire calls; two hook and ladder trucks from around the 1920s were part of the department's equipment. (Courtesy of Judy Vordenbaum.)

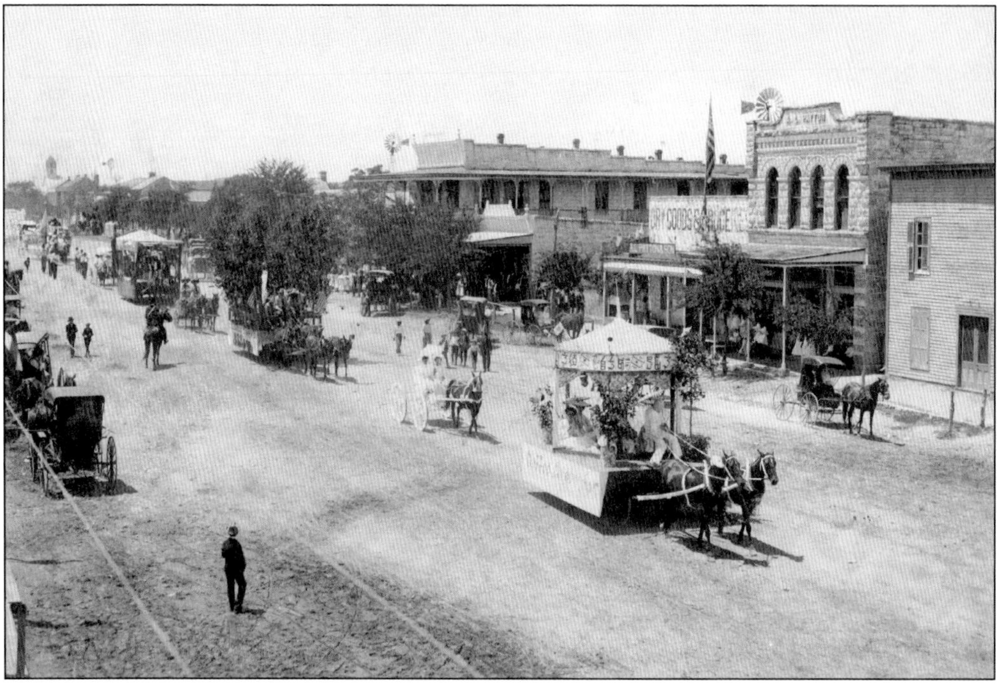

July 4, 1905, is celebrated with a parade of elaborately decorated floats and buggies (shown here) traveling east in the 200 block of West Main Street. Sanborn maps from 1902 show that this block of Main Street had two saloons, a harness shop, the Dietz Hotel, four general stores, a dry goods business, numerous warehouses, two grocery stores, an ice and beer distributor, a bakery, and a grocery store. (Courtesy of GCHS.)

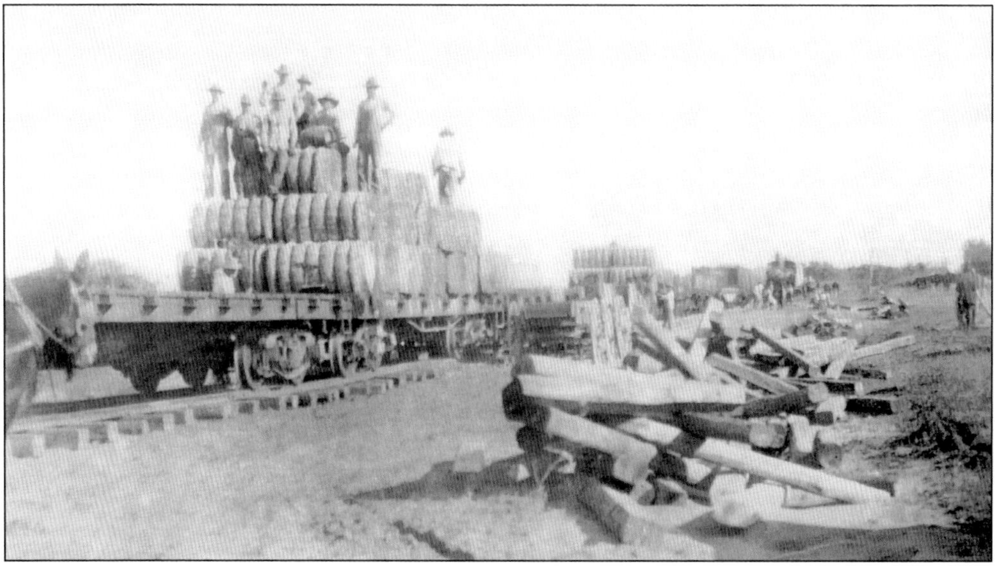

Most communities in Gillespie County had a cotton gin in operation by the turn of the century. Before the railroad came to Fredericksburg in 1913, cotton bales were freighted to San Antonio by wagon. Trips required at least three days, one way, with stops at Comfort and Boerne to rest and water the horses and freighters. Rain, broken wagon spokes, or uncooperative mules could extend the trip to several weeks. (Courtesy of Bill Teague.)

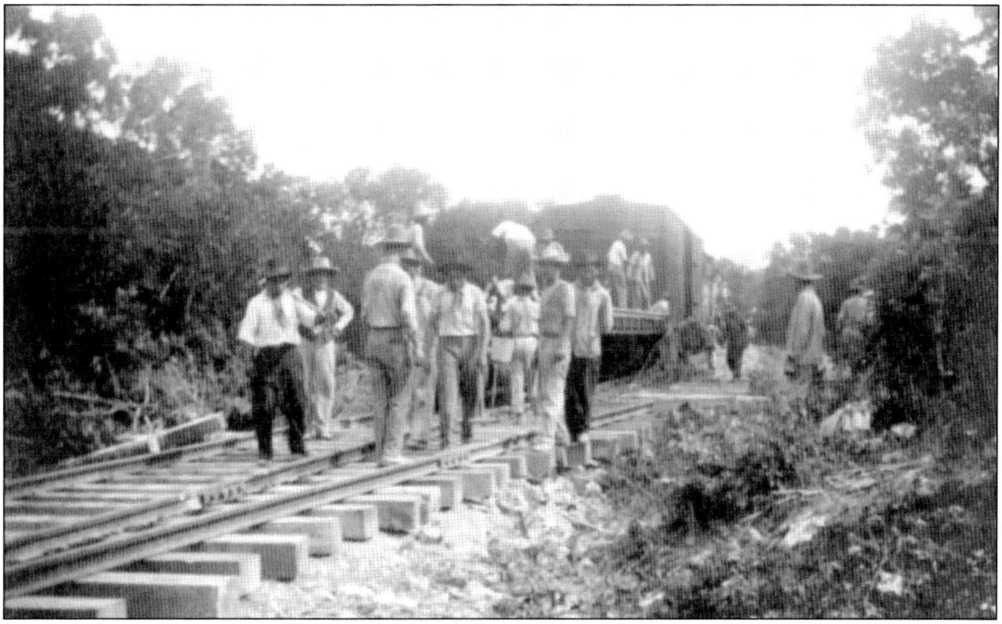

Railroad workers have completed a temporary section of rail line for a loaded boxcar that derailed near Grape Creek. The track to the right is the damaged main line; the boxcar has been moved upright using block and tackle, ropes, jacks and cable, plus the pulling power of a locomotive. The boxcar will be pulled from the temporary rail line back onto the main line. (Courtesy of Kuenemann Collection.)

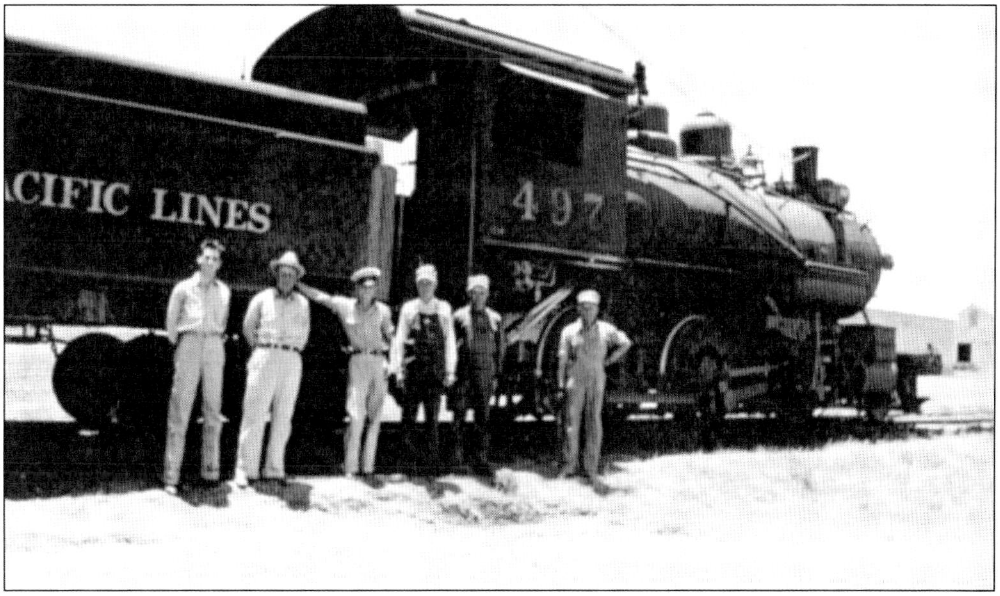

Soon after the railroad had begun runs into Fredericksburg, financial problems brought about by expenses of operating the rail line, bank closures, and the Depression plagued the owners. After World War II started, the rails were dismantled; six carloads of rail were shipped to Australia, where railroads were badly needed. Around the 1930s, the railroad crew includes, from left to right, Olan Price, Bill Teague, Harold Schoenewolf, Franke Goodale, Henry Prochnow, and Ottmar Kaderli. (Courtesy of Bill Teague.)

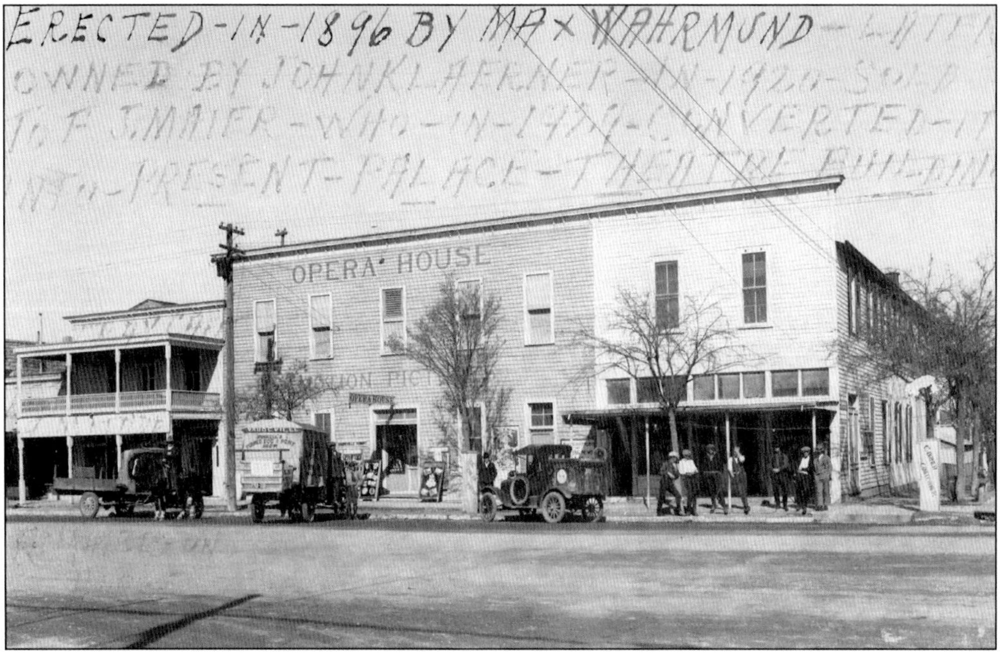

Erected by Max Wahrmund in 1896, and initially operated as Max's Saloon, this frame structure was best known as John Klaerner's Opera House. Beginning as a venue for vaudeville, moving pictures, and local productions, it was later sold to F.J. Maier who, in 1929, converted it into Fredericksburg's first motion picture theater. The Art Deco Palace Theater building is today located where the building on the left is pictured. It no longer serves as a theater. (Courtesy of GCHS.)

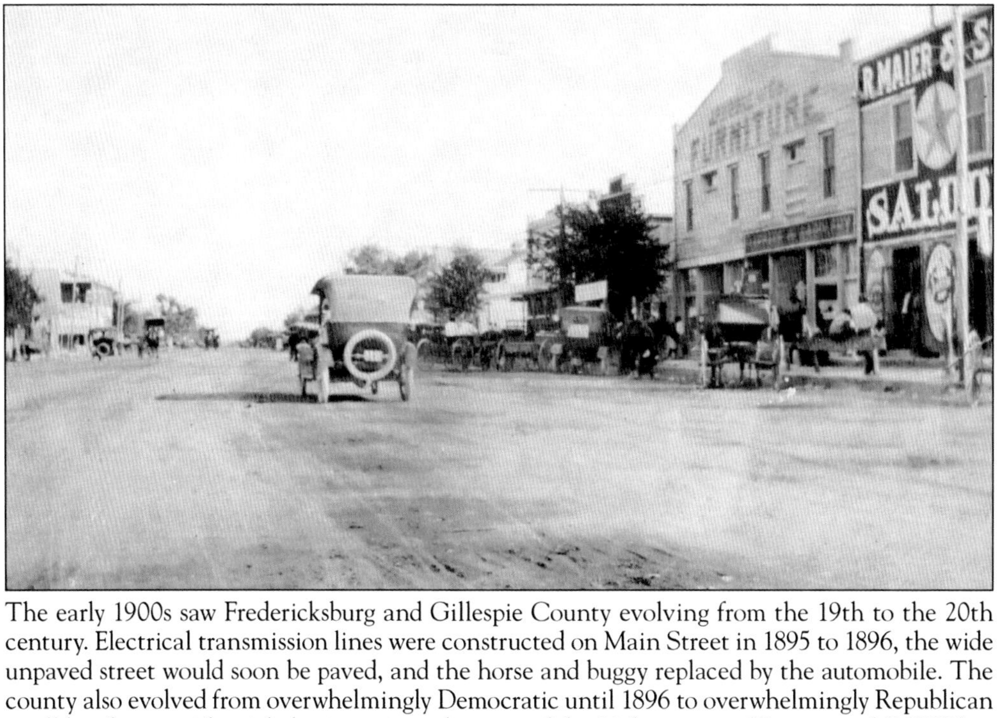

The early 1900s saw Fredericksburg and Gillespie County evolving from the 19th to the 20th century. Electrical transmission lines were constructed on Main Street in 1895 to 1896, the wide unpaved street would soon be paved, and the horse and buggy replaced by the automobile. The county also evolved from overwhelmingly Democratic until 1896 to overwhelmingly Republican in all but four presidential elections since the turn of the 20th century. (Courtesy of GCHS.)

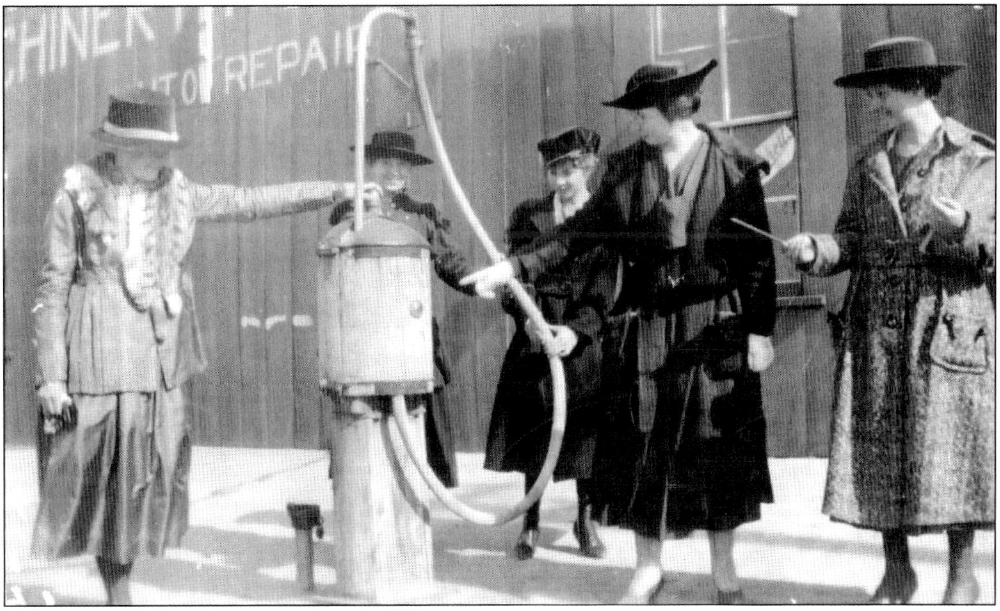

Gasoline was initially stored in overhead tanks that would gravity flow the fuel into vehicles. The first underground gasoline storage tanks with modern pumps were installed in 1918 at the southeast corner of North Adams and East Austin Streets. Wesley Franz owned the building, operating a machinery and auto repair and blacksmith shop; now owned by his descendants, the building remains much the same as it was in 1918. (Courtesy of Bill Teague.)

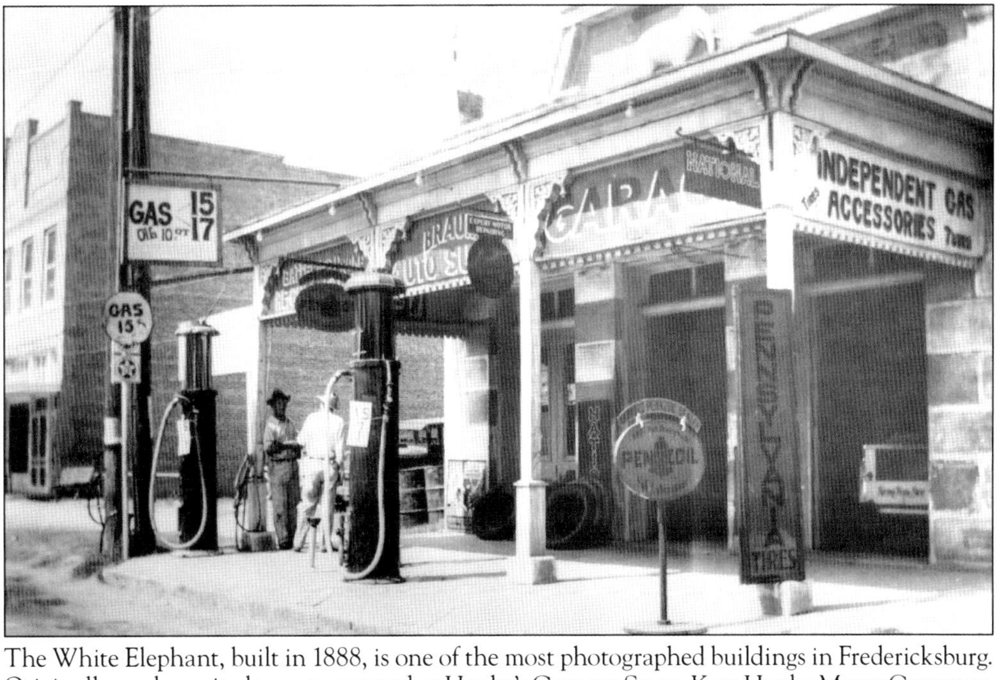

The White Elephant, built in 1888, is one of the most photographed buildings in Fredericksburg. Originally a saloon, it also was operated as Henke's Grocery Store, Kott-Henke Motor Company, Schaefer Tractor and Implement, and (shown here) Brauer Auto Supply and Garage, owned by Gustave "Gus" Brauer around 1950. Gasoline prices displayed are 15¢ for regular and 17¢ for supreme. (Courtesy of GCHS.)

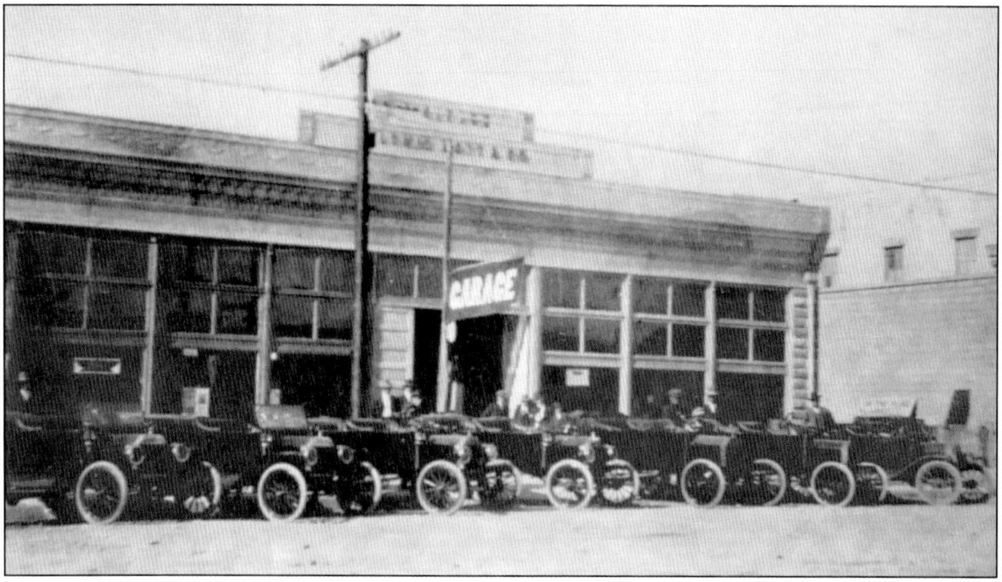

Designed by O'Neil Ford, well-known for his work in San Antonio (Tower of the Americas, La Villita, Trinity University, and UTSA), this 1946 structure is one of the first post–World War II buildings in Fredericksburg. Built by Benno Weiss, the structure was operated as Hill Country Implement Company, the local dealership for International Harvester Farmall tractors and Buick automobiles. (Courtesy of Bill Teague.)

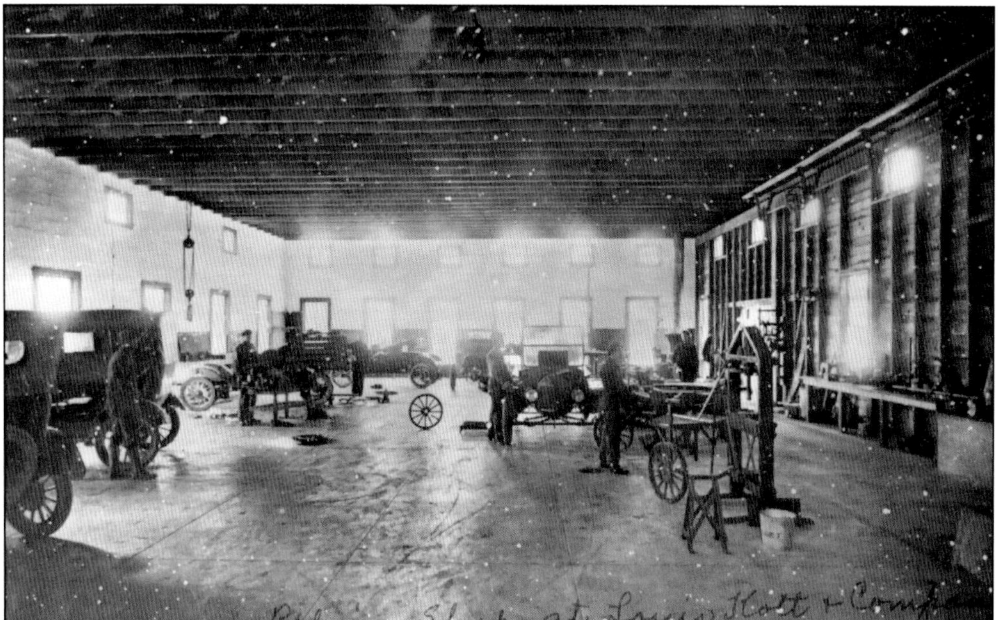

Louis Kott started his business in 1911 in the White Elephant building. In 1914, he built the structure located at 245 East Main Street and moved his business across the street. There, he operated his garage and first authorized Ford sales and service in Gillespie County. In a 1921 advertisement, Louis Kott & Co. publicizes for sale "Ford—the Universal Car," listing the Touring Car for $360, the Runabout for $345, and the Chassis for $325. (Courtesy of Doris Eckert.)

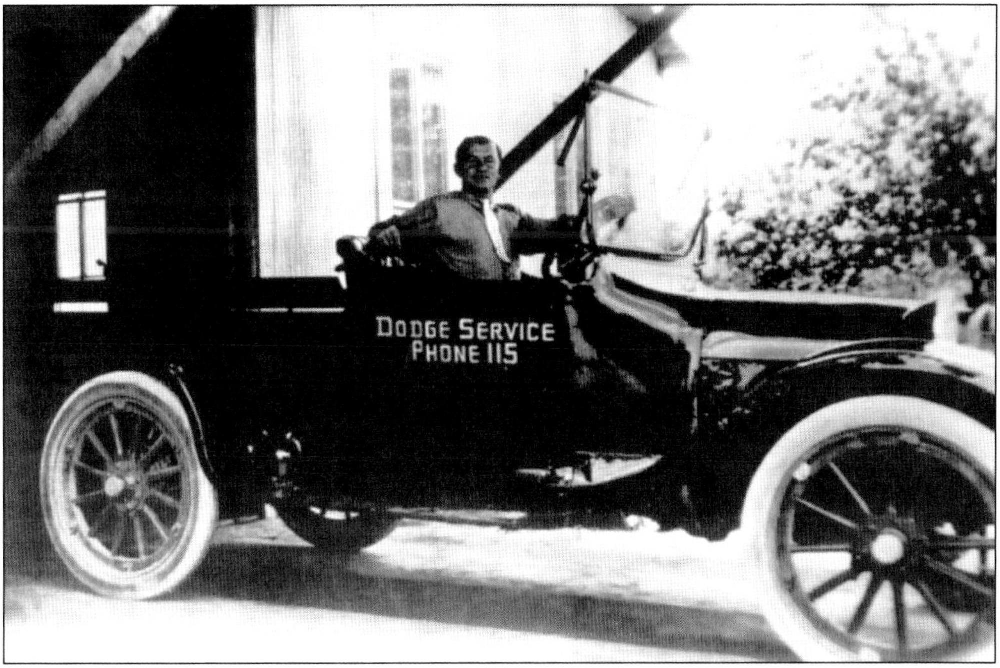

Fritz Joseph and his brother Max emigrated from Germany in 1888; they, along with their parents and seven siblings, were quarantined at Ellis Island before being allowed to move to Texas. They began their business career in Fredericksburg when they opened a blacksmith shop. In 1916, they became dealers for Dodge cars and operated the Joseph Bros. Garage until November 9, 1945, when they sold the business and retired. (Courtesy of Bill Teague.)

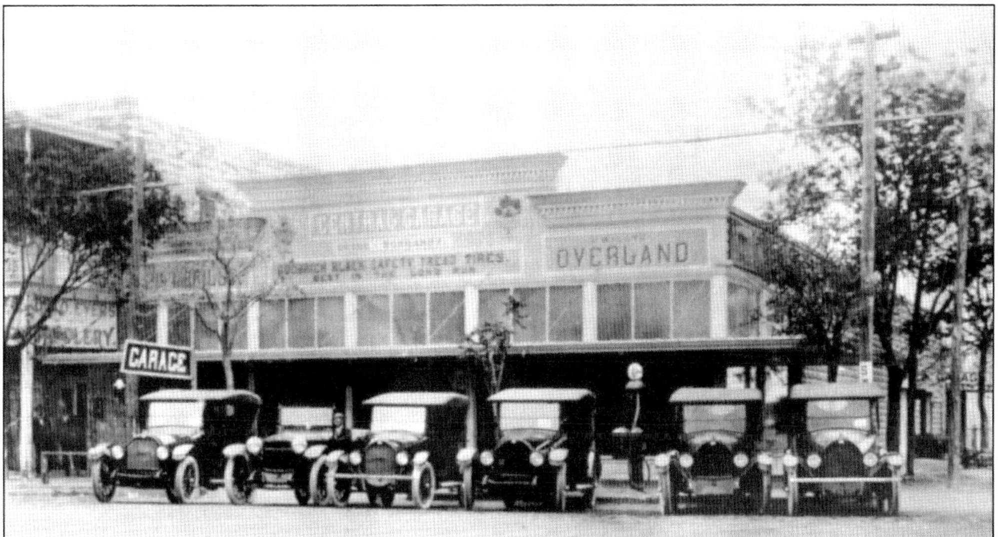

In 1896, Sanborn Fire Insurance Maps describe the Central Garage Building, located at 201 East Main Street, to be of log and stone construction; 1910 maps show the building having the same footprint but modified to stone, most likely a stone facade. Central Garage, an authorized dealer for the Hupmobile, built from 1909 through 1940, and the Overland, built from 1908 to 1926, was one of Fredericksburg's earliest automobile dealerships. (Courtesy of Bill Teague.)

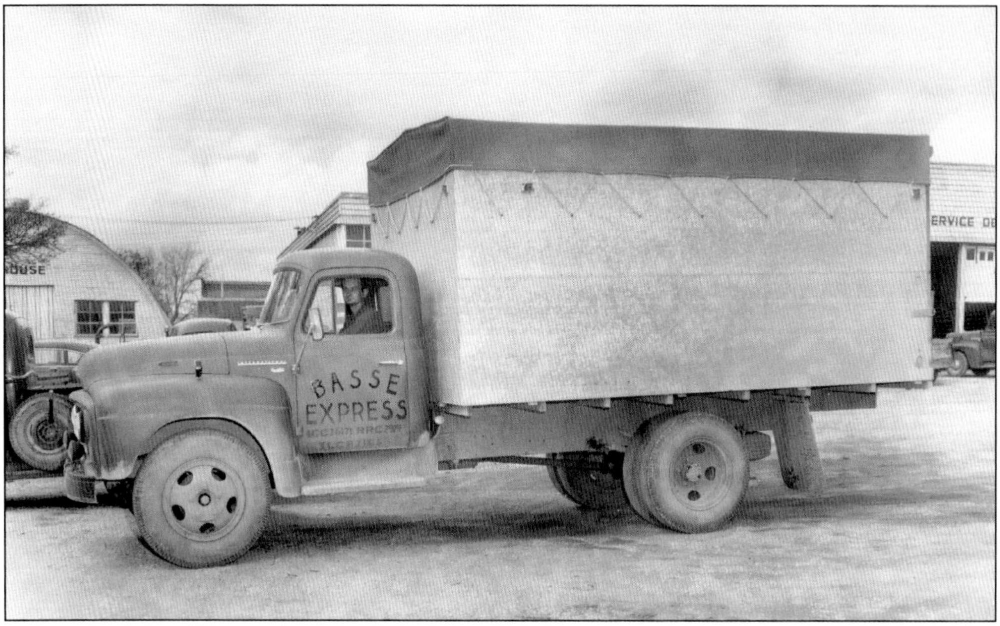

Basse Express and driver Elgin Herbort offered "safe dependable service in a minimum of time" around 1957. The business was started in the 1930s by Alma Hopf Basse, and provided service from San Antonio to Fredericksburg, as well as service to Llano, San Saba, Cherokee, Lampasas, and Lometa. Arrangements for pickup or delivery could be made by calling the local terminal, phone number 109, at 315 East Main Street. (Courtesy of Dietel Collection.)

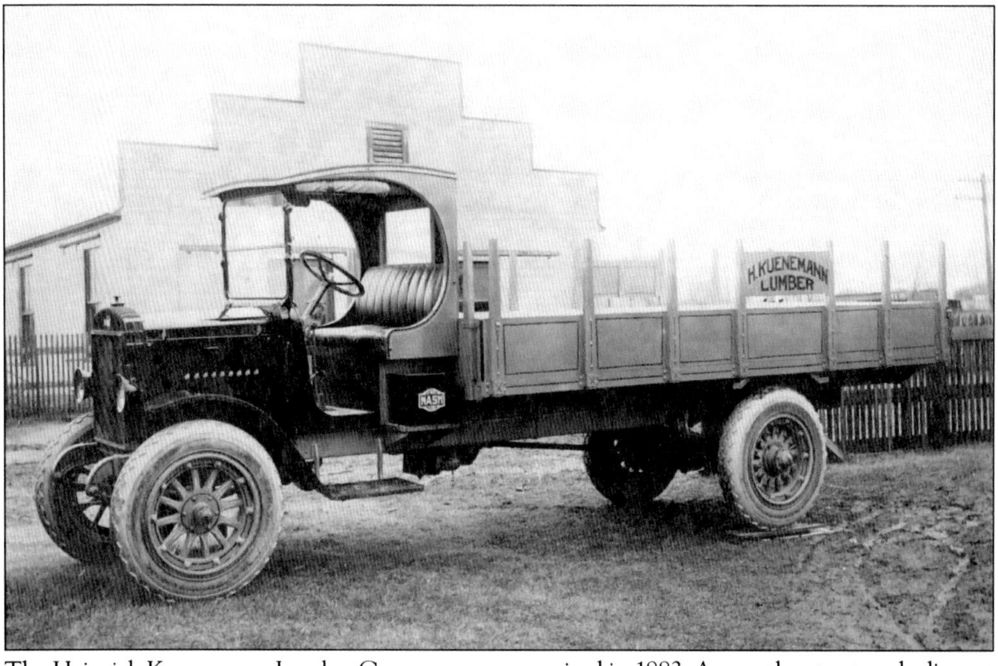

The Heinrich Kuenemann Lumber Company was organized in 1883. Across the street and adjacent to the family's home, Heinrich built the lumber mill, sheds, and lumberyard, a two-story structure housing the furniture shops and offices for the business, as well as homes for six of his children. The complex covered an entire block on Creek Street. (Courtesy of GCHS.)

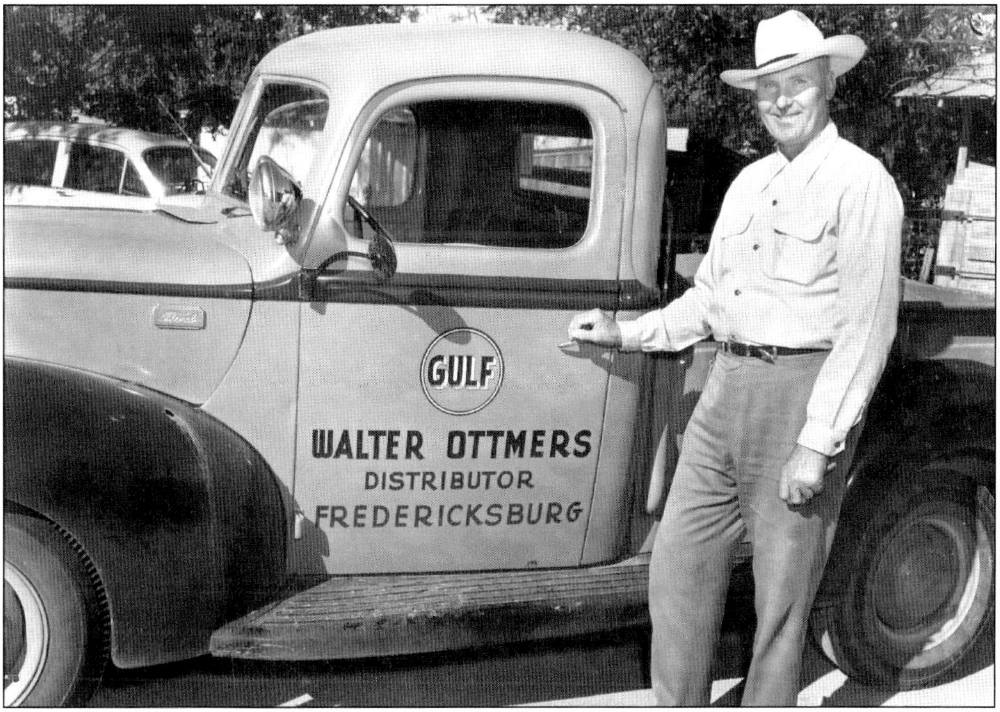

In 1924, Walter Ottmers went to work as a delivery boy for A.W. Stahl, the local consignee of Gulf Oil products. He purchased the business from A.W. Stahl in 1936. Seen here in 1954, Walter hosted a barbecue supper "stag party" on his 30th anniversary with the company and in appreciation for his 30 dealers. Walter retired from Gulf Oil in 1965. (Courtesy of Dietel Collection.)

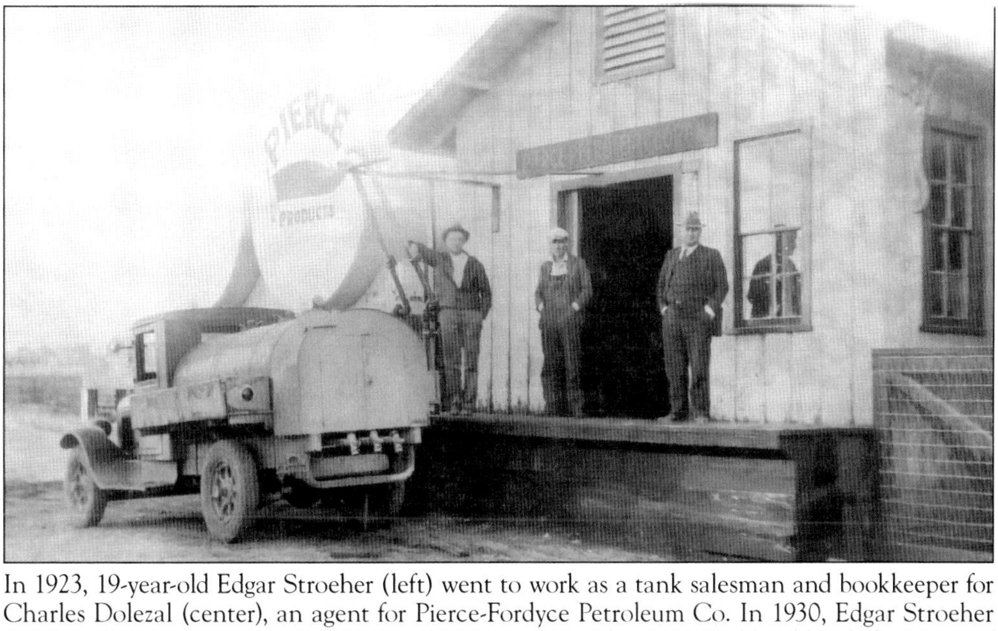

In 1923, 19-year-old Edgar Stroeher (left) went to work as a tank salesman and bookkeeper for Charles Dolezal (center), an agent for Pierce-Fordyce Petroleum Co. In 1930, Edgar Stroeher purchased the agency, then Pierce Petroleum Company, from Reinhold Eckhardt for a sum of $1,000. It later became known as Stroeher and Houy and continues operation today as Stroeher and Son, Inc. (Courtesy of Roy Stroeher.)

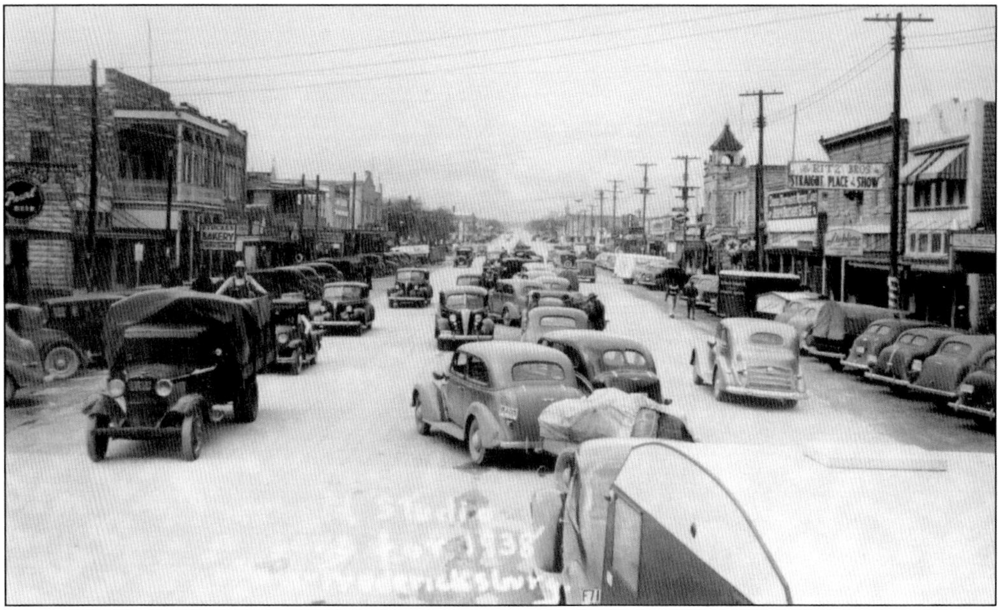

Hunting season has long been one of the busiest times of the year for Gillespie County merchants. In 1938, a view of downtown Fredericksburg from the 100 block of Main at Llano Streets looking west shows all parking spaces filled. Until the 1950s, the overflow of vehicles parked down the center of Main Street; traffic negotiated the lanes past cars, trucks, campers, and trailers loaded with camping gear. (Courtesy of Bill Teague.)

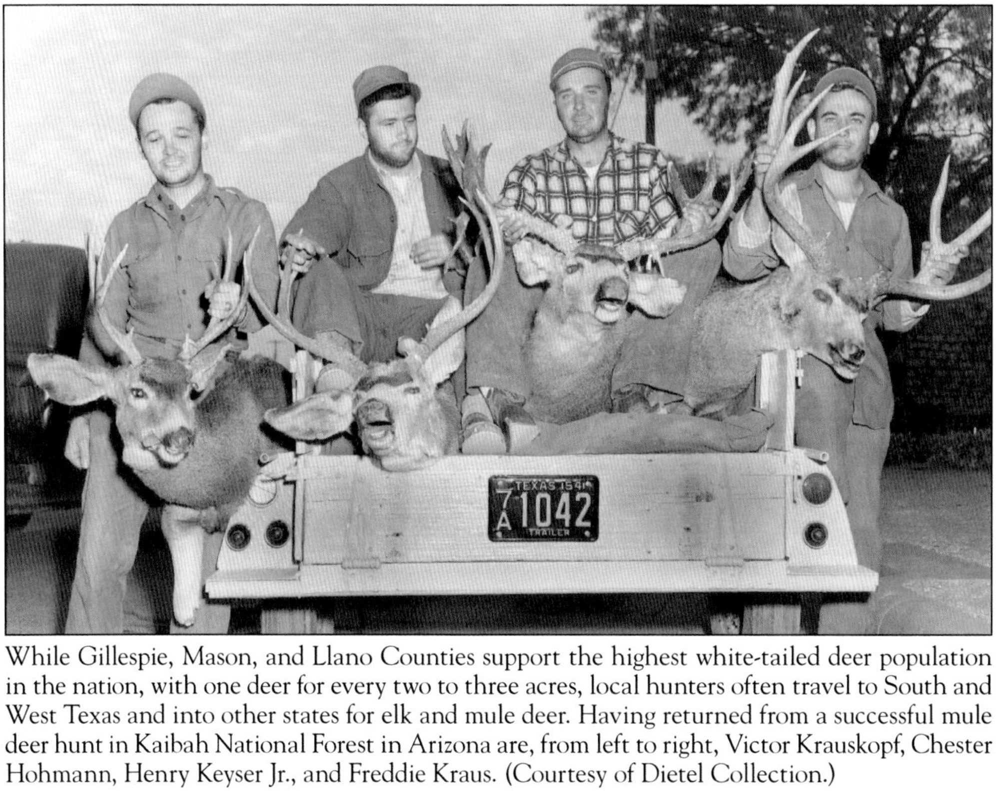

While Gillespie, Mason, and Llano Counties support the highest white-tailed deer population in the nation, with one deer for every two to three acres, local hunters often travel to South and West Texas and into other states for elk and mule deer. Having returned from a successful mule deer hunt in Kaibah National Forest in Arizona are, from left to right, Victor Krauskopf, Chester Hohmann, Henry Keyser Jr., and Freddie Kraus. (Courtesy of Dietel Collection.)

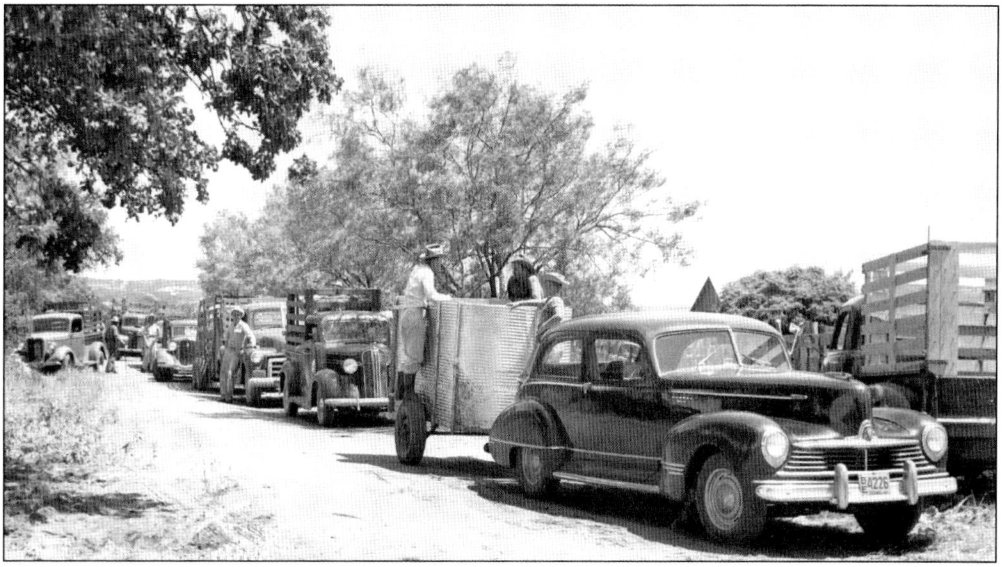

Since the earliest years of Fredericksburg's existence, livestock has been of major importance to the community and its economy. In 1847, cattle were driven from Fayette County to supply the immigrants with much-needed meat. In 1957, local ranchers are lined up to sell cattle, sheep, and goats at Gillespie Livestock, then owned by Gordon Geistweidt, Dan Hoerster, Walter Wallendorf, and Ernest Geistweidt. (Courtesy of Dietel Collection.)

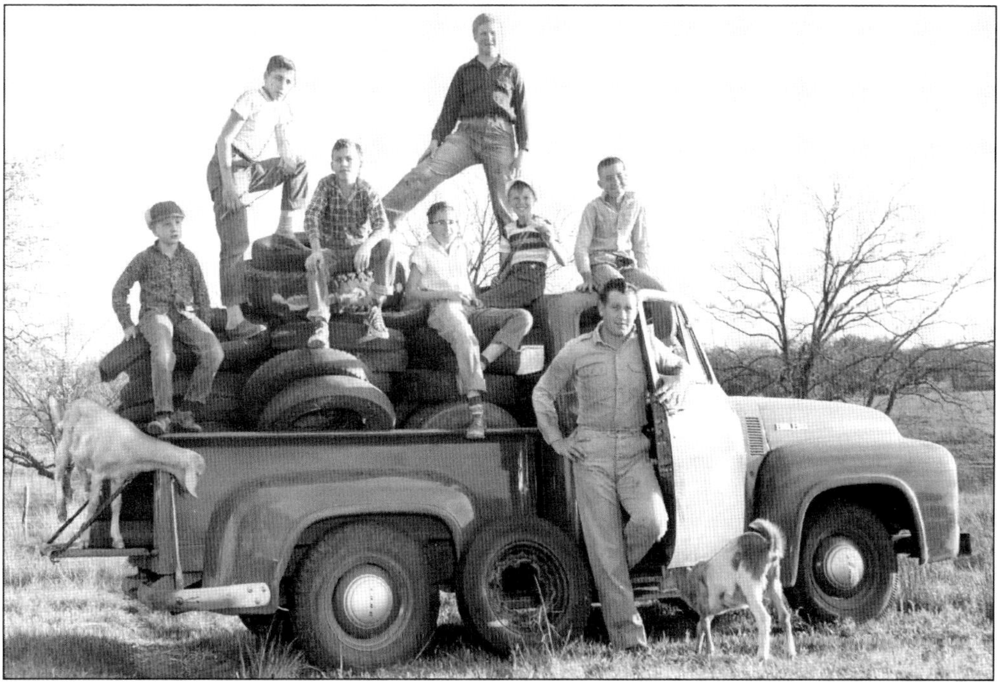

The annual Easter Fires Pageant was a reenactment of the 1847 peace treaty between the German colonists and Comanche Indians. As part of the event, Boy Scouts, with Scout leader R.L. Frantzen (standing at pickup door), prepare to build the fires that would be ignited during the program. From left to right are (seated) Bruce Wittig, Kermit Boos, Buford Durst, Spriggles Enderlin, Lester Frantzen, and (standing) Kermit Gold and Arthur Wittig Jr. (Courtesy of Dietel Collection.)

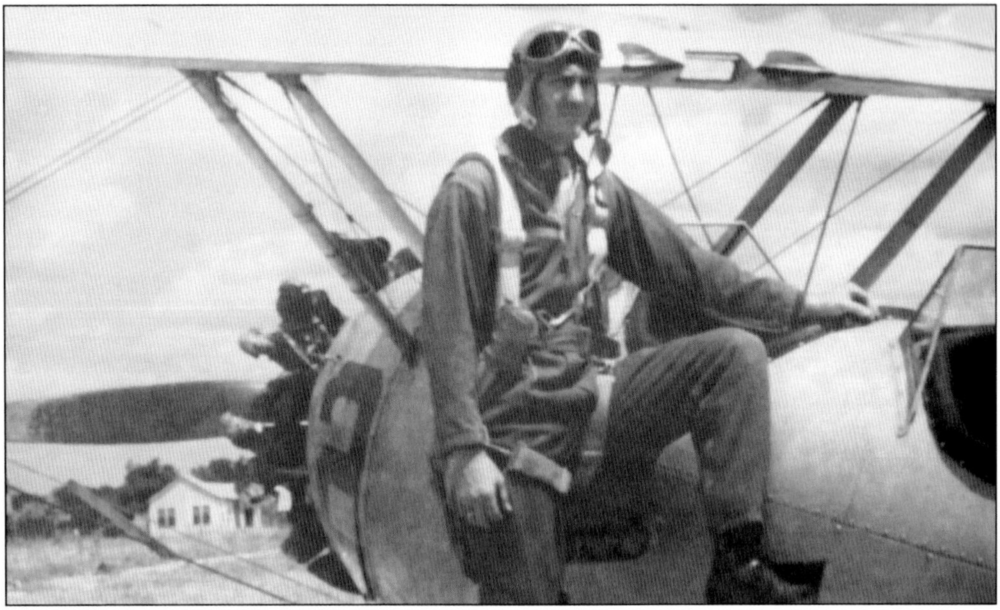

During World War II, Hans Hannemann was responsible for instructing Naval cadets in basic flight training in Kerrville. In 1948, he and William "Red" Schroeder were instrumental in securing property for the Gillespie County Airport and Oak Crest Park (Lady Bird Johnson Park). Hans continued to be involved in each aspect of the airport expansion, considering it a vital part of economic development for the area. (Courtesy of Dorthy Hannemann.)

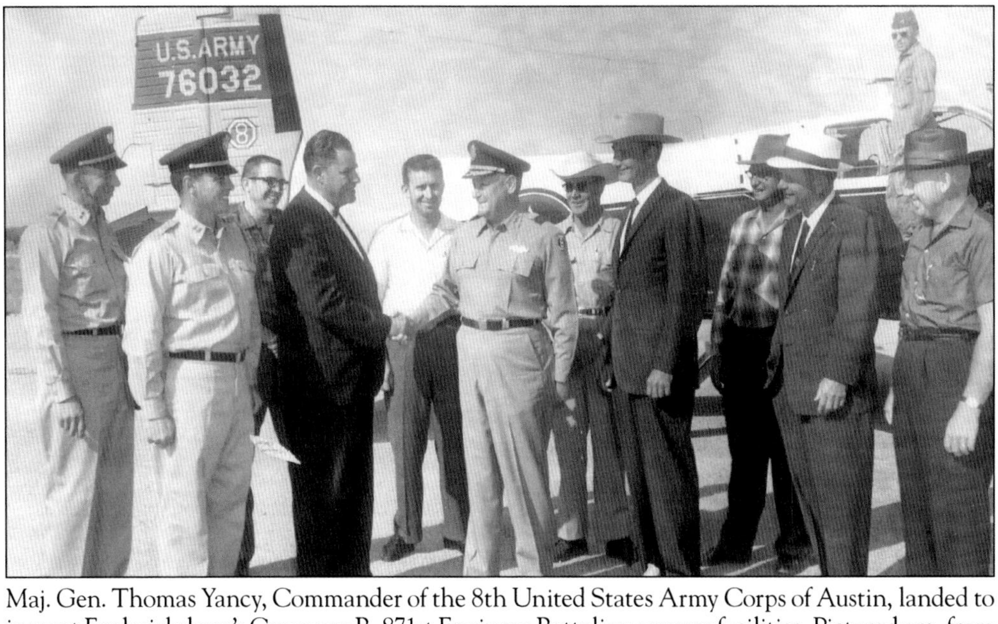

Maj. Gen. Thomas Yancy, Commander of the 8th United States Army Corps of Austin, landed to inspect Fredericksburg's Company B, 871st Engineer Battalion armory facilities. Pictured are, from left to right, Warrant Officer Leonard Lott (local reserve unit head), Capt. Alton Oehler (local reserve unit head), Jerry Follis (chamber of commerce) Mayor Sidney Henke, Hilmar Weinheimer Jr. (chamber of commerce), Maj. Gen. Yancy, City Commissioner Gilbert Kaderli, County Judge Victor Sagebiel, County Commissioner Levi Rosenbusch, Allen Keller (contractor), and County Commissioner Marvin Roos. (Courtesy of Dietel Collection.)

Four

HOME AND FAMILY

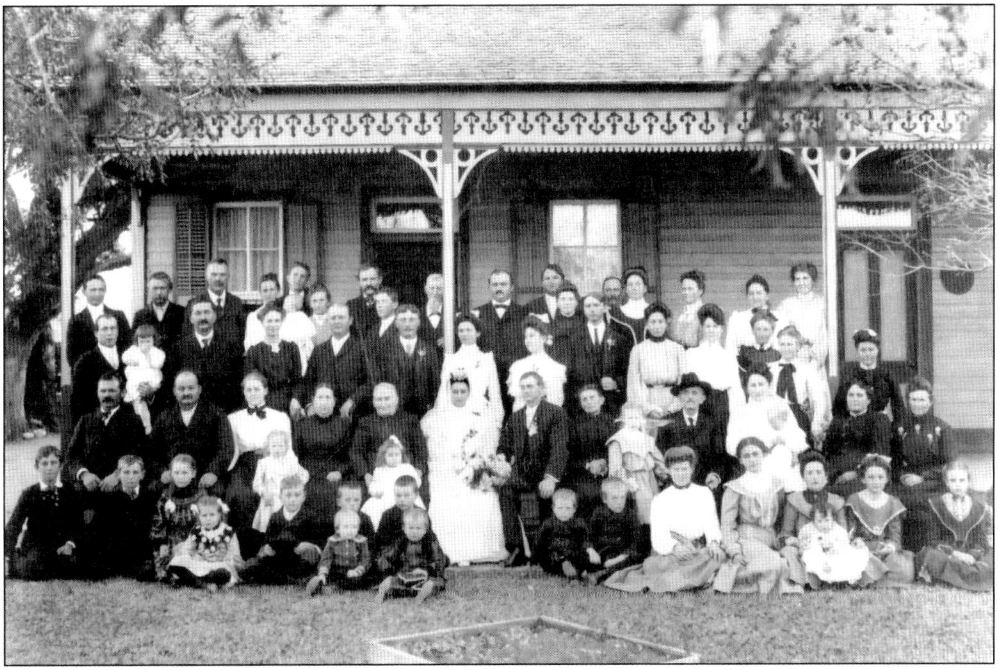

The newlyweds, Felix Reinbach and Elisa Henke, and their guests pose for a wedding photograph on November 22, 1904. Elisa was an aunt to future Adm. Chester Nimitz. The future admiral's mother is the third woman to left of the bride and wearing a large bow. The photograph was taken at the admiral's grandparents' house, the Heinrich Henke home. (Courtesy of GCHS.)

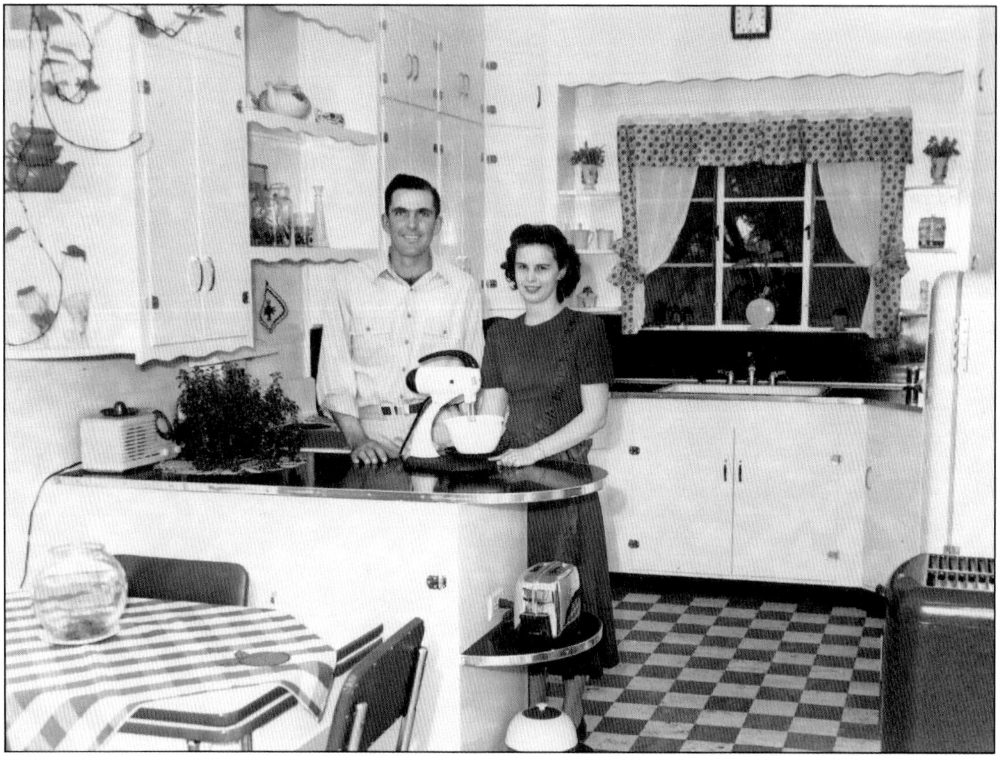

Calvin and Irene Jenschke Weinheimer stand in their 1950 kitchen, typical of postwar style, with a chrome dinette set, Formica tabletops and countertops, linoleum in bold geometric patterns, and floral patterns often with cherries or apple prints in tablecloths and curtains. The modern electric Mixmaster replaced manual labor. Weinheimer bought the property including the 1917 house when he and Irene were married in 1949. (Courtesy of Dietel Collection.)

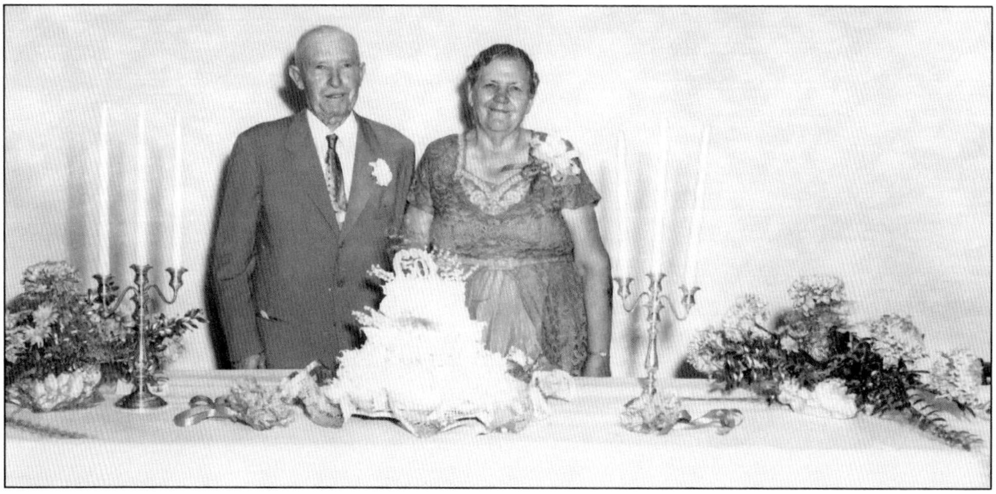

Edward and Olivia Roos celebrated their golden wedding anniversary with an impressive church service and reception with their six children. They were married on September 28, 1905, in the home of her parents, George and Emma Ottmers, and farmed in the Crabapple and Palo Alto communities. He was the son of Fritz and Martha Roos. In addition to farming, Edward was a carpenter and in 1919 started Roos Cement Yard. (Courtesy of Dietel Collection.)

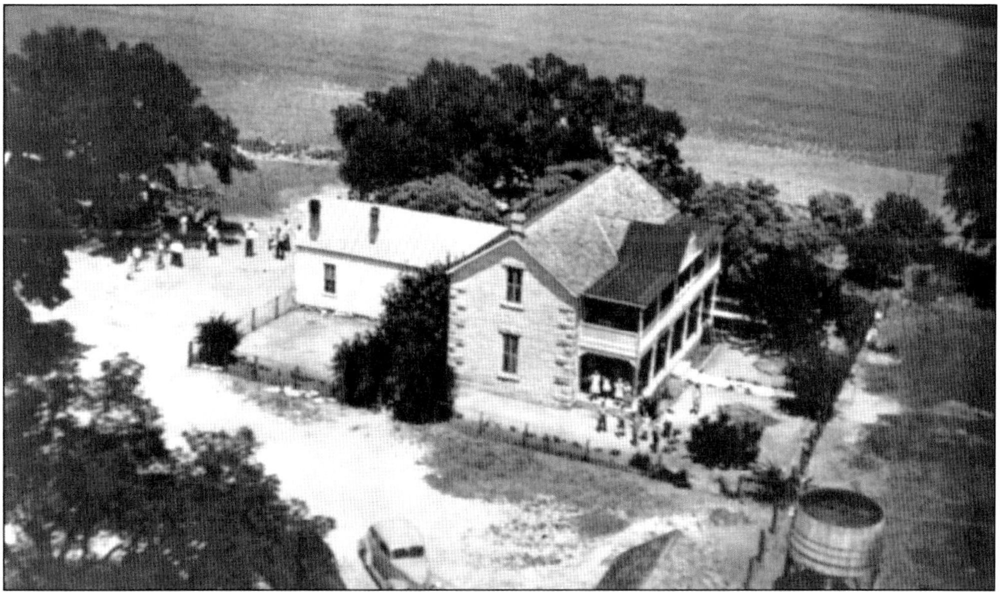

Families gathered to celebrate wedding anniversaries at home. In May 1946, Hugo and Anna Gold Crenwelge celebrated their 50th wedding anniversary at their residence, built in 1916. Festivities included a meal and reception for the family and friends of the Willow City community. Outdoor games were enjoyed by the family's youngsters. (Courtesy of Linda Langerhans.)

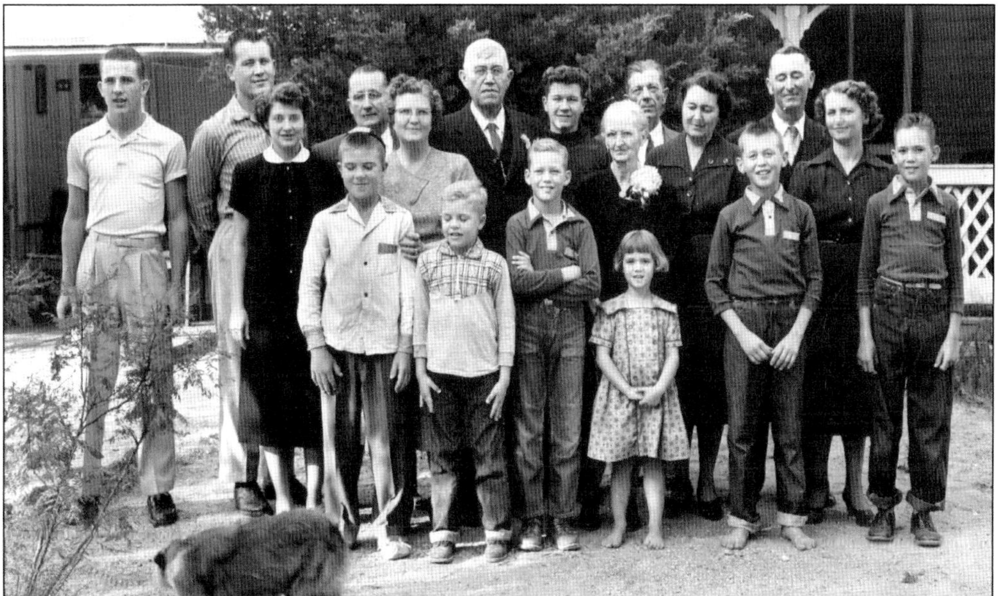

Reinhard and Amalia Frantzen celebrated their golden wedding anniversary with immediate family on November 16, 1954. Pictured are, from left to right, (first row) Lester Frantzen, Gary Scheele, Joe Frantzen, Betty Frantzen, Patrick Frantzen, and Curtis Frantzen; (second row) Cleo Frantzen, Laura Herbort Frantzen, Reinhard Frantzen, Amalia Enderlin Frantzen (Reinhard's wife), Wera Frantzen Scheele, and Norma Wendel Frantzen; (third row) Henry J. Frantzen, R.L. Frantzen, Alex R. Frantzen, Olin Scheele, Edgar Scheele, and Henry R. Frantzen. (Courtesy of Dietel Collection.)

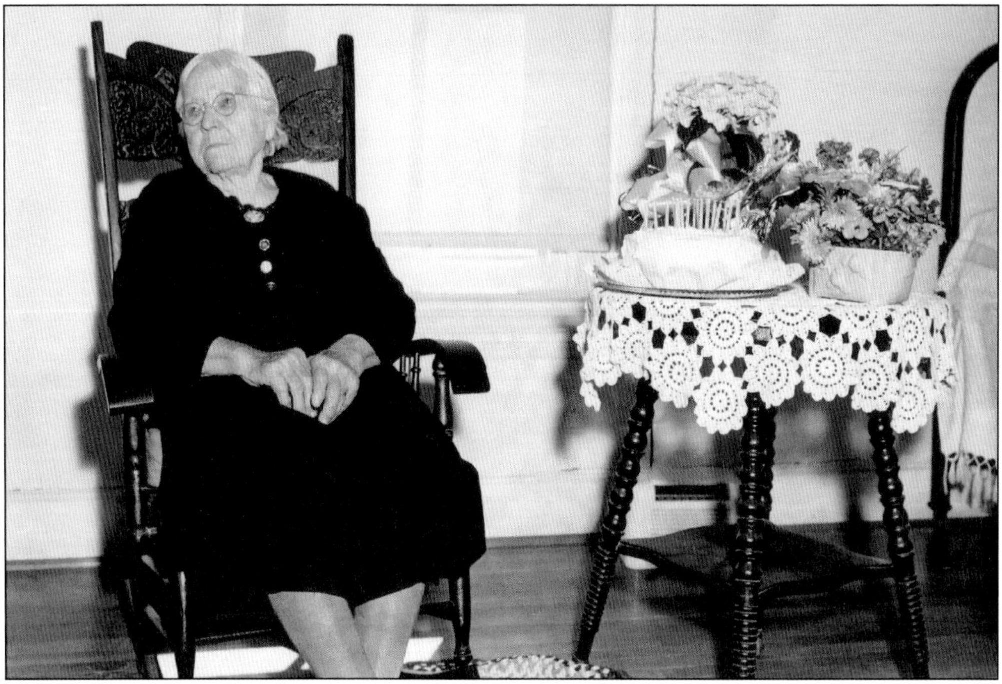

Ida Lang Eckert celebrated her 90th birthday on April 7, 1955, with cake and flowers presented to her for the occasion. One of 13 children, she was the daughter of Heinrich and Minne Lang of the Cherry Spring community and a lifelong resident of Gillespie County. Even at the age of 90, she was renowned for growing beautiful flowers in her yard. (Courtesy of Dietel Collection.)

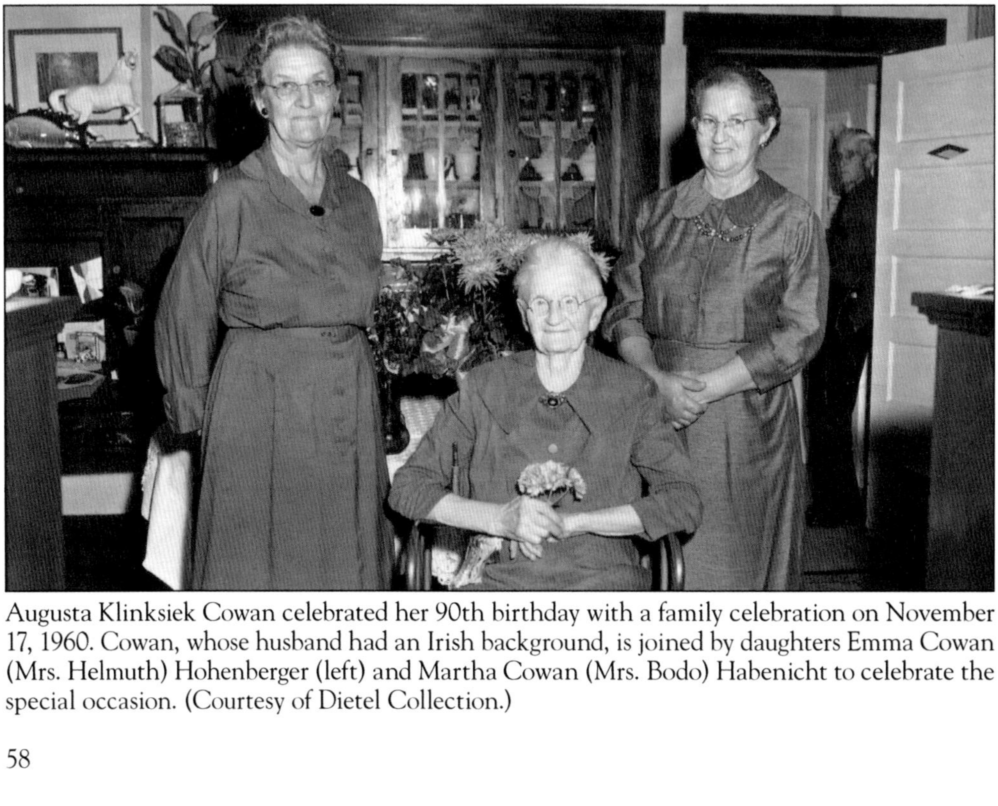

Augusta Klinksiek Cowan celebrated her 90th birthday with a family celebration on November 17, 1960. Cowan, whose husband had an Irish background, is joined by daughters Emma Cowan (Mrs. Helmuth) Hohenberger (left) and Martha Cowan (Mrs. Bodo) Habenicht to celebrate the special occasion. (Courtesy of Dietel Collection.)

These family members are identified by an inscription on the back of the photograph as the "Family of August Kothmann" in 1911. The family is standing outdoors near the tank house and grape arbor. (Courtesy of Jentsch Collection.)

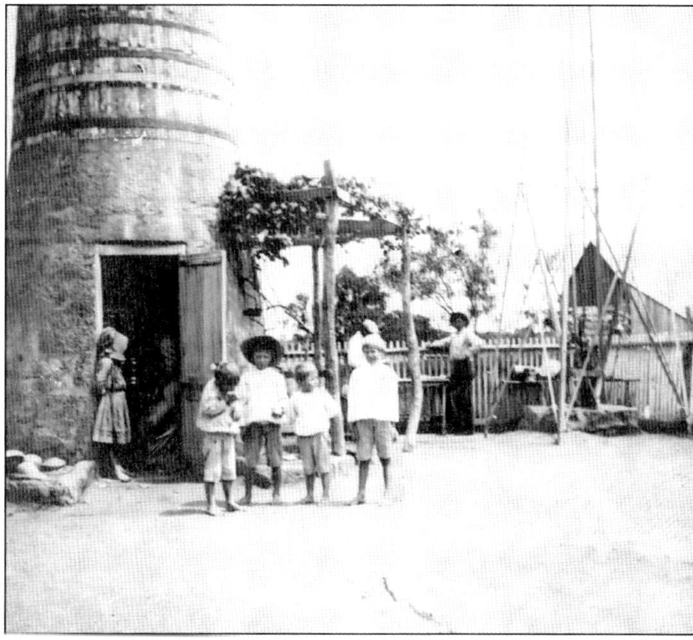

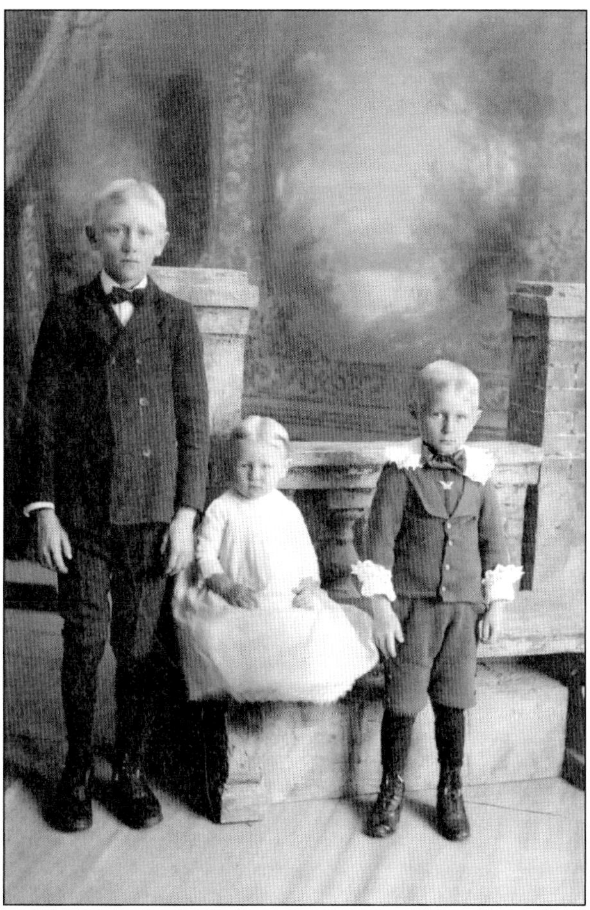

The children of Louis and Augusta Feller Lehne are dressed in their Sunday best for the rare opportunity of a family portrait. Photographed around 1906, they are, from left to right, Alfred, Christian, and Emil. Christian, born in 1904, is wearing the traditional dress worn by young boys until about the age of four, when they progressed to their first pair of long pants. (Courtesy of Kuenemann Collection.)

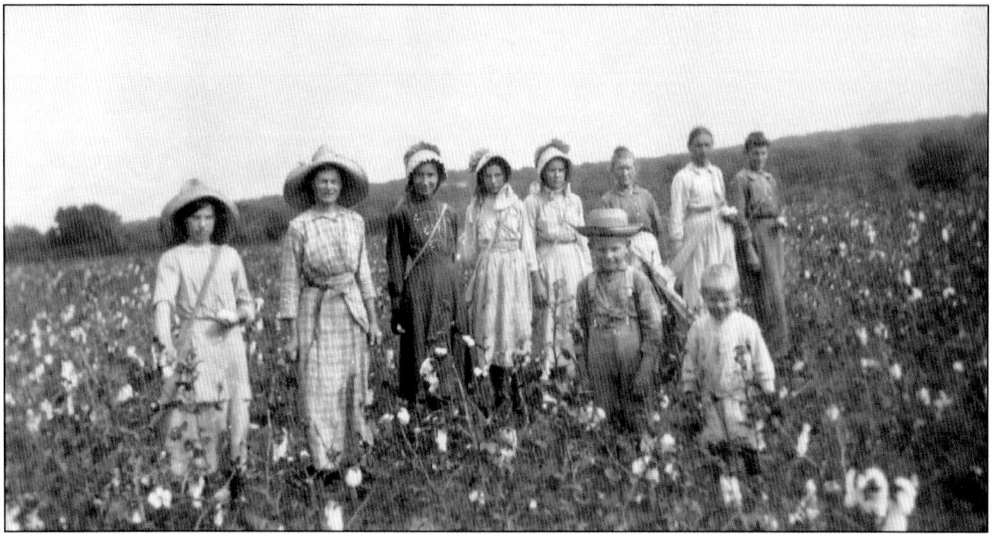

The Heimann extended family of Bear Creek worked together in the cotton field. The younger family members worked in the fields with the parents, picking for part of the day. To endure the heat and the sun's rays, the women and children wore long-sleeved dresses or shirts and bonnets or large hats. (Courtesy of Gertrude and Harvey Land.)

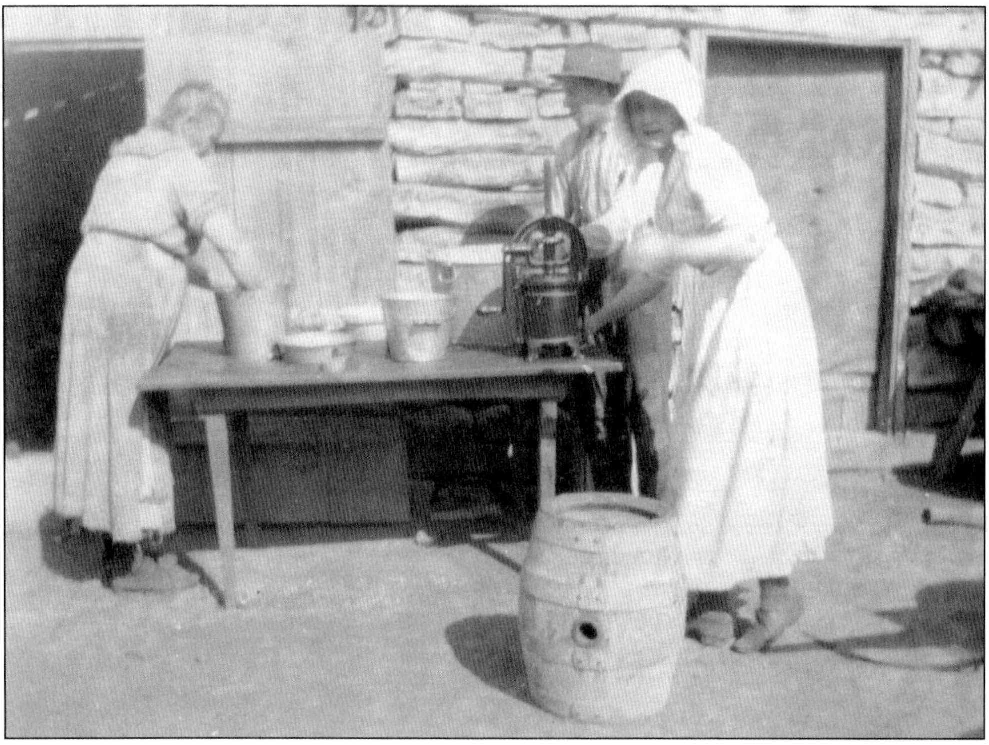

Sausage-making was part of meat processing. Families would spend the most part of a week carrying out the entire process. Large tubs, buckets, and the sausage stuffer on the table were essential items in sausage-making. The woman on the left appears to be preparing the casing for stuffing with sausage meat from the large tub. The meat is put in the stuffer to be pressed into the casing. (Courtesy of Arthur Grobe.)

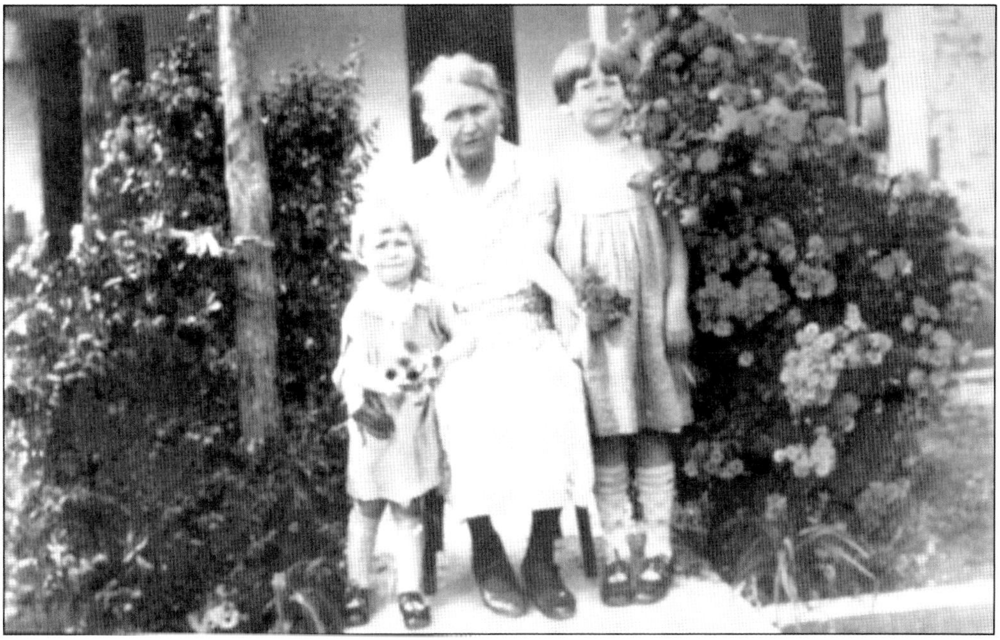

The beautiful roses that Grandmother, or "Oma," proudly planted and nurtured are the backdrop for this photograph of Bertha Ellebracht Grobe with two of her grandchildren at her side. The Grobe homestead was located on North Llano Highway, 16 North. (Courtesy of Arthur Grobe.)

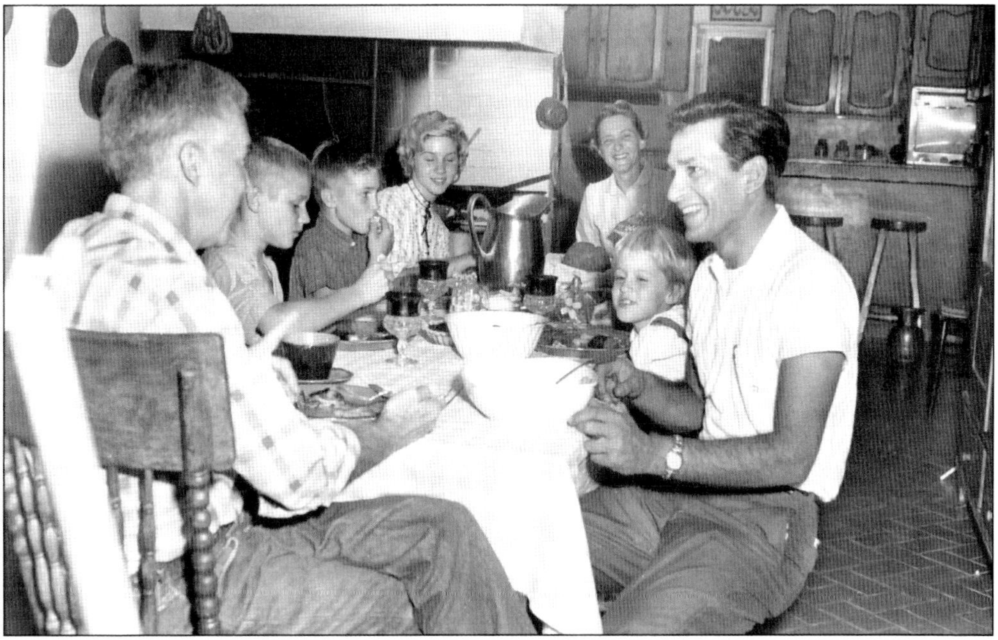

Helen "Schatzie" Crouch prepared a sumptuous fried sausage dinner at their country home in their typical German kitchen, with flames shooting from the logs in the hearth, for a *National Geographic* reporter preparing for a feature article on Texas in a future issue of the magazine in September 1959. Pictured, from left to right, are the Crouches—Hondo, Juan, Kerry, Becky, Schatzie, and Chris—and reporter Tom Nebbia. (Courtesy of Dietel Collection.)

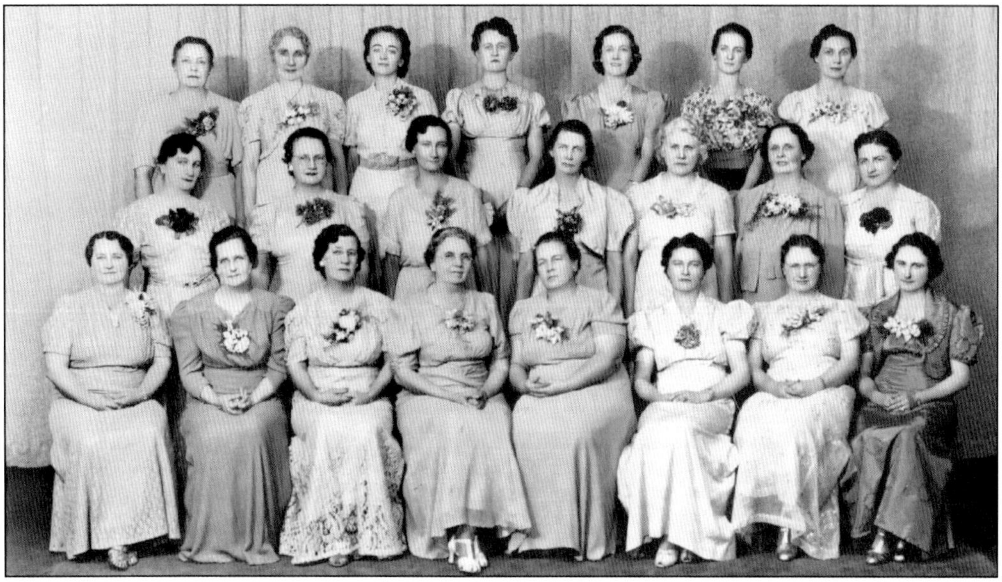

On January 27, 1941, some 40 members of the Choral Club of Parent Teacher Association of Fredericksburg Schools observed its 10th anniversary. The club's purpose was to serve Fredericksburg Schools, foster a music spirit and good fellowship in schoolchildren and their musical mothers and friends, and assist in any worthy cause within Texas. Pictured are, from left to right, (first row) Anna Stahl, Christine Brodie, Cora Henke, Nannie Striegler, Hildegarde Haag, Helen Kolmeier, Anna Hahn, and Lillie Bierschwale; (second row) Emily Kuenemann, Selma Hahn, Elsie Lochte, Adele Kneese, Effie Hohnmann, Meta Houy, and Hattie Bierschwale; (third row) Selma Ottens, Julia Estill, Alma Pfeiffer, Annie Mangelberger, Violet Kirchhoff, Lilly Peterson, and Lydia Bernhard. (Courtesy of Bierschwale Collection.)

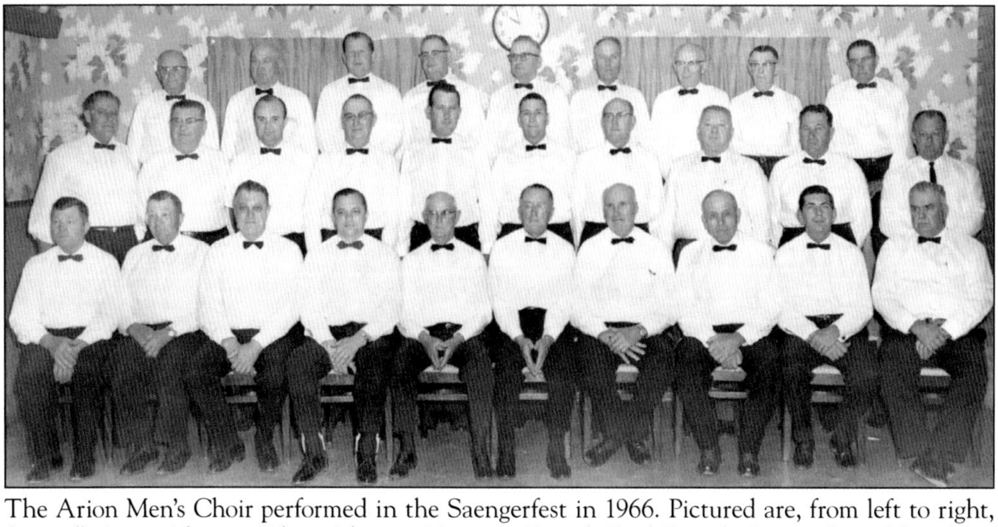

The Arion Men's Choir performed in the Saengerfest in 1966. Pictured are, from left to right, (seated) Arno Ahrens, Edgar Ahrens, Norman Dietel, Fred Dietel, Gustav Jenschke, Alex Frantzen, Walter Ottmers, Hugo Mueller, Roy Stroeher, and Erwin Rusche; (second row) Sidney Henke, Edgar Stroeher, Dick Dorer, Henry Frantzen, R.L. Frantzen, Tony Hartmann, Gilbert Kunz, Hugo Klaerner, Ewald Schaefer, and Milton Oehler; (third row) Felix Pehl, Eddie Schaefer, Rudy Olfers, Louis Durst, Benno Stehling, Guido Klett, Felix Heep, Edgar Marshall, and Edgar Durst. (Courtesy of Arion Men's Choir.)

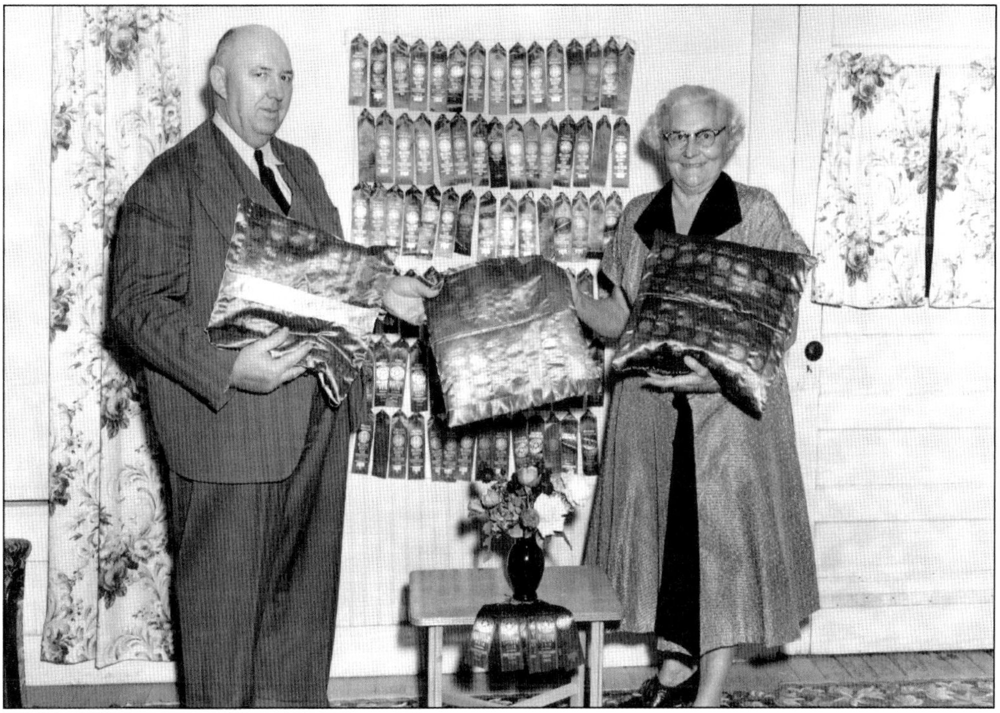

Meta Mund is congratulated by Bill Petmecky of the Gillespie County Fair Association for the amazing number of county fair ribbons she had won by 1954. For years, Mund would bake, cook, and do handwork that she would bring to the fair in August to be exhibited in the respective departments. She was one of the many housewives who would display products of their expertise. (Courtesy of Dietel Collection.)

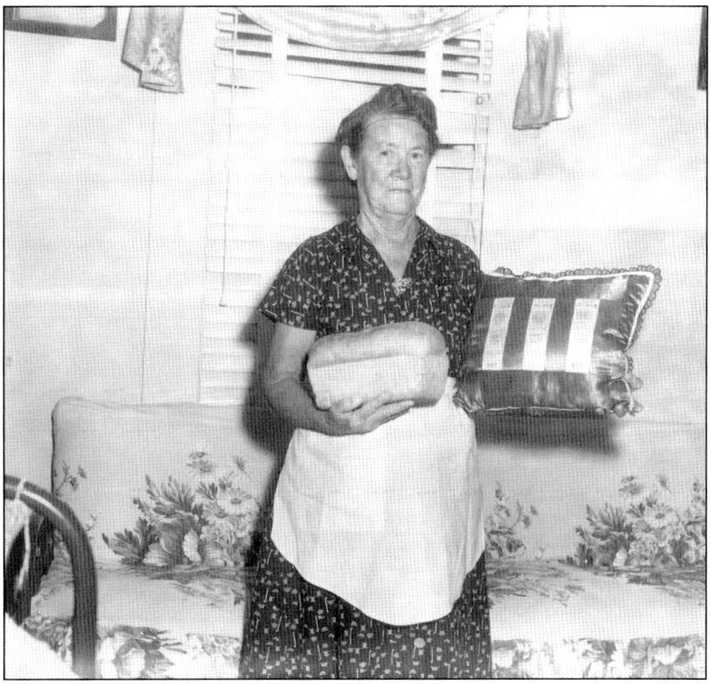

Alma Schmidt was a devoted housewife, mother, and grandmother, the way many "omas" are lovingly remembered. Here, she is displaying a throw pillow she created from the many ribbons she won by baking bread like the loaf she is holding and other entries she took to the Gillespie County Fair in August up until 1956. (Courtesy of Dietel Collection.)

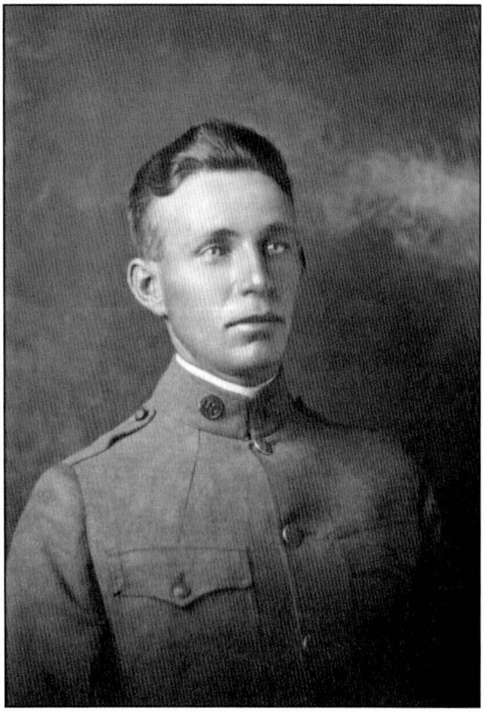

Hilmar J. Lott, listed as a private in World War I on his military record, was born August 26, 1890, and died April 16, 1982. He was one of the Gillespie County veterans who answered the call to fill the county's quota and withstood the highest mental and physical tests, a fine tribute to their inherited qualities and proper training. (Courtesy of Schumann Collection.)

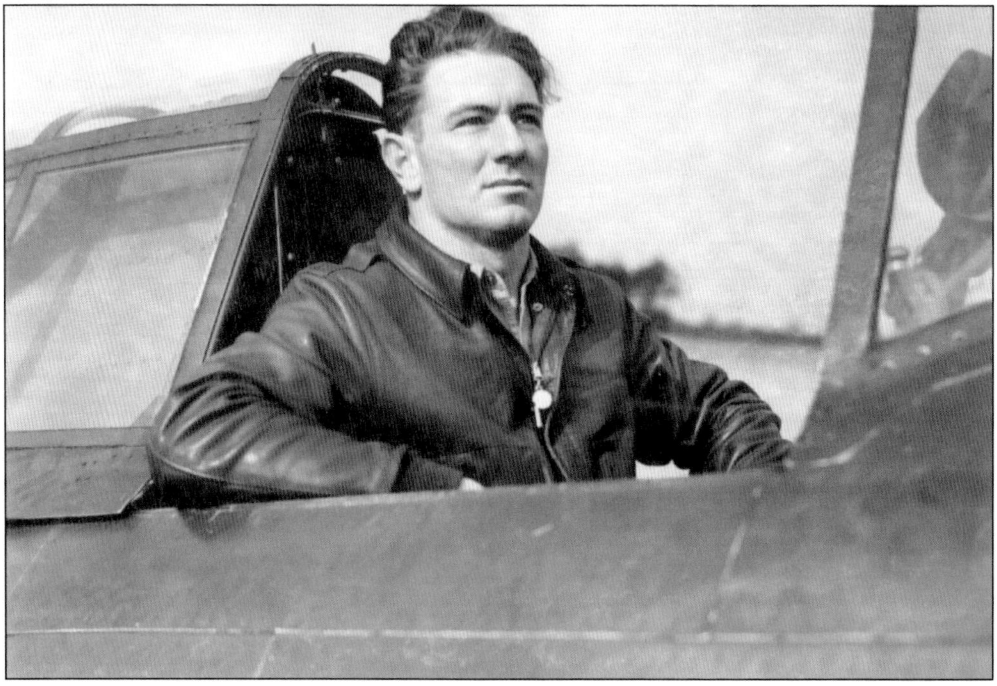

Gillespie County boys were proud to serve in the war. Lt. Clifford B. Hahn completed his 60th mission over Europe in January 1944 and was the holder of the Distinguished Flying Cross and the Air Medal with three Oak Leaf Clusters. The son of Willie Richard and Milda Hahn, he was presumed dead by the War Department and listed as "missing in action" on January 24, 1944. (Courtesy of Dietel Collection.)

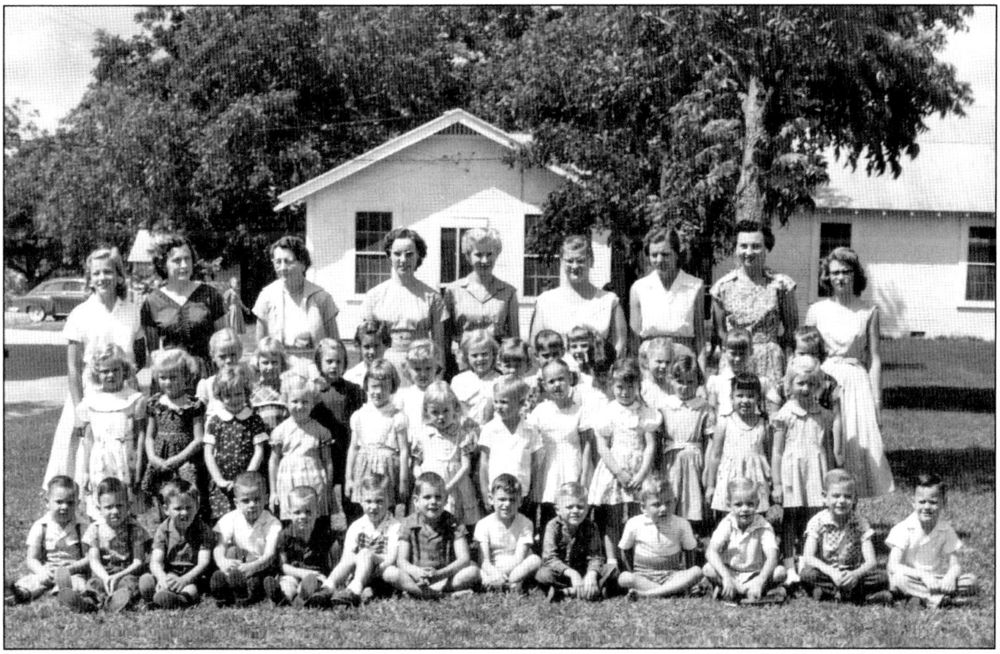

Generally in June of each year, churches of different denominations would have Vacation Bible School. This group of preschool students and their teachers attended Holy Ghost Lutheran Church Vacation Bible School in 1957. Behind them is the Sunday school house, which is still in use by that congregation at 110 East San Antonio Street. (Courtesy of Dietel Collection.)

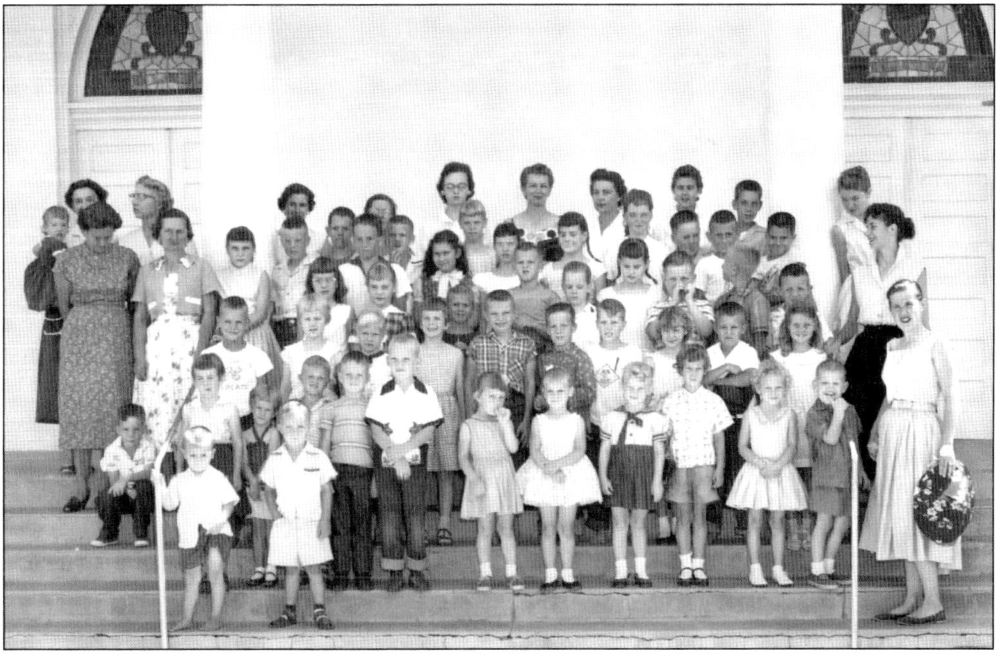

The First Methodist Church Vacation Bible students pose for the camera in June 1957. The students of various ages attended class at the church at 312 West San Antonio Street. The building was purchased by the Gillespie County Historical Society in 1970, and the church is now referred to as the Historic Sanctuary. (Courtesy of Dietel Collection.)

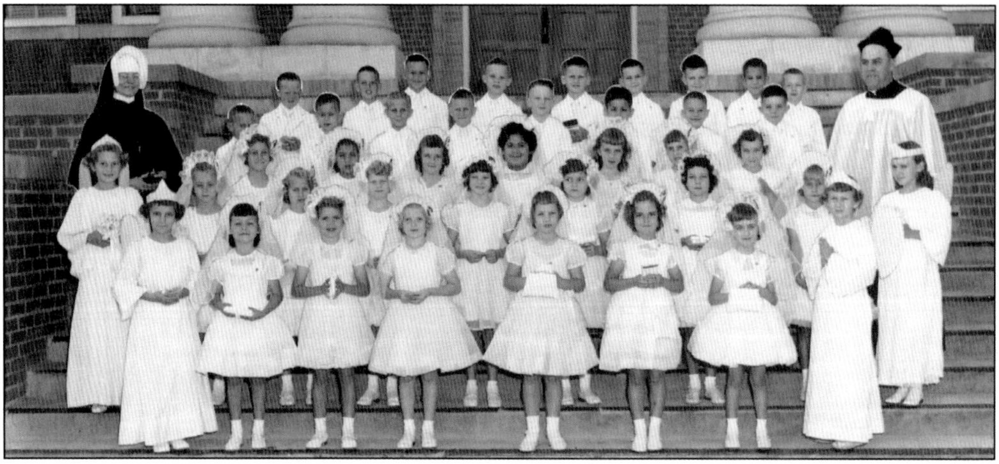

St. Mary's First Communicants are posing in front of the St. Mary's School Building on May 5, 1955. Pictured are, from left to right, (first row) Gladys Scott, Phyllis Pape, Janet Jenschke, Eunice Wallendorf, Delores Jenschke, Cris Jung, Linda Wallendorf, and Myrtle Tatsch; (second row) Charlotte Weber, Glendene Klaerner, Carolyn Usener, Sharon Seelig, Janet Kaiser, Sharon Lang, Bonnibel Crenwelge, Bernadette Schneider, and Jeanette Wilson; (third row) Sister Leona Marie, Sandra Hohmann, Helen Sanchez, Theresa Ottmers, Julia Cancino, Mary Beth Ottmers, Genevieve Pehl, Carolyn Moritz, Father J.J. Hildebrand (priest); (fourth row) Daniel Svatek, Jeff Henke, Stephen Schmidt, Charles Mazurek, Phillip Tybor, Edward Rendon, Jerry Stehling, and Joseph Kammlah; (fifth row) Gary Kiehne, Lester Schmidtzinsky, David Staats, Larry Pyka, Billy Bryla, Marvin Crenwelge, Jerry Turrentine, James St. Clair, and Rodney Danz. (Courtesy of Dietel Collection.)

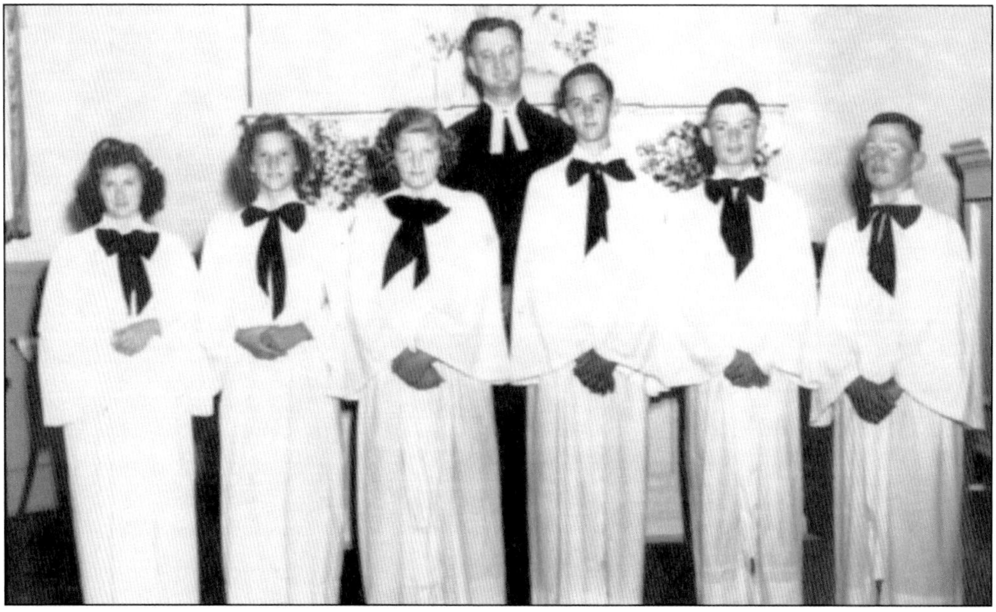

This photograph is from Bethany Lutheran Church confirmation on March 25, 1945. Rev. G.A. Poehlmann stands in back of the confirmands. Pictured are, from left to right, Dulcie Zesch, Dorothy Luckenbach, Carolyn Nichols, Oliver Kowert, Royce Brown, and Clemens Eckhardt. Students attended confirmation classes for about a year and were confirmed on Palm Sunday. (Courtesy of Verdie Pezzaro.)

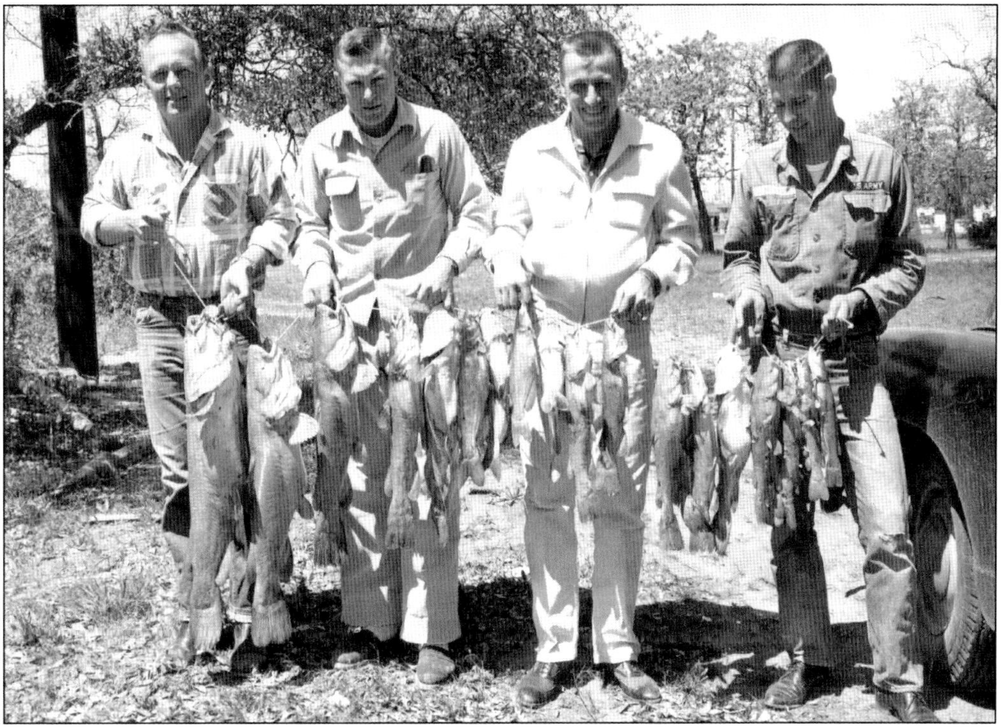

Weekend fishing trips have been a special treat for men in Gillespie County. From left to right, Louis Dietrich, Terry Stehling, Melvin Itz, and Robert "Bob" Metzger show off their 100-pound-plus catch after a weekend trip to the Llano River in April 1961. The largest yellow cat weighed 24 pounds, followed by 16-, 10-, and 7-pounders. (Courtesy of Dietel Collection.)

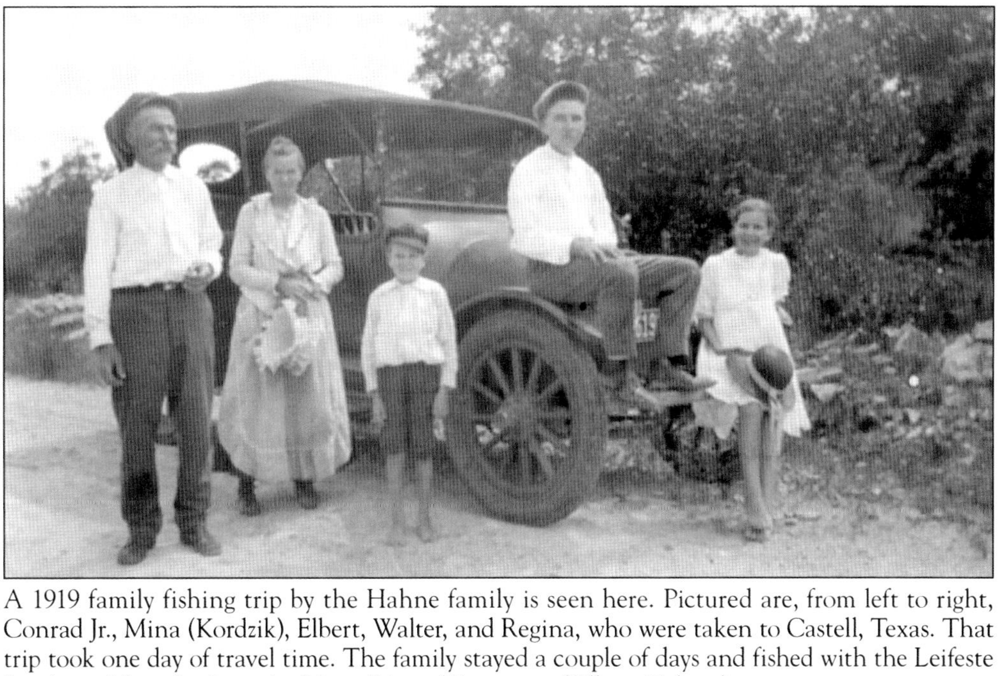

A 1919 family fishing trip by the Hahne family is seen here. Pictured are, from left to right, Conrad Jr., Mina (Kordzik), Elbert, Walter, and Regina, who were taken to Castell, Texas. That trip took one day of travel time. The family stayed a couple of days and fished with the Leifeste family and friends along the Llano River. (Courtesy of Elbert Hahne.)

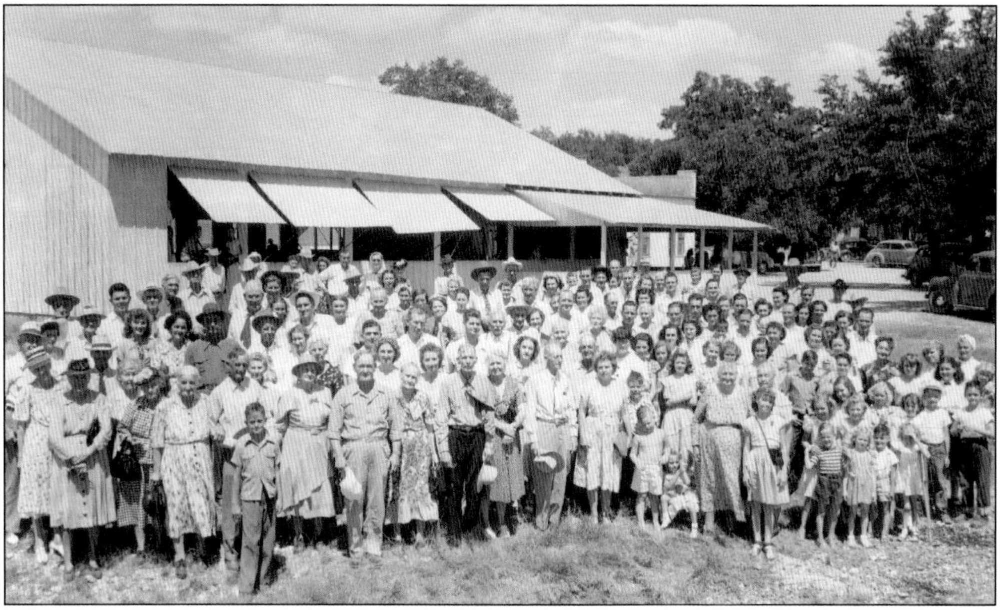

Louis Martin and Hester McDonald family reunion was held at Reeh's Spring Creek Hall on August 15, 1948. The McDonalds had built their home in 1854 near the hall. At the time of the reunion, only three of their nine children were still living. Many of the older reunion attendees were educated from 1877 to 1878 at the rural Spring Creek School. They came from Harper and Barksdale, Texas, and Douglas, Arizona. (Courtesy of Dietel Collection.)

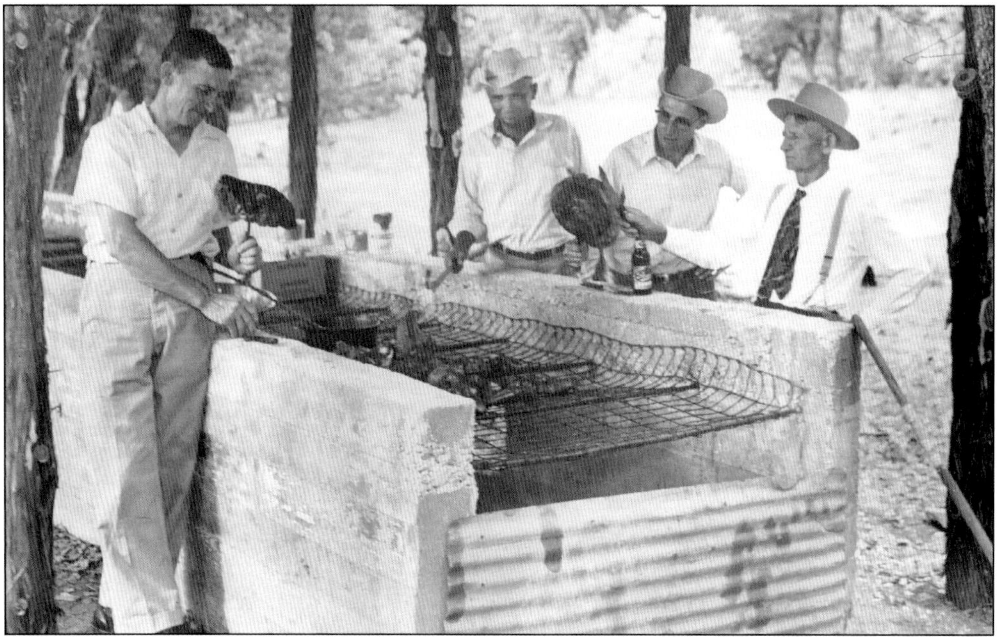

The barbecue pit has always been the spot for the men to gather at any function including a barbecue meal. Here at the George Weber family reunion held in Luckenbach, men who volunteered to make the barbecue are checking for flavor and tenderness before the meal is served to those attending. From left to right, the barbecue cooks are Eugene Weber, Ewald Petsch, George Weber, and Henry Weber. (Courtesy of Dietel Collection.)

The back of photograph is inscribed, "Mrs. Ad. Wehmeyer and daughter/Mrs. Alfred Riley." Wilhelmine Wehmeyer stands behind the baby's carriage, which includes a parasol to shade the baby. Probably called a sleeper cart, it sold for $5 to $10, according to the 1902 Sears, Roebuck & Co. catalog. The house appears to be made of cut limestone, with a wooden railing across the front of the porch. (Courtesy of GCHS.)

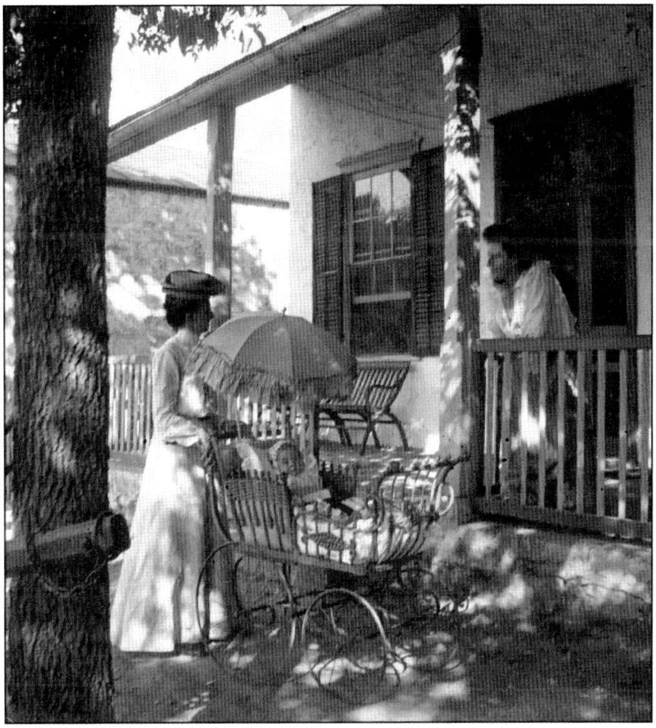

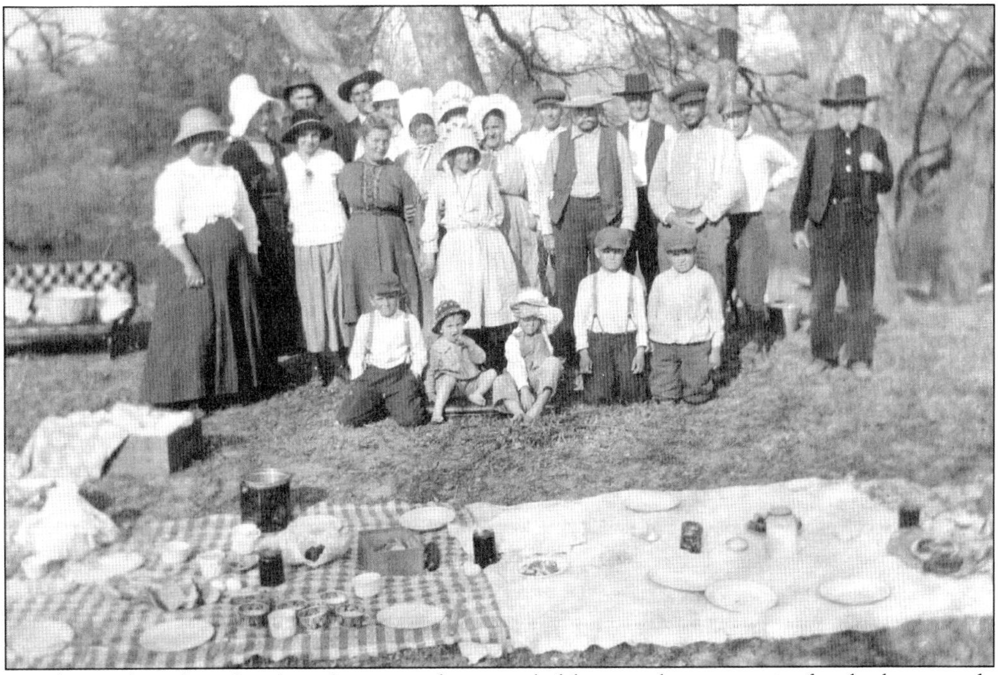

Families gathered on Sunday afternoons for gemütlichkeit, with an appetite for the homemade jellies, breads, jerky, and sausage. Checkered tablecloths as well as plain tablecloths were spread out on the grass and a buggy seat was pulled for sitting or storage. It was the start of what today are known as potluck meals. Each cook would aim to bring her very best samples for all to enjoy. (Courtesy of Arthur Grobe.)

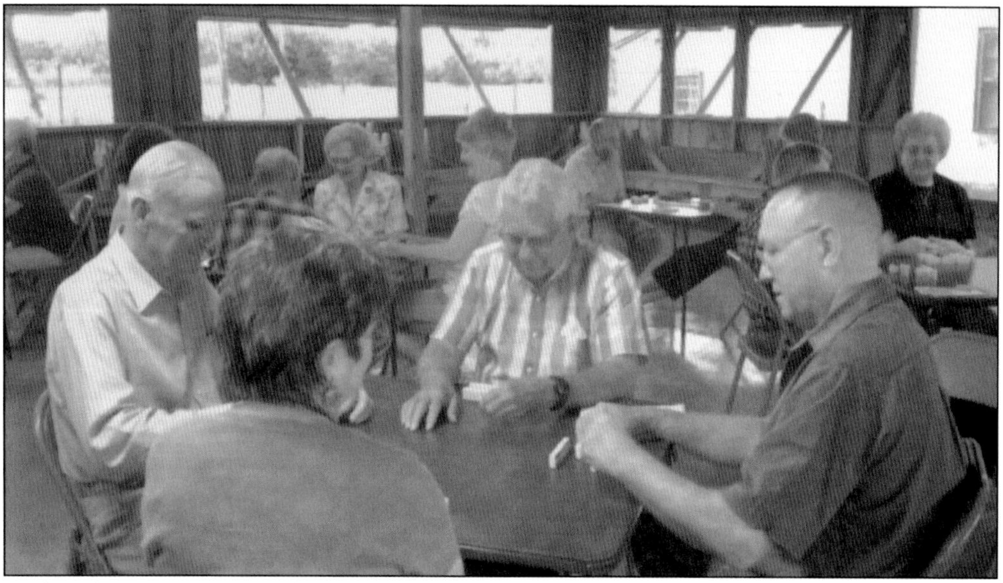

Crabapple Community Club members are enjoying an evening of 42 domino, playing in the pavilion of the Crabapple Country School. The community members gather for work to maintain the schoolhouses and also use the buildings for social events. One of the members, Helen Rusche Wahl, to the left of the post in the center, is 101 years old. (Courtesy of Crabapple Community Club Collection.)

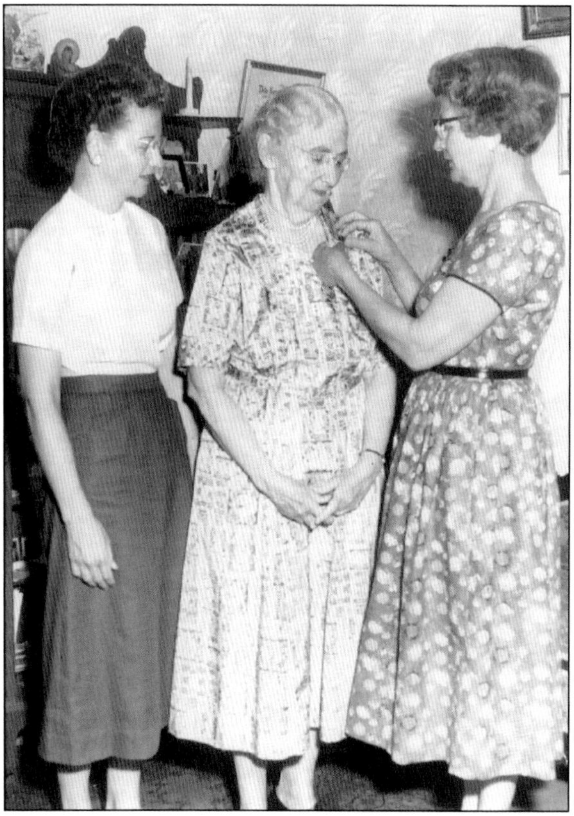

Julia Estill, a retired teacher, was honored as a 50-year member of the Mathilde Keidel Lodge No. 18 of the Order of the Sons of Hermann, represented by Anna Marie Bohnert and Alma Filter. Born in Fredericksburg where she attended school, Julia received her bachelor of science degree in 1904 and a master of science degree in 1905, both from the University of Texas. Her career included teaching English for 36 years and 11 years as high school principal at Fredericksburg High School. (Courtesy of Dietel Collection.)

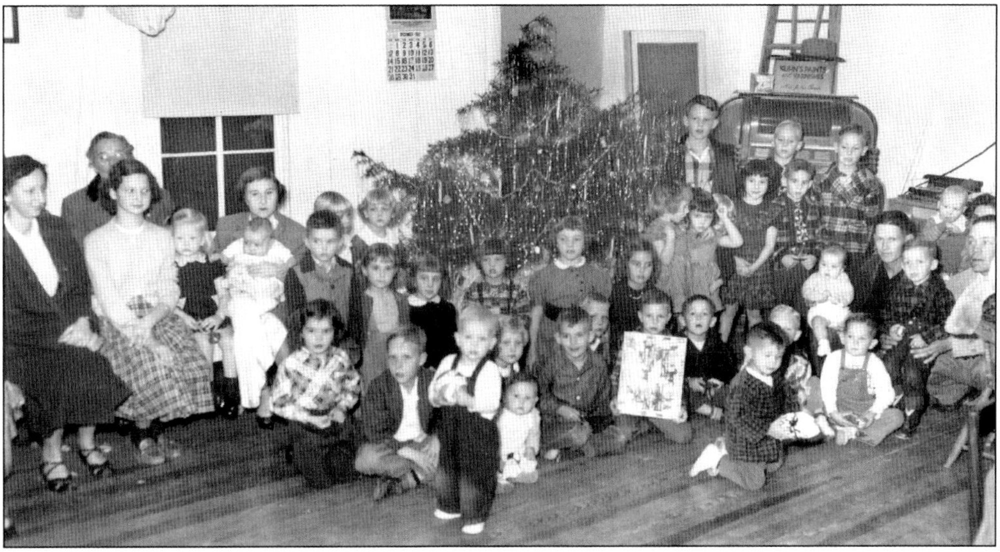

Many local organizations to which parents belonged had Christmas parties in the month of December. This 1952 Christmas party was well attended by the VFW Post 7105 members' children. Children eagerly waited for Santa Claus to distribute goody bags. Mary Louise Heinen played Christmas selections on her piano accordion. Refreshments were served by Florence Zatopek, Estella Wuest, Irmgard Nagel, and Lorenz Bading. (Courtesy of Dietel Collection.)

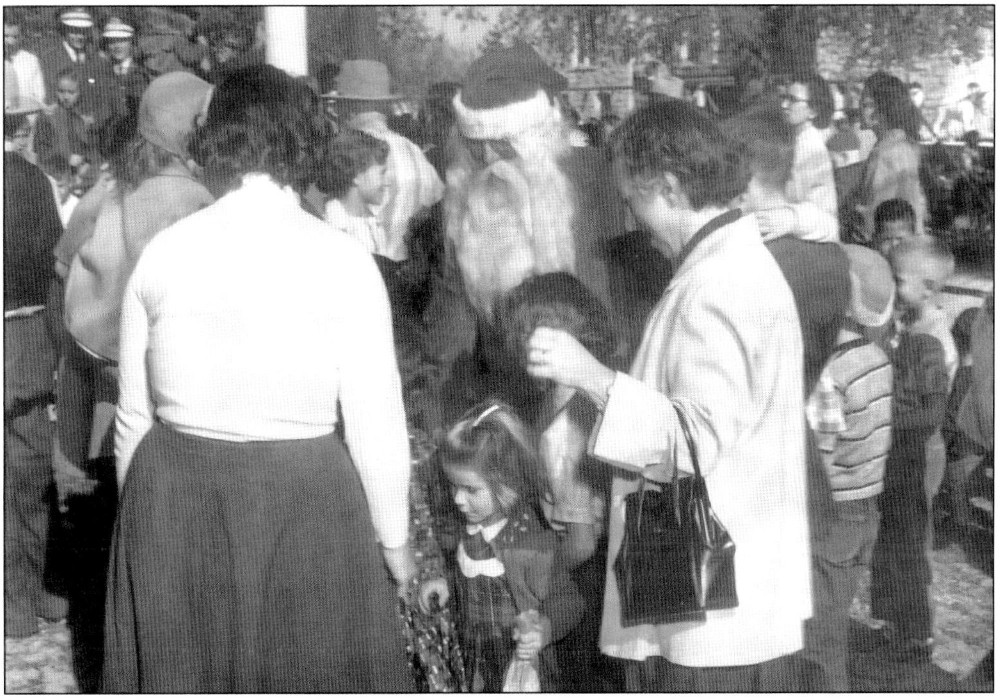

Many Fredericksburg children have experienced Santa Claus Day sponsored by the Fredericksburg Jaycees. After Santa Claus had made his way up and down Main Street in a short 1956 street parade led by the Fredericksburg High School Band, the children eagerly await to visit with the jolly old man at the gazebo behind the courthouse and collect their bags of goodies. (Courtesy of Dietel Collection.)

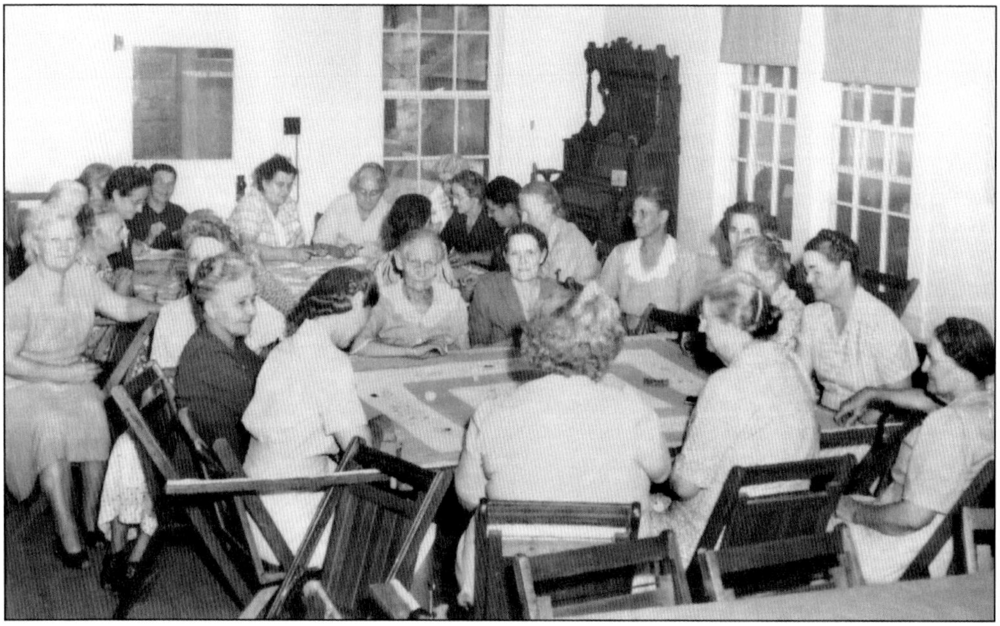

Traditionally, quilting was learned by young women as a method of providing warmth and comfort for their families. A beautiful handmade quilt could become a treasured wedding gift, handed down through generations. Since 1921, the Holy Ghost Lutheran Church "quilting ladies" have met weekly to make quilts, as ordered, as a form of stewardship, as a means to raise funds for the church, and for Christian fellowship. (Courtesy of GCHS.)

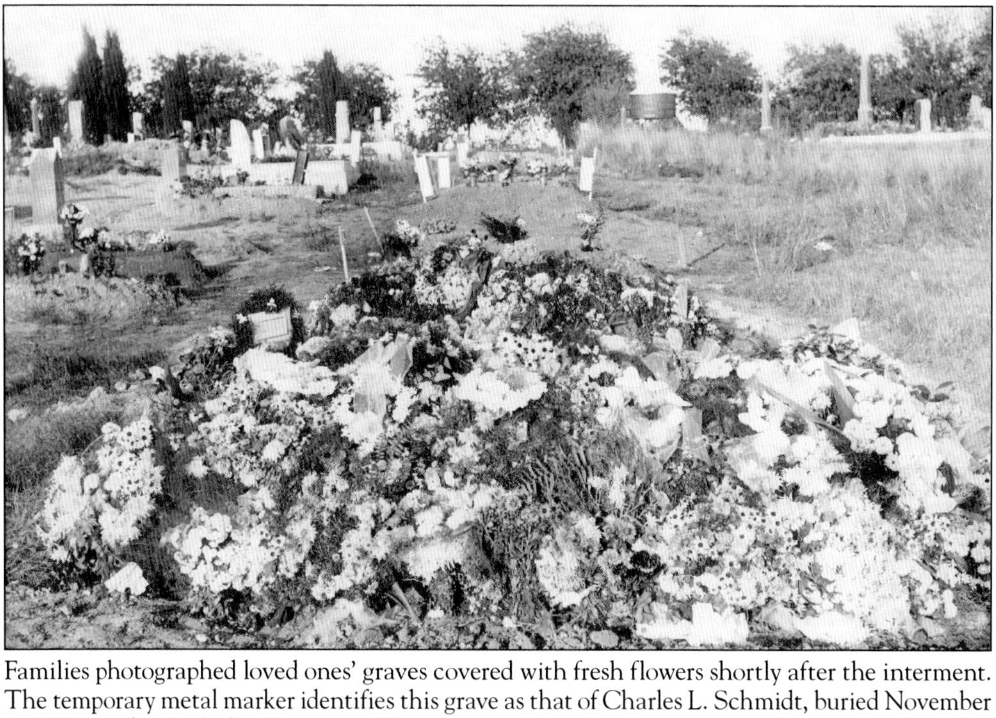

Families photographed loved ones' graves covered with fresh flowers shortly after the interment. The temporary metal marker identifies this grave as that of Charles L. Schmidt, buried November 8, 1920, in the Catholic Cemetery. The water tank in the distance is on the north side of the cemetery. (Courtesy of GCHS.)

Five

EDUCATION

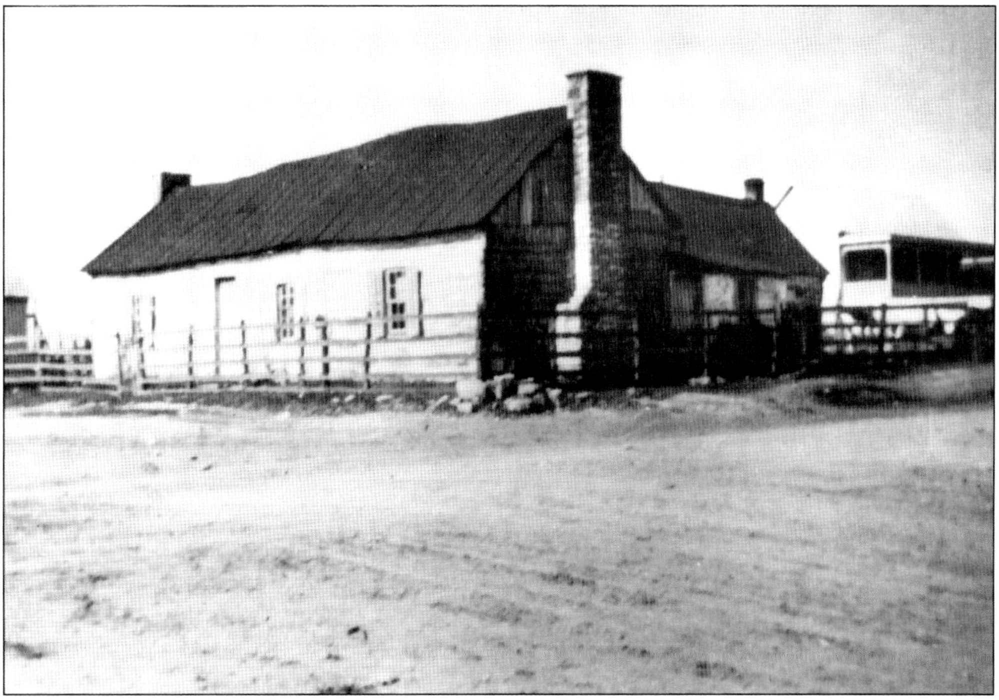

In November 1856, the Catholics, through the parish committee—Johann Metzger, Johann Fritz, and Anton Kraus—bought two lots with log cabins on them for $250. The school was started in this building in December 1856. Both houses were joined together to form the schoolroom and teacher's living quarters on what in 1921 was known as Straube's Place at the corner of South Milam and West San Antonio Streets. (Courtesy of GCHS.)

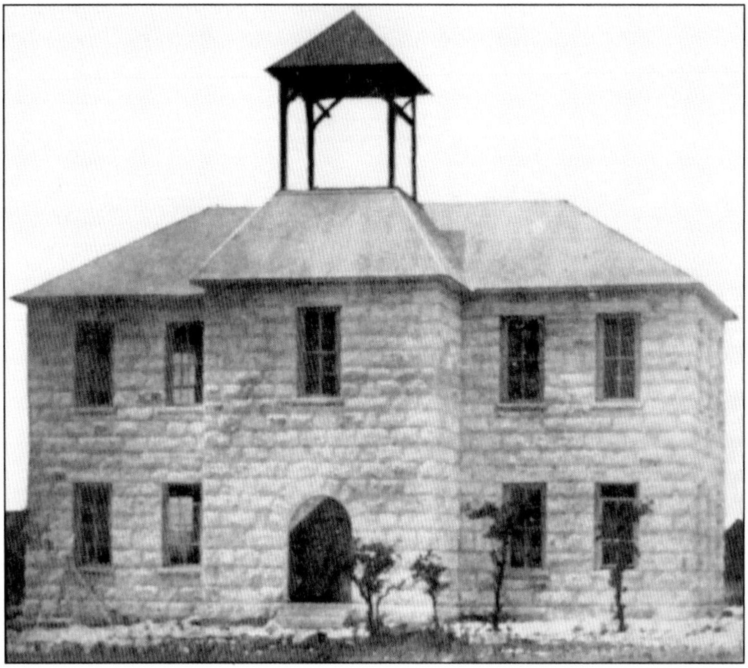

The Harper School was established in 1884. The original schoolhouse burned in 1906. This new two-story stone building was erected after unanimous voter approval of a $3,000 bond issue and first occupied in 1908. Part of the north wall of this structure was incorporated into the new school building, which was constructed in 1940. (Courtesy of GCHS.)

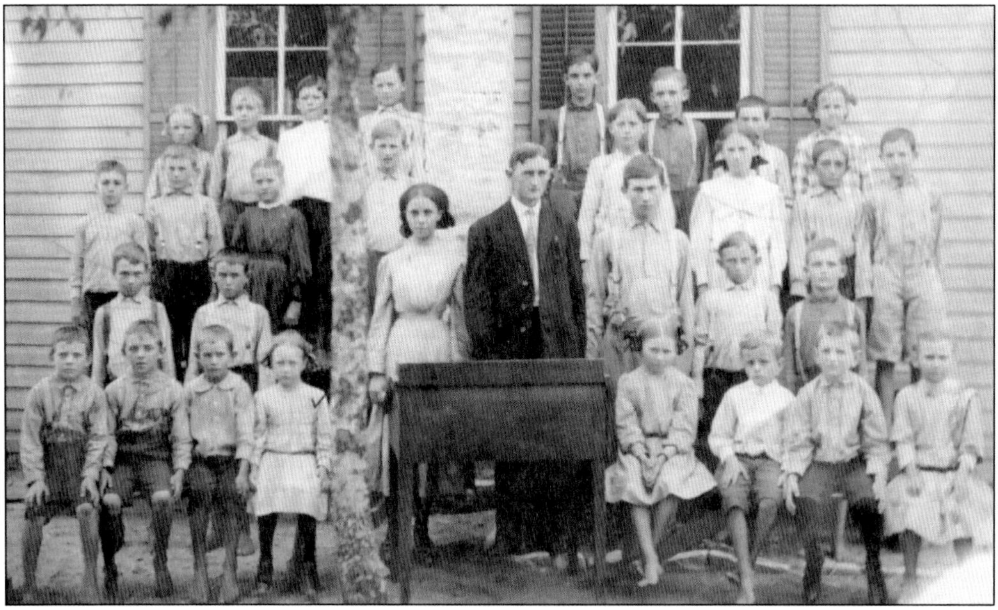

These children pose next to the frame structure the Meusebach School community built in 1897 on the first acre of land owned by the school; it was the third school building constructed. Pictured are, from left to right, (first row) Edmund Weinheimer, Hilmar Weinheimer, Hugo Heimann, Dora Kott, Erna Braeutigam, Alfred Weinheimer, Edgar Stroeher, and Elfrieda Braeutigam; (second row) Edwin Moellering, Arno Heimann, Tekla Heimann, Alfred Heimann, teacher; Fritz Braeutigam, Johnnie Rausch, and Wolfgang Weinheimer; (third row) Erno Bonn, unidentified, Ida Bonn, Charles Braeutigam, Walter Kuhlmann, Emma Braeutigam, Emil Heimann, and Emil Lochte; (fourth row) Selma Lochte, Harry Moellering, Harry Bonn, Harry Heimann, Walter Weinheimer, Leo Weinheimer, Walter Braeutigam, and Louise Kott. (Courtesy of Doris Eckert.)

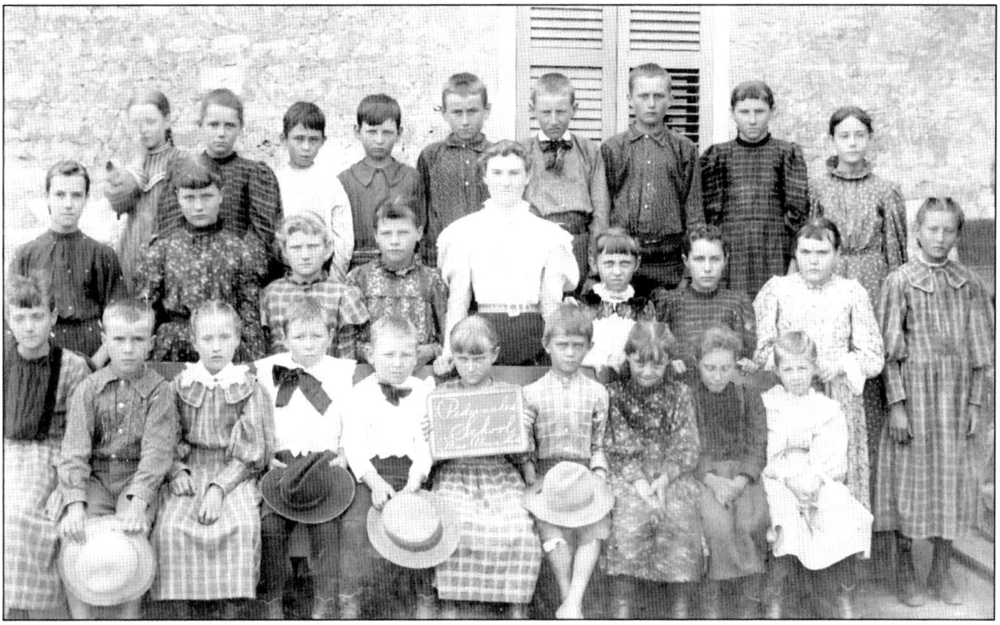

This is Alma Koch's class at the Pedernales School. Koch was the first female teacher at the school in the late 1890s and she preceded Ernst Schmidt. The Pedernales School is now a beautifully restored residence located about seven miles southwest of Fredericksburg on the north bank of the Pedernales River and alongside South State Highway 16. (Courtesy of GCHS.)

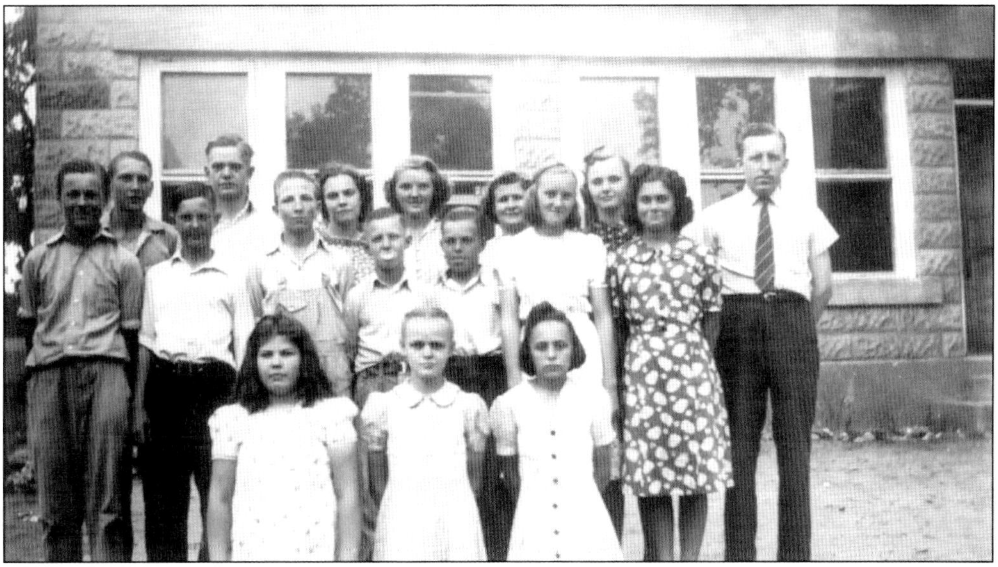

The Knopp School on Knopp School Road was consolidated with Fredericksburg Independent School District before the 1950s. These pupils from the 1940s are, from left to right, (first row) Margaret Beyer, Leola Dietrich, and Helen Houy; (second row) Kurt Kuhlmann, Roland Kuhlmann, Erwin Segner, Raymond Dietrich, Jonathan Beyer, Ottilie Kuhlmann, and Minerva Durst; (third row) Logan Peschel, Martin Beyer, Dora Dietrich, Anita Kuhlmann, Ruth Grobe, Lorene Dietrich, and teacher Robert Klett. (Courtesy of Opal Treibs.)

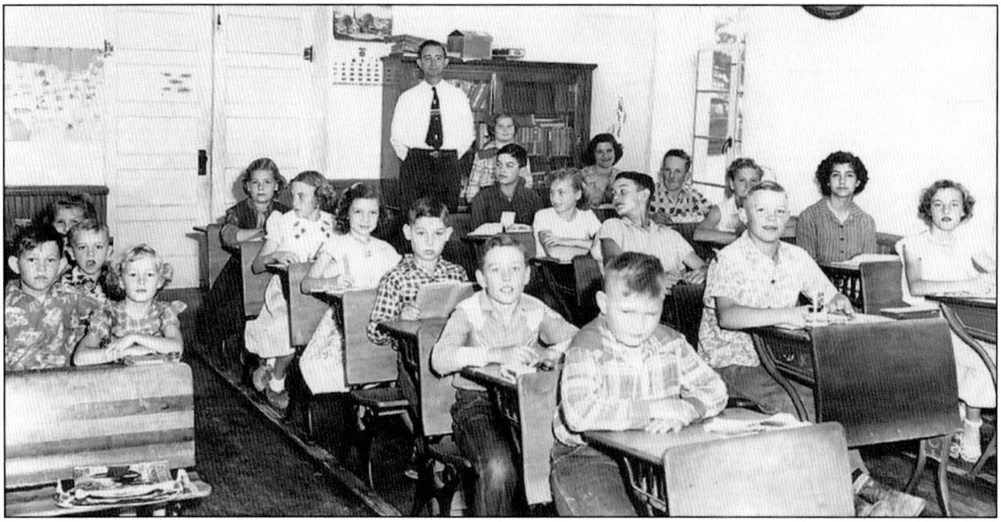

The students of the Crabapple School are, from left to right, (first row) Daniel Sagebiel, Carol Feller, Vernon Staats, and Virginia Sagebiel; and, from front to back, (second row) Dietrich Sagebiel, Belton Feller, Dennis Schneider, Marjorie Alberthal, Florine Ersch, and Beverly Rabke; (third row) Vernon Ahrens, Clinton Alberthal, Marlene Staats, and Elmer Tatsch; (fourth row) Joyce Feller, Mable Schneider, Jeanette Itz, Freddy Goehmann, Jewell Welgehausen, and Arlene Moellering, standing next to Joe Weinheimer, a teacher in the 1950s. (Courtesy of Crabapple School.)

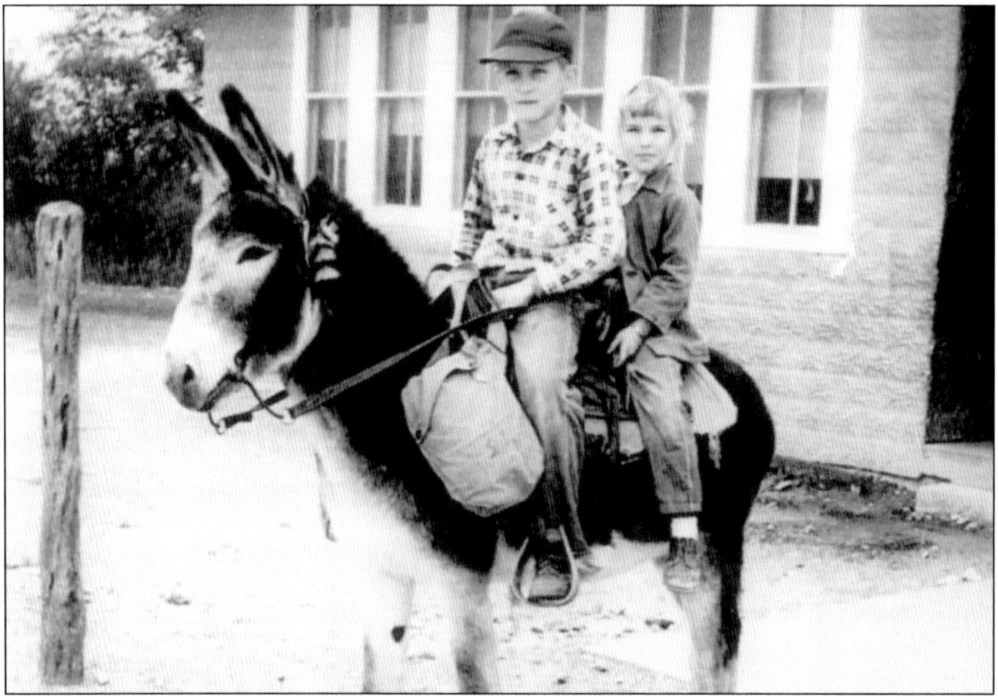

No school bus was available to convey children to the Pecan Creek School. Jinny the donkey took Calvin Friedrich and his sister Sandra Friedrich Kammlah to school and home each day. Along with their books, they carried their lunch in a saddlebag (duffle). This photograph appears in the *Fredericksburg Standard* from February 18, 1953. Sandra was in the second grade, and Calvin was in the fifth grade.(Courtesy of Pecan Creek School.)

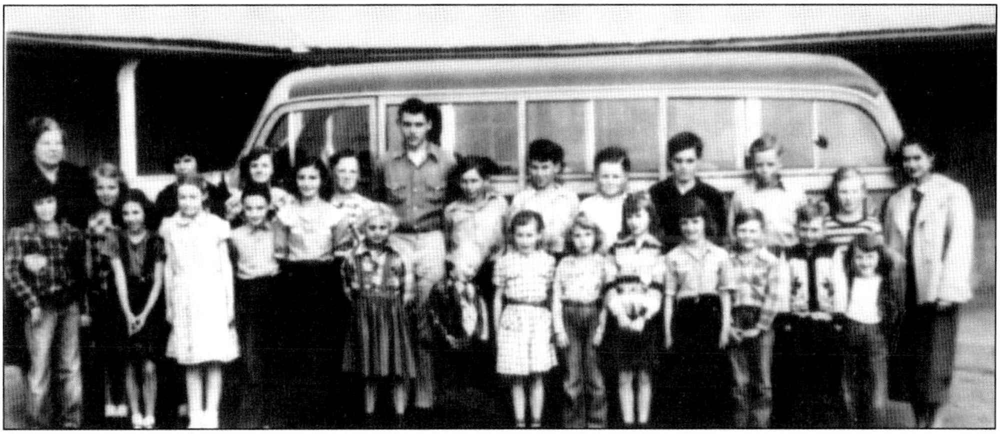

In 1885, through a combined community effort, the Rocky Hill School was erected without any aid from the state. Rocky Hill School's first school bus, for when the school consolidated with Grapetown and Cain City in 1950s, meant an added responsibility for the teacher becoming the bus driver. Located on Highway 290 east of Fredericksburg, the school building was constructed for $196.02. Pictured are, from left to right, (first row) Charlotte Doebbler, Deborah Oehler, Bobbie Nell Abbott, Susan Kaiser, Evelyn Klinksiek, Madge Pehl, Carolee Kallenberg, Beatrice Hansen, Lynette Hohenberger, Roxie Jennings, Victoria Klinksiek, Harvey Moellering Jr., Jacob Schmidt, and Marlene "Janie" Doebbler; (second row) teacher Alma Mosel, Clara Schmidt, Marian Doebbler, Leola Schmidtzinsky, Thomas Doebbler, Joe Kaiser, Daniel Moellering, Conrad Doebbler, Elmer Schmidtzinsky, Barry McHalek, Roy Schmidtzinsky, Elmer Hansen, and teacher Leota Moellering. (Courtesy of GCHS.)

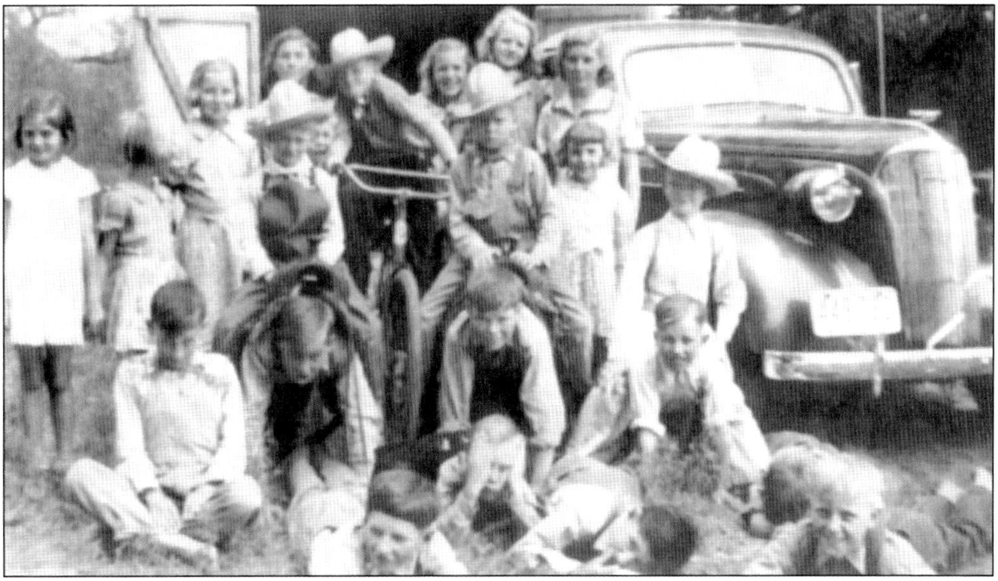

In the 1940s, transportation to country schools included saddle horses, bicycles, and Chevrolet automobiles. Pictured, from left to right, are (first row) Clarence Behrends, Rubin Wehmeyer, Marvin Behrends, unidentified, and Dayton Kuhlmann; (second row) Rubin Barsch, Alvin Behrends, Willie Wehmeyer Jr., and Calvin Beckmann; (third row) Elgin Kusenberger, Bobby Wehmeyer, Paula Frantzen, and Levy Kusenberger; (fourth row) Virginia Barsch, Betty Luckenbach, Irene Beckmann, Elenora Frantzen, Frank Wehmeyer, Helen Luckenbach, Lorene Baag, and unidentified. (Courtesy of Bernice Kunz Weinheimer.)

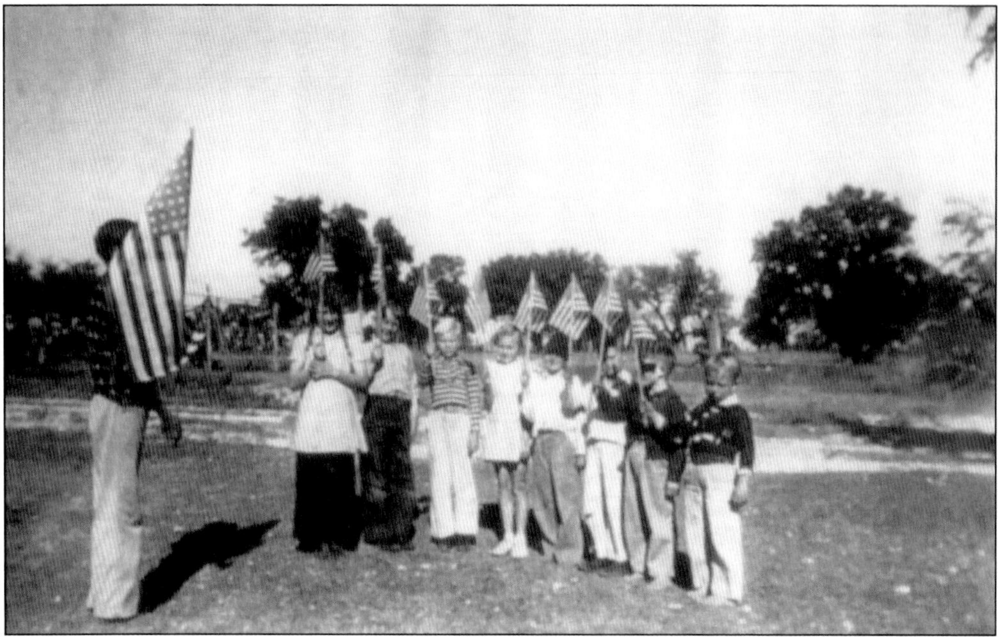

White Oak students with flags performing at a school closing are, from left to right, William Kunz (with the large flag), Betsy Brandon, Alta Lee Baumann, Clint Seelig, Shirley Kunz, Dayton Klein, Kermit Roeder, August Lott, and Stanley Feller. The students represent grades one through eight attending White Oak School. (Courtesy of Charles Feller.)

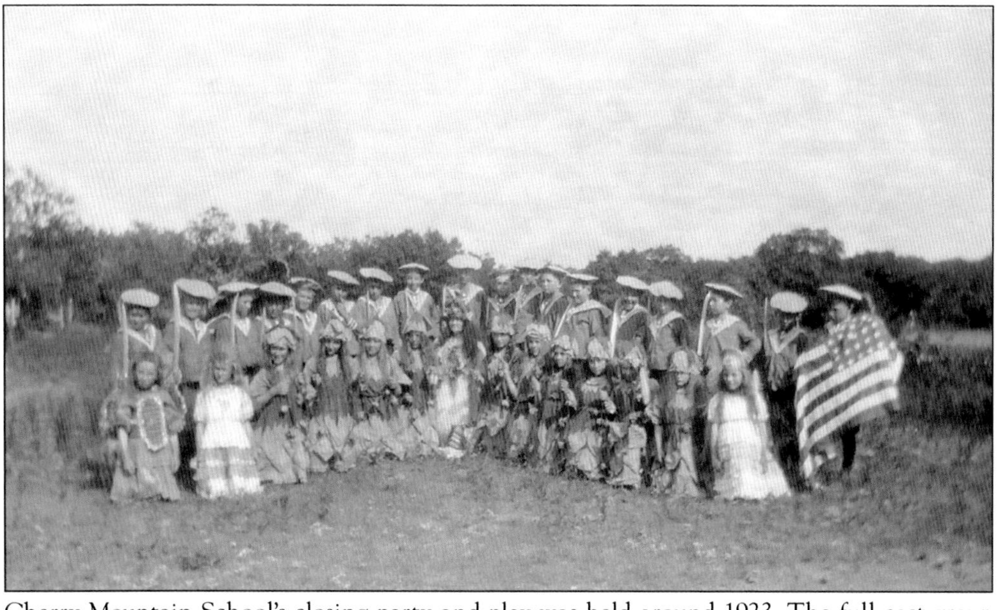

Cherry Mountain School's closing party and play was held around 1923. The full cast group pictured on the flat of the Herman Durst property performed on a platform stage with a makeshift curtain. Homemade ice cream and lemonade were served. Alma Thiele made all these costumes except the sailor outfits. (Courtesy of Clara Ahrens.)

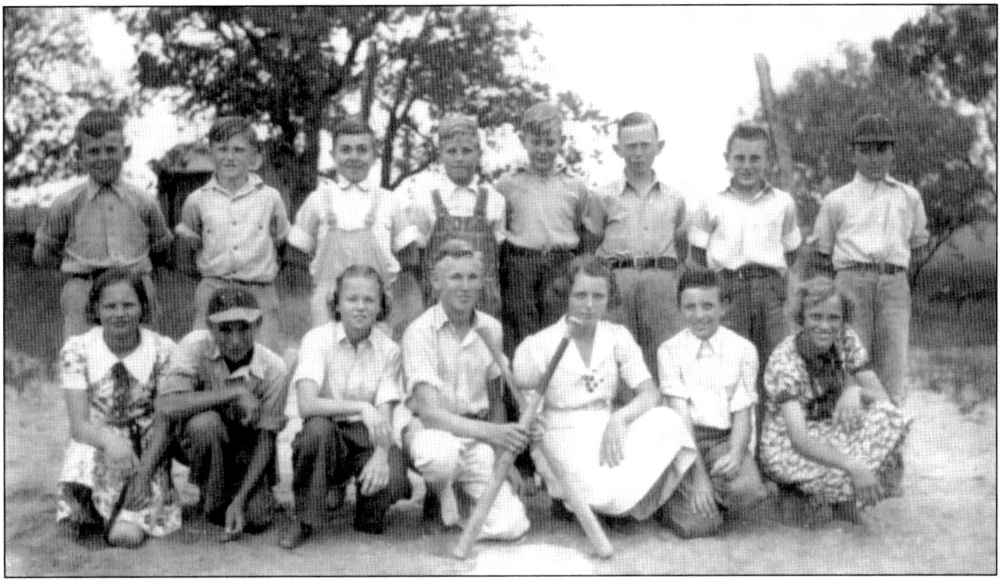

The Meusebach baseball team photograph includes, from left to right, (first row) Ellen Lochte, Gilbert Kuhlmann, Bernice Striegler, Warren Hahn, Virginia Lochte, Marvin Heimann, and Bertha Klinksiek; (second row) Victor Eckhardt, Reuben Gold, Johnny Braeutigam, Conrad Elack, Jackson Wiemers, Alvin Eckhardt, Milton Meier, and Harry Barsch. This photograph was taken in front of the baseball backstop of Meusebach School. (Courtesy of Meusebach Creek School.)

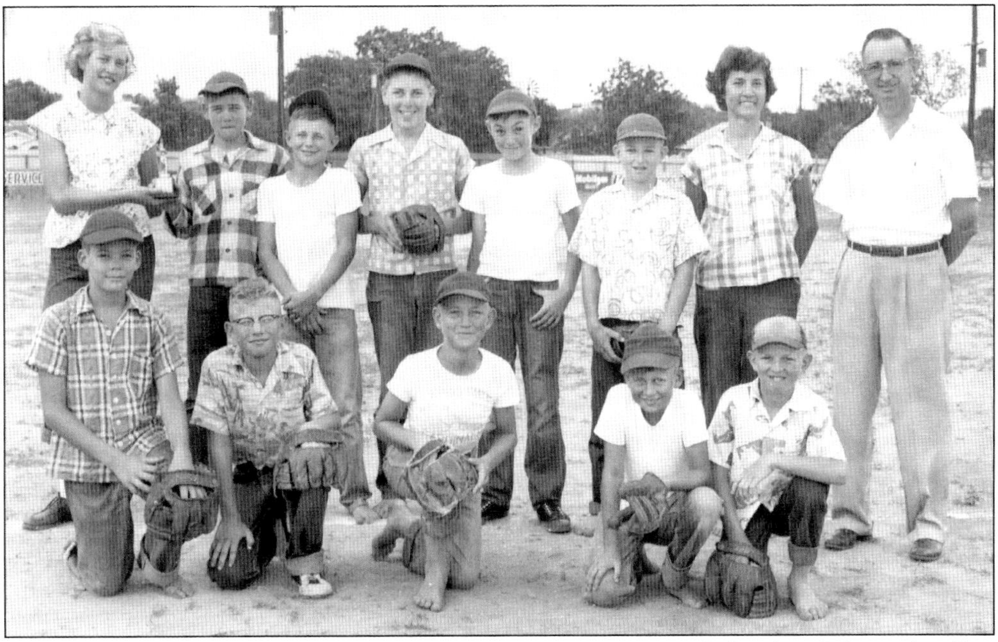

The Morris Ranch School softball team photograph in May 1955 includes, from left to right, (first row) pitcher Daniel Fritz, Chester Ahrens, Larry Heinemann, Delton Feller, and Leslie Klein; (second row) Helen Heinemann, Clayton Klein, Billy Roeder, Harvey Klein, August Brandon, Freddy Klein, Maxine Heinemann, and Joe Weinheimer (teacher.) Each country school would play in the tournament with other country schools. Many times, the teams traveled between schools in the bed of a pickup truck. (Courtesy of Dietel Collection.)

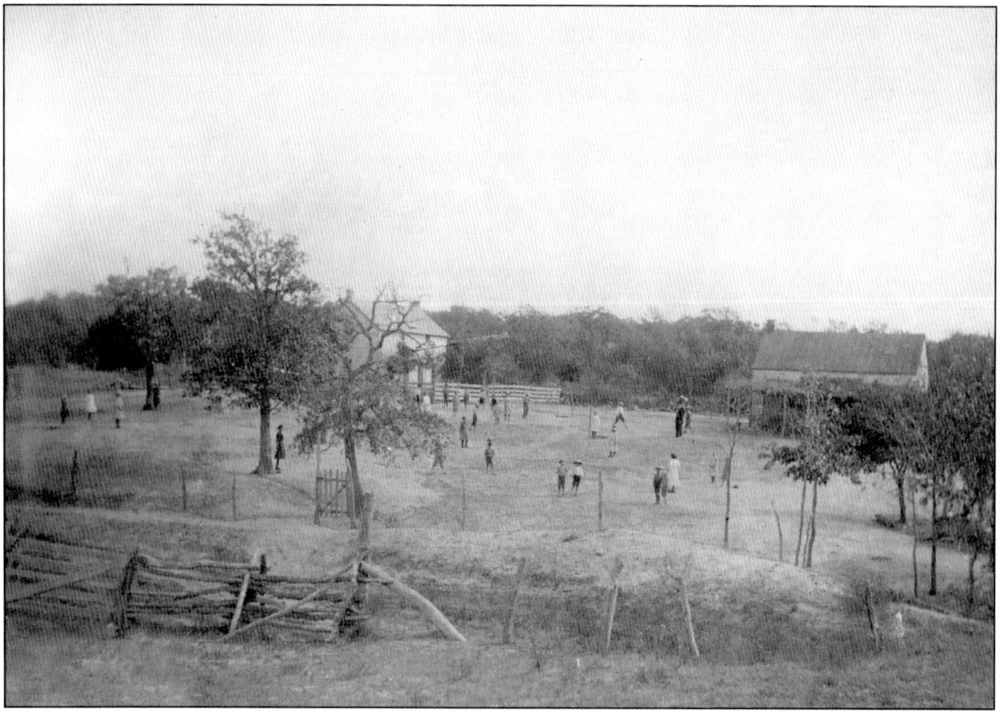

Children of various ages are seen playing at recess in the Palo Alto schoolyard around 1907. The school year started in late September and lasted eight months or till the end of May or early June. Subjects varied, but usually reading, writing, grammar, arithmetic, penmanship, German, English, and history were taught. (Courtesy of Jentsch Collection.)

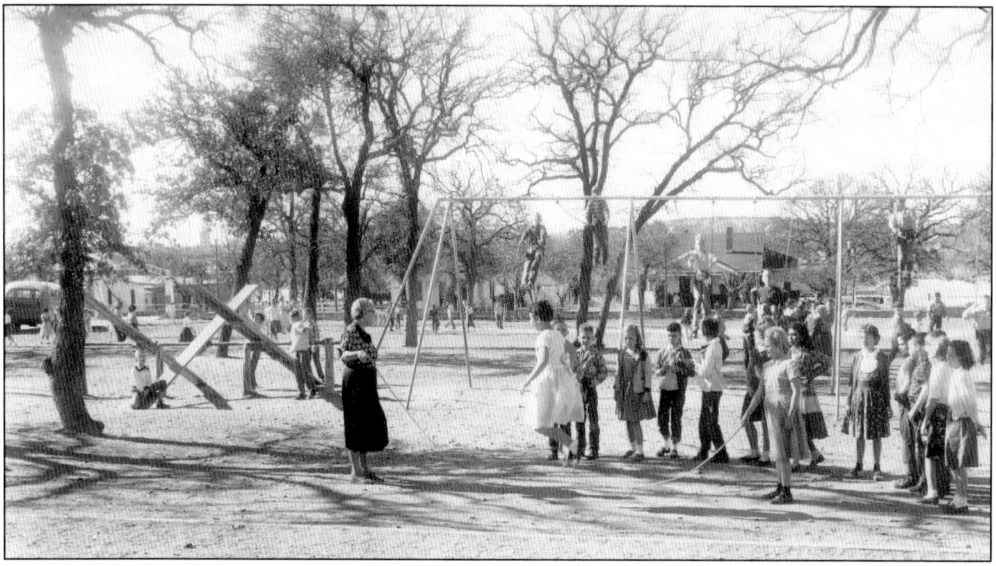

Fourth-, fifth-, and sixth-grade students are at play on the Fredericksburg Elementary School Campus. The photograph was taken to be included in a "Public School Week Issue" published in March 1957 by *The Radio Post*. The seesaws, slides, and swings were popular items on the playgrounds. Currently, this site is the middle school campus on West Travis Street. (Courtesy of Dietel Collection.)

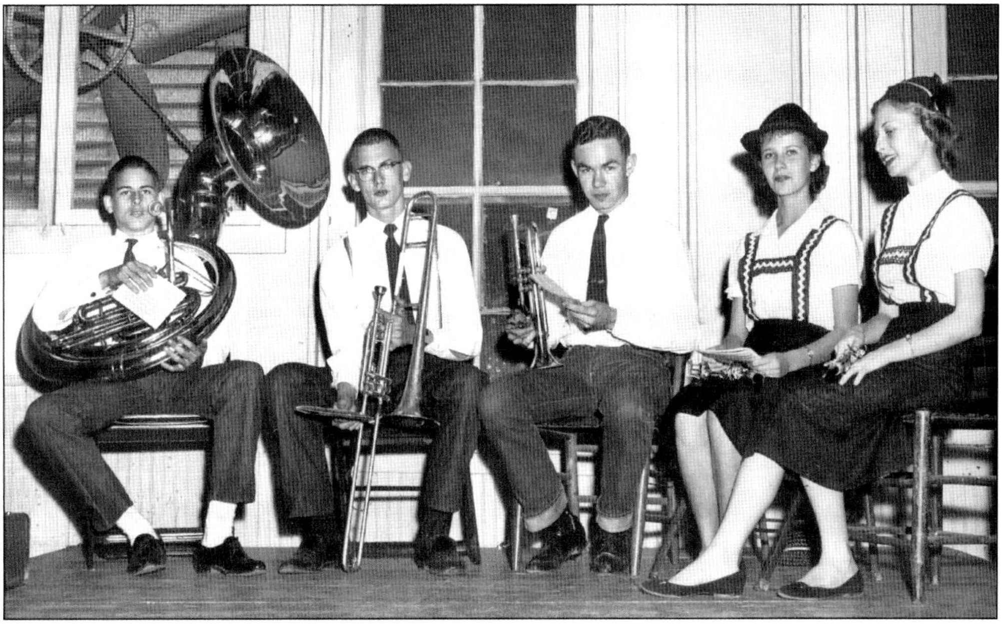

The Alpenveidchen Band composed of Fredericksburg High School band students played at the Girl Scout Round-Up in 1958 at the Turner Hall. From left to right, playing the bass horn was Jim Stephenson, on the trombone was Bruce Kowert, with E.W. Hallford on cornet, and playing clarinets were Iris Itz and Elaine Crenwelge. (Courtesy of Dietel Collection.)

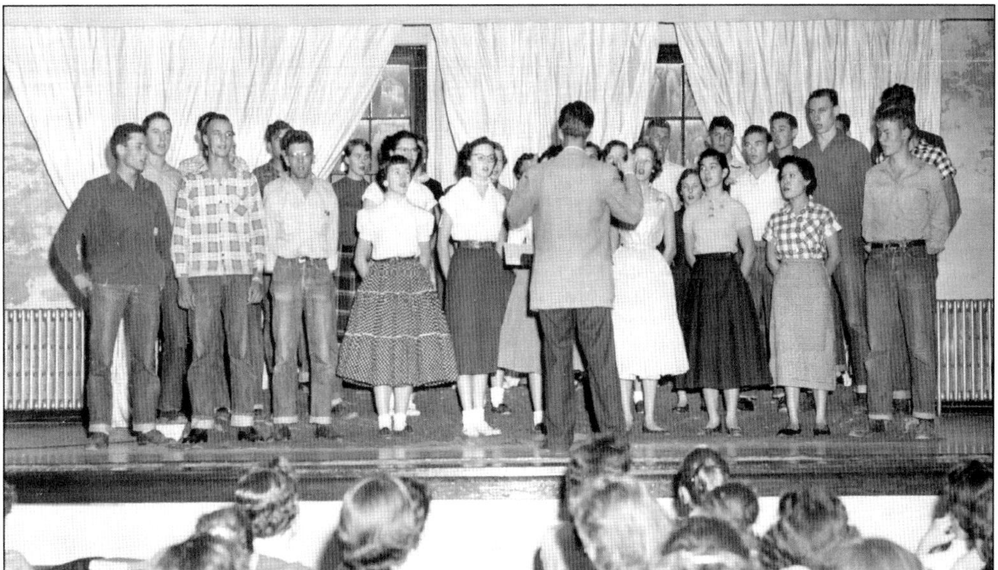

The Fredericksburg High School choir performs in March 1954 under the direction of Hilmar Wagner, the band and choir director, while singing for the student body. Pictured are, from left to right, (first row) Marvin Grosenbacher, Travis Langehennig, Donald Ottmers, Lottie Helen Gold, Martha Virden, Beverly Boening, Kitty Smith, Suzy Bartholmae, Joyce Feller, Mabel Schneider, and Rosita Castillo; (second row) Clarence Beckmann, Marlene Huebner, Vernell Treibs. Willard Dearing, Roy Woerner, Curtis Merz, Robert Houy, Billy Petmecky, and Charles Humes. (Courtesy of Dietel Collection.)

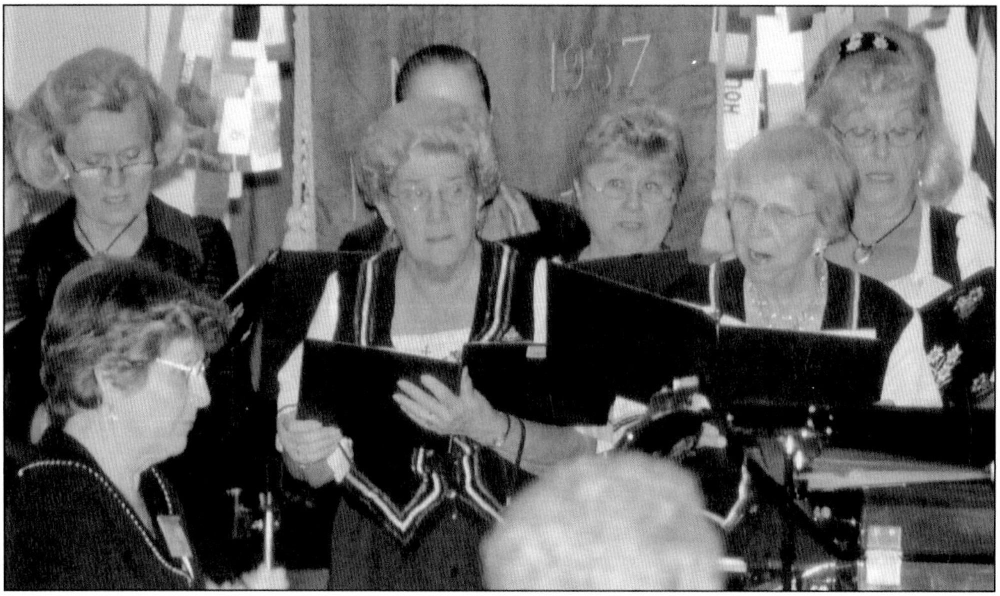

The Herman Sons Mixed Choir was started in 1934. Today, its director is Mark Heirholzer. In this photograph, local ladies in the center are Frances Hartmann (left), Carol Woitalla (center), and Elsa Rode, who are taking part in a sing-along with other members of the Saengerfest choir during the annual Saengerfest in 1987 . (Courtesy of Frances Hartmann.)

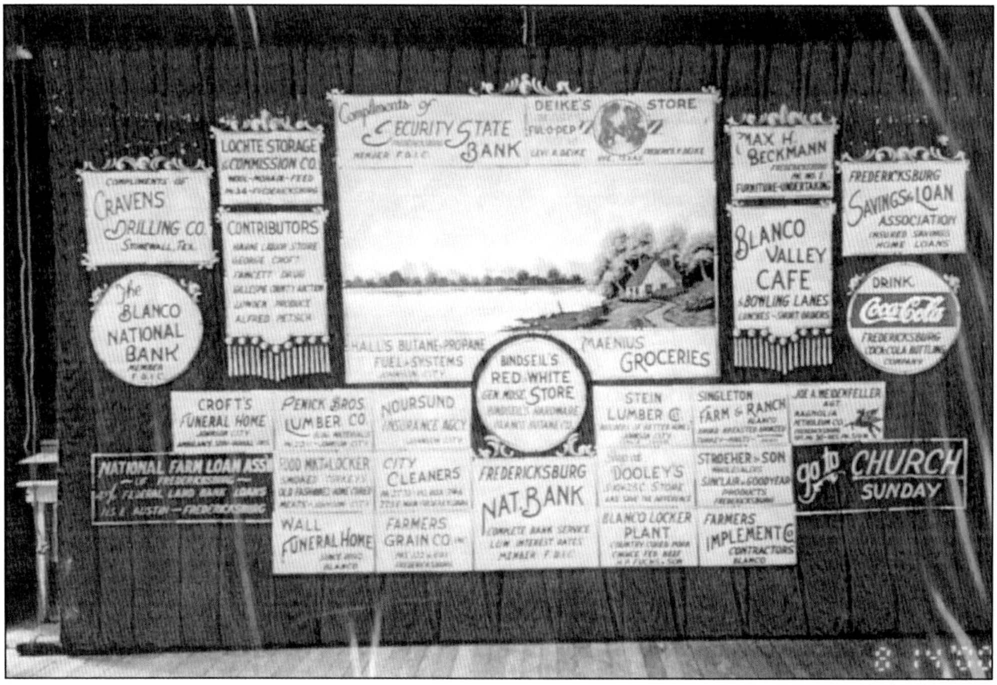

Williams Creek School in Albert had a canvas curtain for the stage, which was used at Christmas and school closing plays presented by the students. The curtain was painted by the Gordon Studio, of Austin, Texas, which was owned by Julia E. Gordon, an interior decorator. Each school sought donations from various businesses in the community to pay for the curtain. (Courtesy of Albert Community Club Collection.)

Albert 4-H girls are learning to sew clothing for the dress review project starting sewing projects at the early age of nine. Mothers served as leaders to teach taking measurements, placing and cutting pattern pieces from a cloth selection, and completing the outfit. Girls in the photograph include Shirleen Schumann, Elaine Schumann, Ellen Maenius, Carolyn Jenschke, Emmie Lou Itz, Laverne Ottmers, Peggy Schumann, Annie Lou Mayer, Carolyn Schumann, Josiepha Kunz, and Cheryle Maenius. (Courtesy of Albert Community Club Collection.)

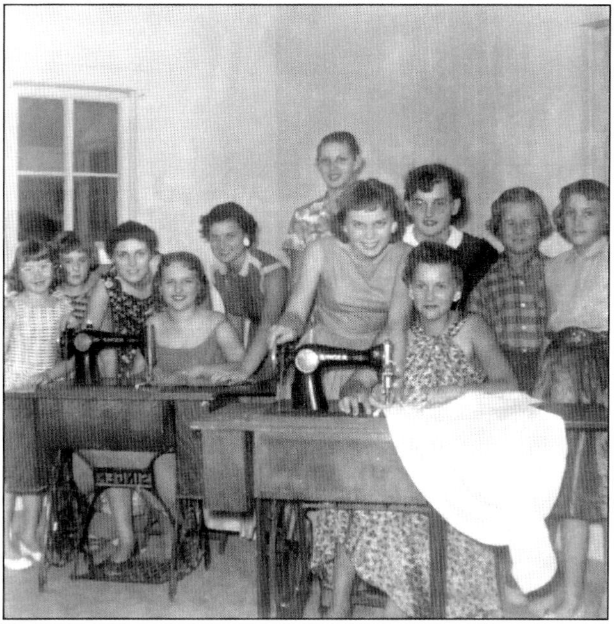

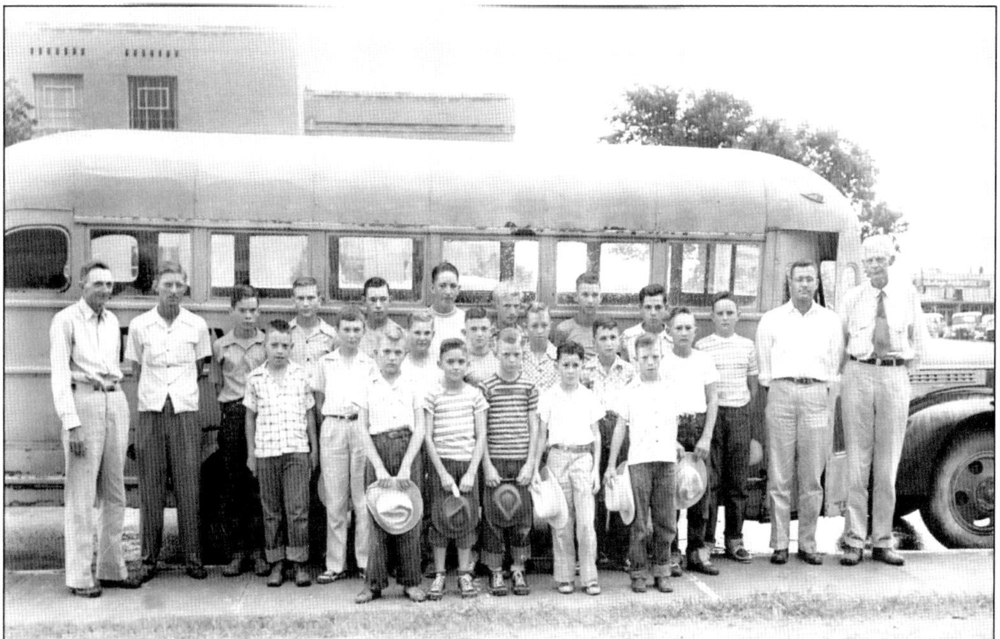

The 4-H Club boys enjoyed an annual outing to Bandera in 1949 for a three-day encampment at the Latter-day Saints reunion grounds. Posing next to the bus used for transportation are, from left to right, (first row) Marlin Schumann, Charles Burg, Henry J. Burg, Samuel Baethge, and Harvey Friedrich; (second row) Luther Baethge, Freddie Hartmann, Alton Meyer, James Eckhardt, Clemens Friedrich, James Hartmann, and Alvin Schumann; (third row) Lawrence Hartmann, Simon Burg, Ronald Doebbler, Stanley Ernst, Elroy Ransleben, Kermit Lochte, Hayden Grona, Rueben Heinemann, Stanley Meier, Kelton Lange, A.V. Garrett, and H.F. Grote, the county agent. (Courtesy of Dietel Collection.)

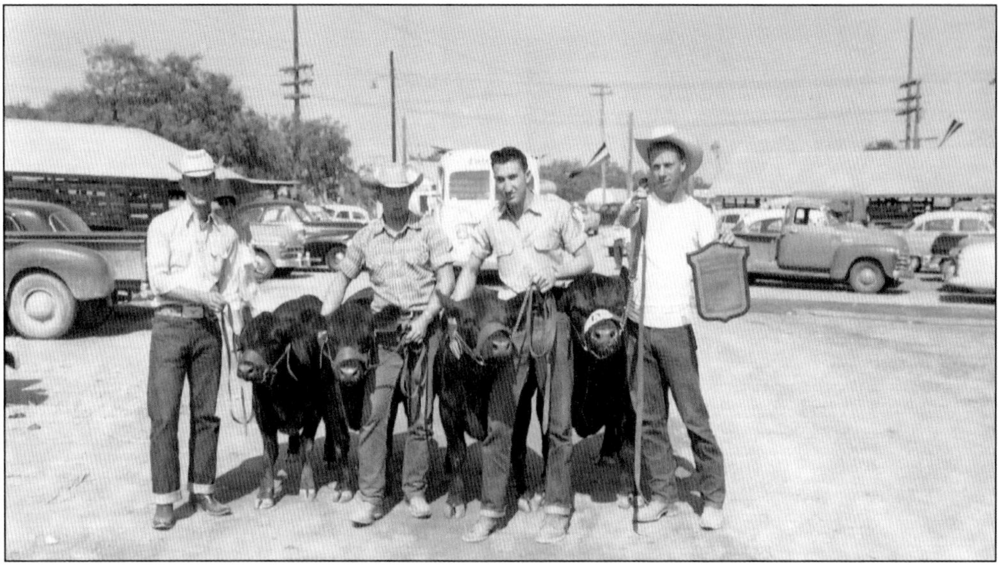

During the 22nd Annual Gillespie County FFA and 4-H Stock Show on January 23, 1954, these FFA boys showed Angus show calves. Boys and girls worked many hours in the months prior to feed, train, and practice grooming the animals before showtime. These FFA boys are A.C. Kast, Bill Teague, James Welgehausen, and Dudley Althaus. (Courtesy of Bill Teague Collection.)

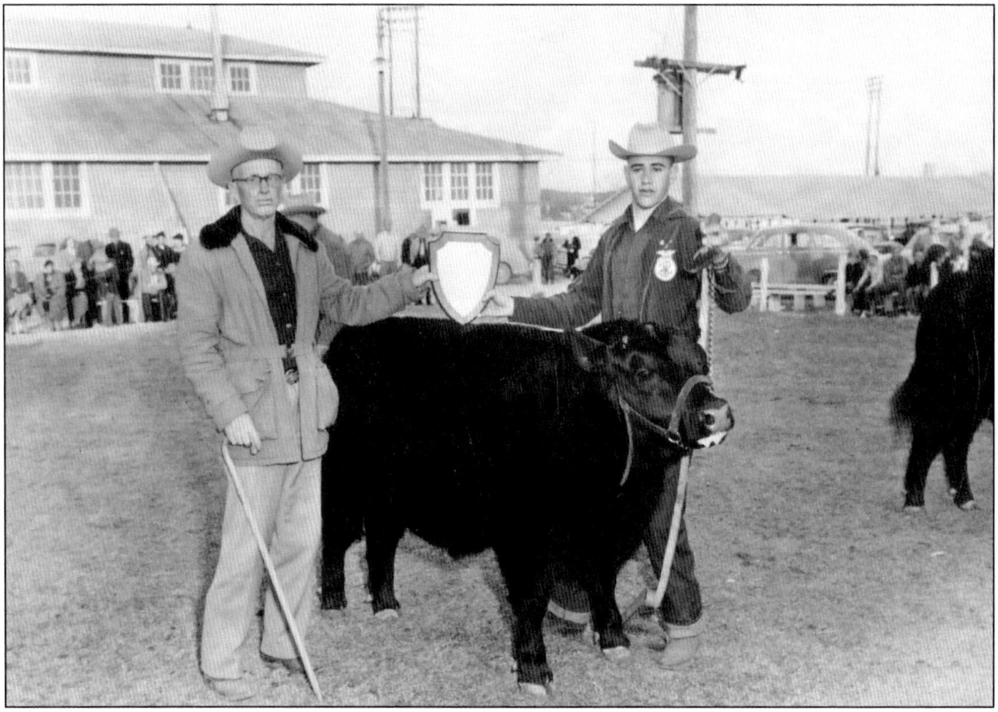

Atlee Lochte, Fredericksburg FFA member, showed the champion Angus steer at the 22nd Annual 4-H FFA Stock Show on January 23, 1954. Nolan Althaus, a registered Angus breeder, presented a plaque from the Hill Country Angus Breeders Association for Atlee's outstanding achievement. The stock show was held at the old fairgrounds at the corner of South Adams and Park Streets, the site now occupied by HEB. (Courtesy of Dietel Collection.)

Wilburn Pfeiffer exhibited the grand champion turkey tom at the 22nd Annual 4-H FFA Stock Show in 1954. "Willie" purchased and fed the turkey as a 4-H project. He sold the turkey at the auction, which followed the judging. His brother, Archie, showed the reserve grand champion tom. (Courtesy of Dietel Collection.)

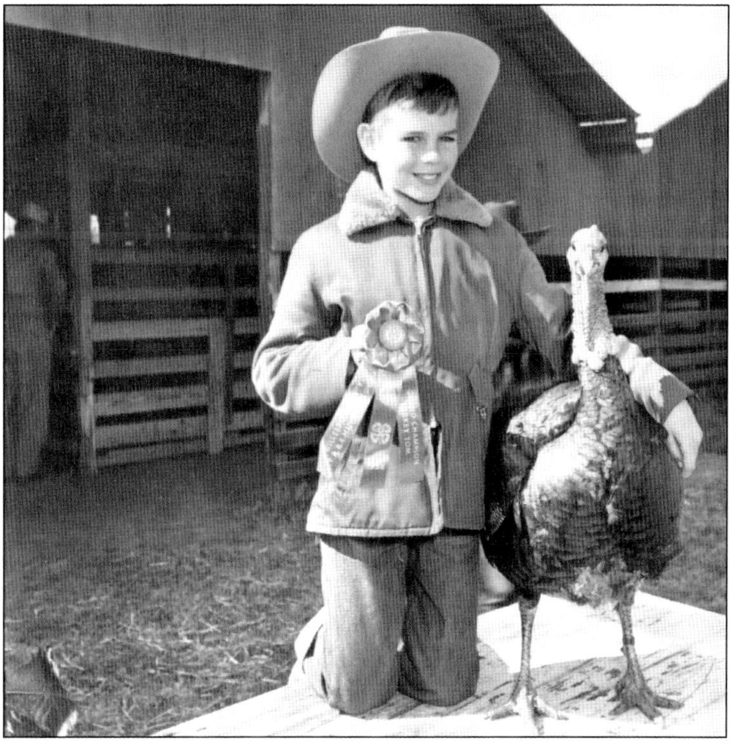

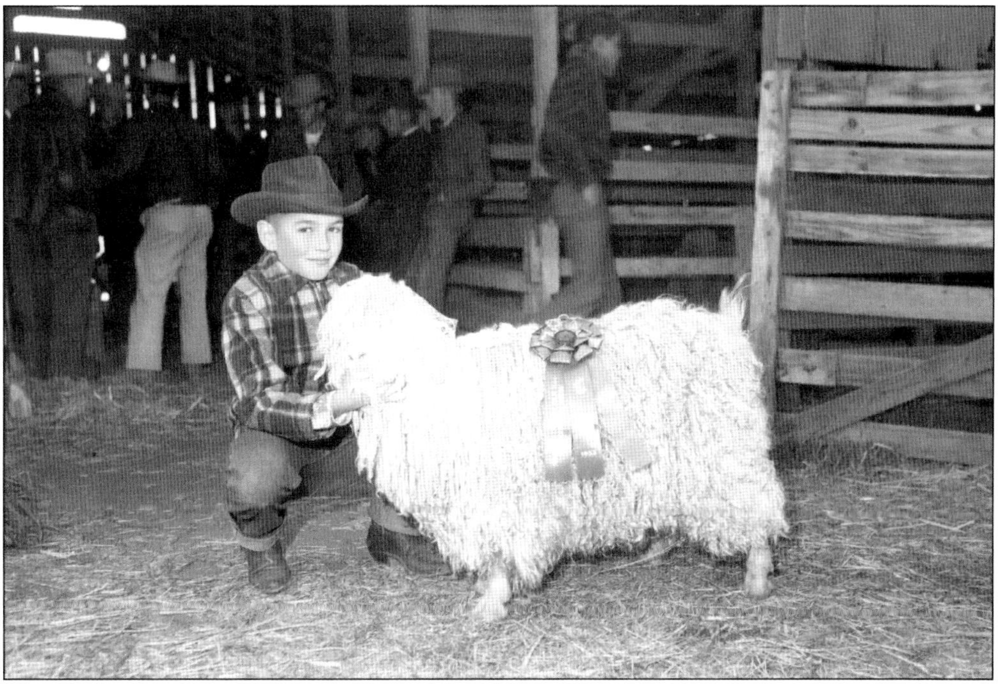

Carlton Wendel shows his prize-winning Grand Champion Billy Angora goat during the 21st Annual Youth Stock Show in January 1953. Wendel was a member of the Harper 4-H Club and the son of Victor and Johanna Wendel. The photograph was taken in the barn area of the old Gillespie County Fairgrounds, where HEB Food Store is now located. (Courtesy of Dietel Collection.)

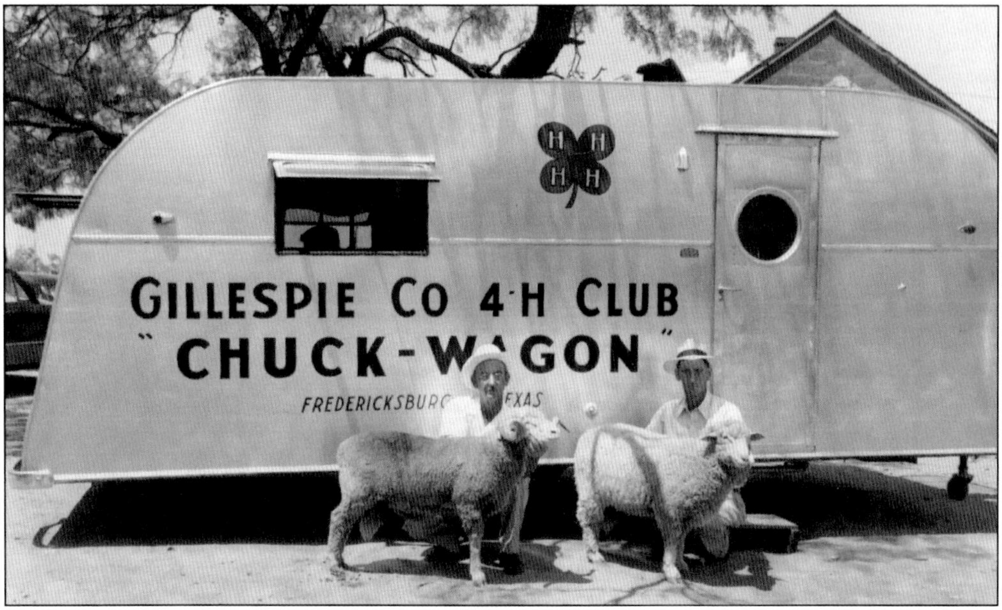

The Gillespie County 4-H Club acquired a 25-foot house trailer on June 15, 1950, appropriately called the "Chuck-Wagon." It was used by 4-H Club members and the FFA, under the jurisdiction of the 4-H Club, for attending stock shows, tours, and trips. The club sold chances for a registered Rambouillet ram, held by Emil Sauer, and a registered Corriedale ram, held by Otto Spaeth, at the county fair to help pay for the Chuck-Wagon. (Courtesy of Dietel Collection.)

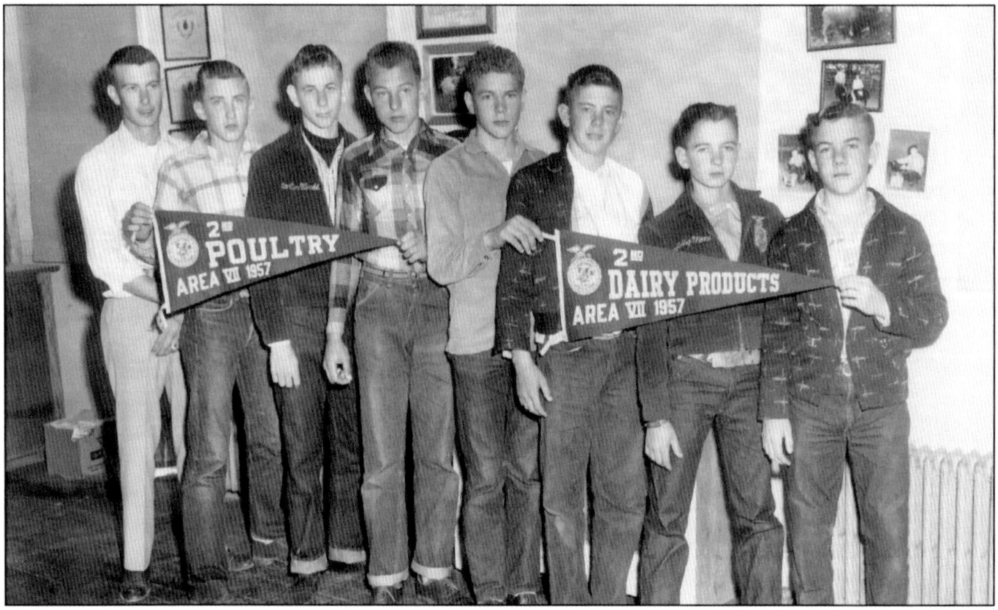

These young men are on Fredericksburg High School's Future Farmers Association Poultry and Dairy Products Judging teams in April 1957. The boys selected to the team had demonstrated their judging expertise and built confidence and pride in their own decision-making. Pictured are, from left to right, vocational ag instructor Ken Killion, Calvin Friedrich, Martin Wendel, Calvin Ransleben, Davis Schumacher, Billy Roeder, Bobby Monk, and J. Duderstadt. (Courtesy of Dietel Collection.)

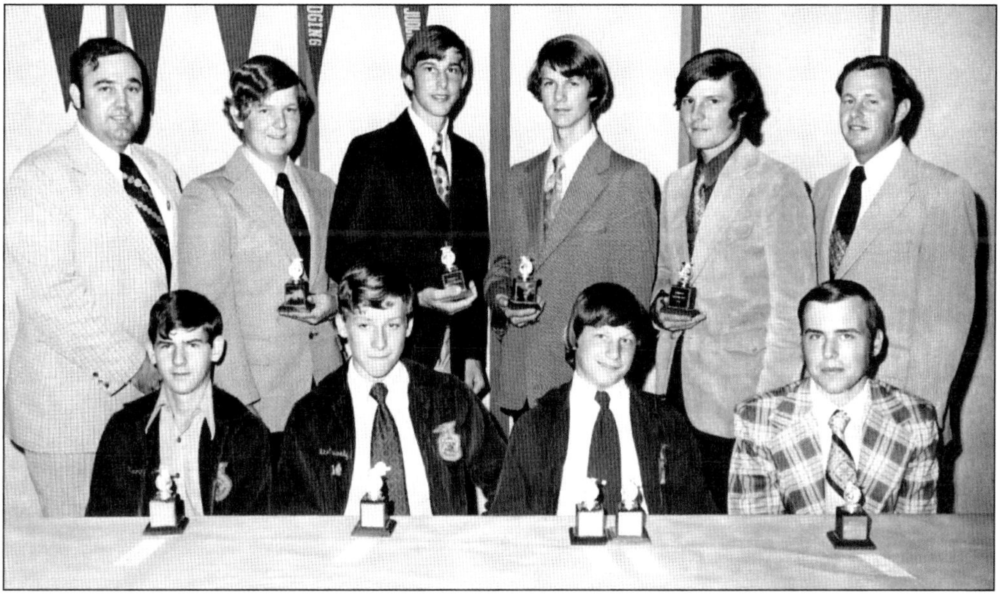

Future Farmers Associations across America include members who are enrolled in classes to promote agriculture and involve students in agriculture. The 1975 awards banquet was held in May to honor those boys who had been top competitors at contests. Pictured are, from left to right, (first row) Larry Meier, Dale Crenwelge, Glenn Jung, and Darrell Mohr; (second row) Albert Usener (agriculture teacher), Robert Beckmann, Barrett Klein, Daniel Woerner, Lyle Malechek, and Roger Crenwelge (agriculture teacher). (Courtesy of Jeanette Beckmann.)

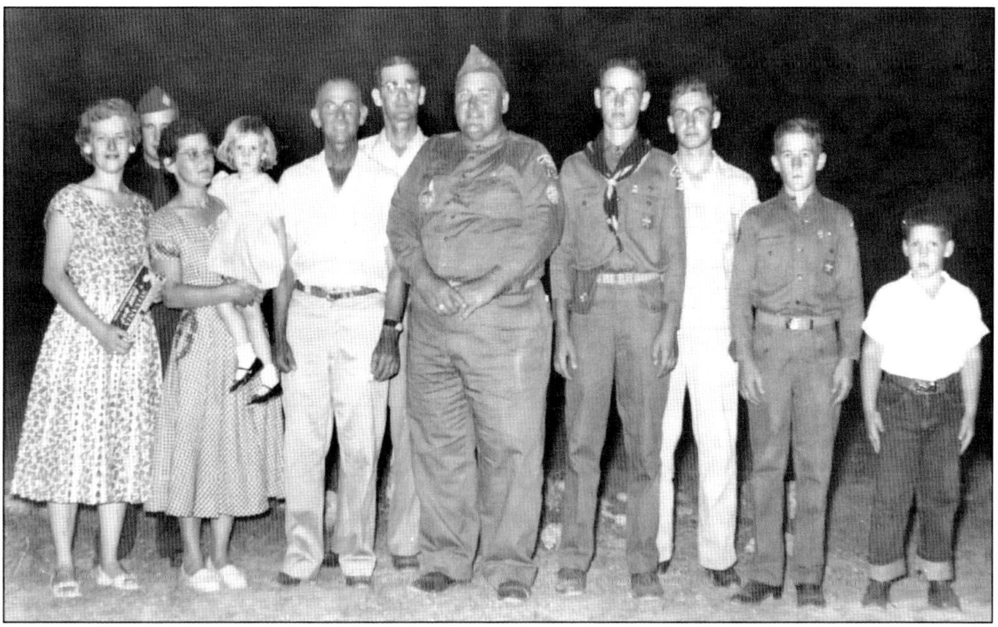

Family members formed the Doss Delegation for the tapping out ceremonies for candidates for membership in the Order of the Arrow at Camp Tom Wooten on July 18, 1957. Members of the Doss Scout troop and families are Shirley Lange, Gordon Sauer, Marie Sauer holding Cindy Sauer, Emil Sauer, Otto Spaeth, Scoutmaster Harry Wahrmund, Clifford Spaeth, Marion Baethge, Tony Sauer, and Rodney Sauer. (Courtesy of Dietel Collection.)

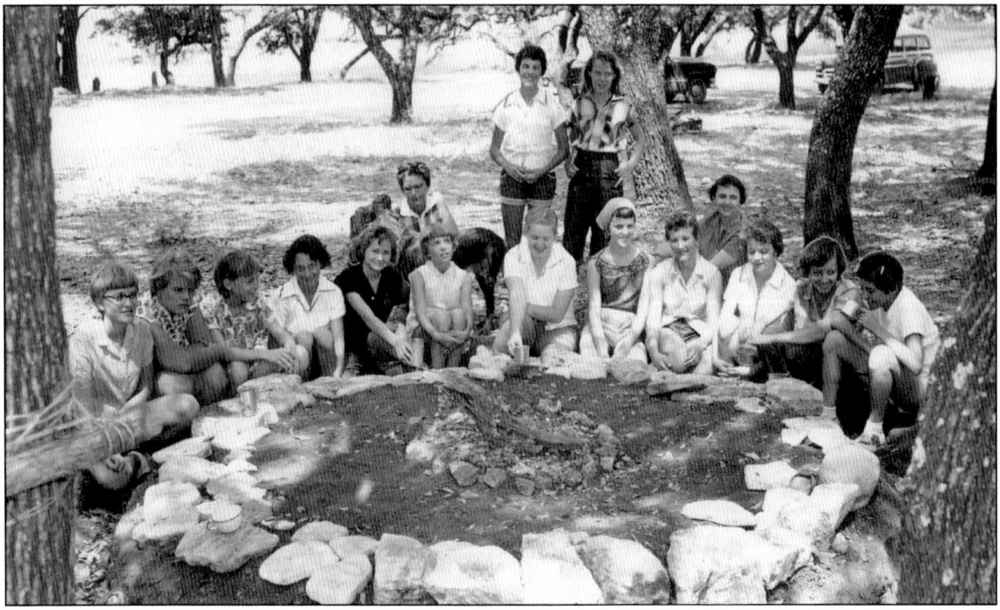

Girl Scout Unit VI, Pioneer Unit with May Cox, leader, and assistant leaders DeRose Schoenewolf, Dora Stein, and Ruth Boerner built a Danish table. The table was made by digging trenches and piling dirt on a flat center. Big rocks were laid around the center to eliminate getting plates dirty. (Courtesy of Dietel Collection.)

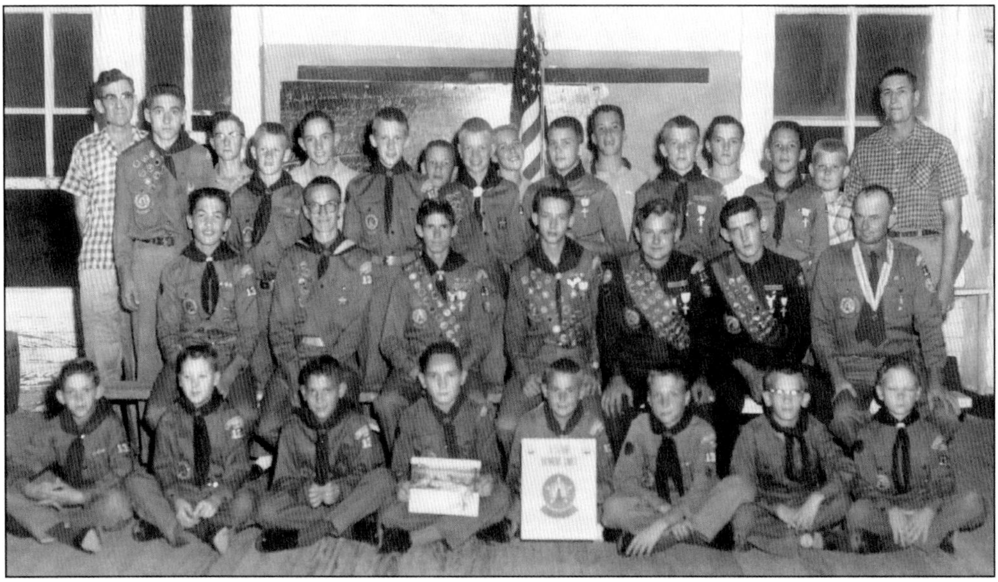

This photograph of Boy Scout Troop 134 includes, from left to right, (first row) Gary Itri, John Paul Weidenfeller, Eugene Hartmann Jr., Patrick Heep, Greg Kaiser, Vernon Meurer, Gary Pyka, and Wesley Giesbers; (second row) Bruce Eckhardt, Douglas Moritz, Donald Itri, Danny Kaye Heep, Billy Kruse, Michael Weber, Bill Kruse (Scoutmaster); (third row) Hugo Giesbers (troop committeeman), Douglas Sollohub, David Tatsch, Charles Mazurek, Anthony Heep, Ricky Hext, Donald Rink, Anthony Moritz, Barry Kaiser, John Walch, David St. Clair, John Hext, Daniel Heep, James St. Clair, Freddie Kruse, and Anthony "Tony" Hartmann (assistant Scoutmaster). (Courtesy of Dietel Collection.)

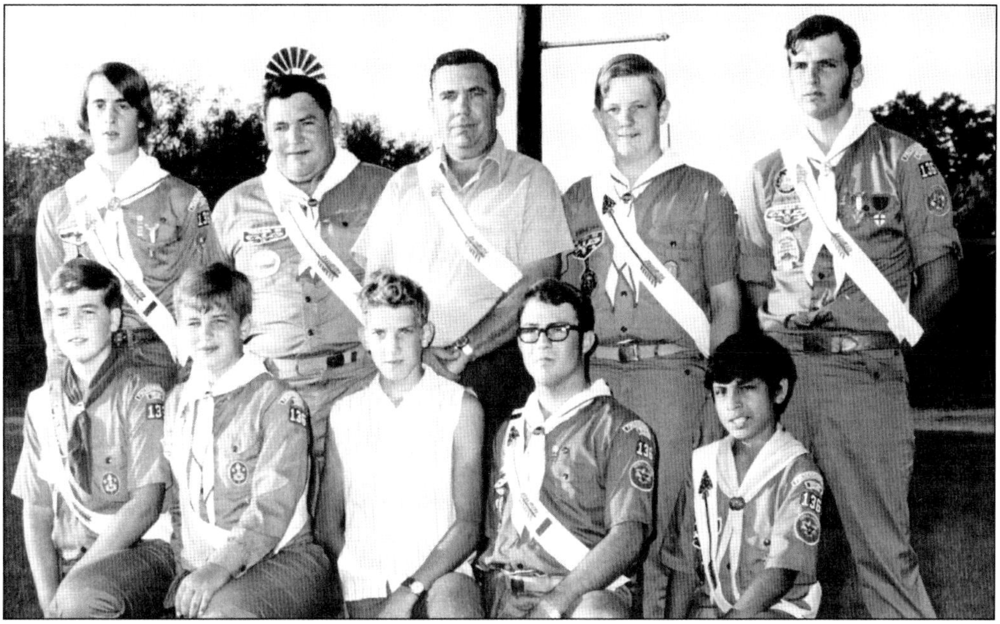

In 1973, Boys Scout Troop 136 were inducted during the ceremony awarding the Order of the Arrow from the Boy Scouts of America. Pictured are from left to right, (first row) Dennis Crenwelge, Wilbert Hazelett, Carlos Moellering, David Hannemann, and Joe Martinez; (second row) William Brown, Don Hazelett (Scoutmaster), Melvin Beckmann (chairman), Robert Beckmann, and Eugene Whitehead. (Courtesy of Jeanette Beckmann.)

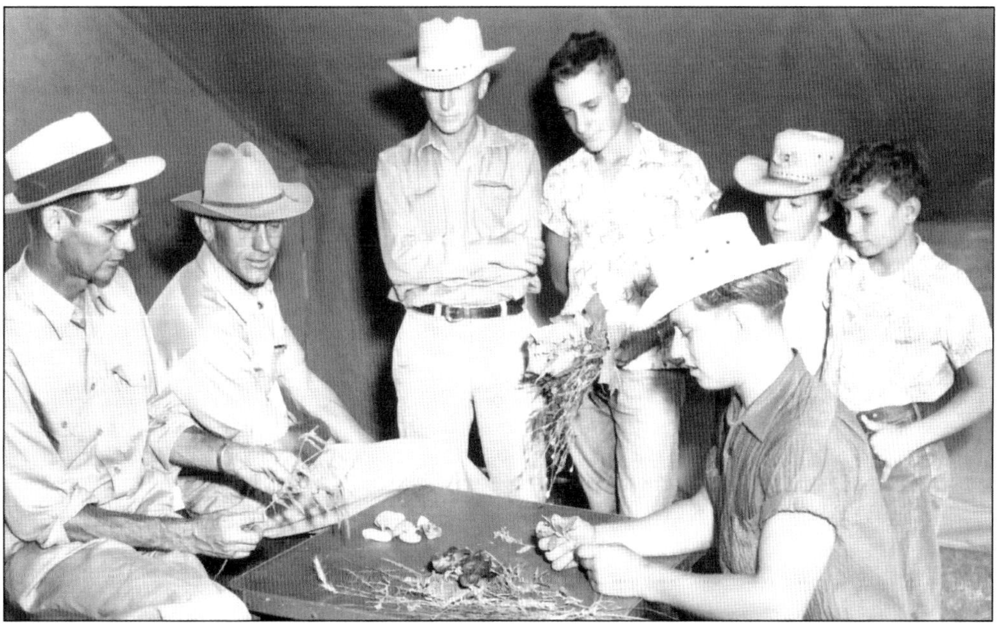

Doss Boy Scouts and counselors pose for a photograph at camp held on the Herman Evers Ranch at Beaver Creek. In order to earn a nature merit badge, they had to identify plants and geological specimens in the Scout training program. Identifying plants are, from left to right, Otto Spaeth, Albert Ellebracht, Albert Sieckmann, Sidney Ellebracht, Kermit Friedrich, Billy Mund, and an unidentified visitor. (Courtesy of Dietel Collection.)

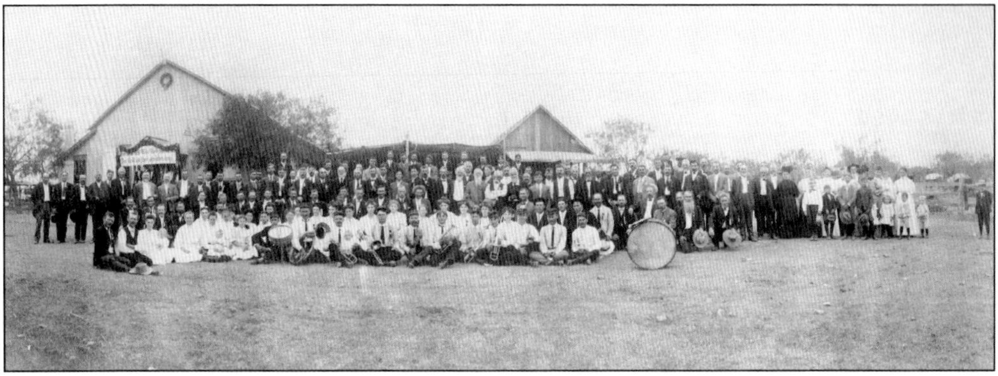

The German phrase on the building at left reads: "*Wer nicht liebt wein, weib, und gesang, Der bleibt ein Narr sein leben lang*" (He who does not love wine, woman, and song remains a fool his life long). The 1896 Saengerfest members held their annual meeting, which usually took place in September or October, for two to four days, with communities from as far away as San Antonio and New Braunfels taking turns as hosts. (Courtesy of Saengerfest.)

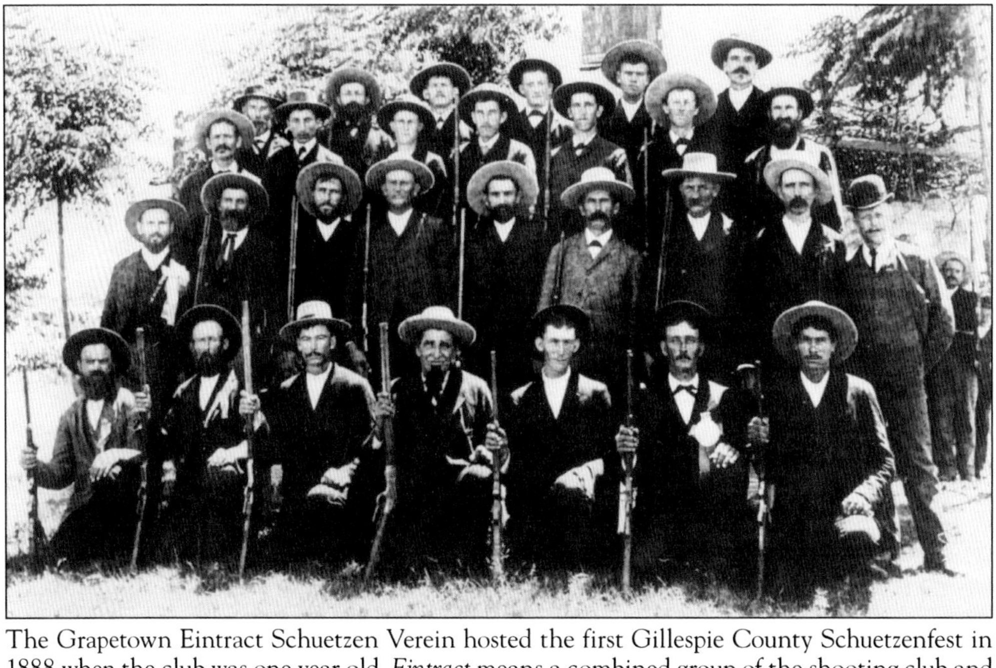

The Grapetown Eintract Schuetzen Verein hosted the first Gillespie County Schuetzenfest in 1888 when the club was one year old. *Eintract* means a combined group of the shooting club and the singing group. Pictured are, from left to right, (first row) Wm. Kallenberg, Carl Enderlin Sr., Carl Tatsch, August Hoffmann, Robert Rausch, William Rausch Sr., and Emil Doebbler; (second row) W. Dettlefson, Ferdinand Gellerman Sr., Alfred Doebbler, Louis Kuhlmann Sr., Theodore Hohenberger, John Knopp, Henry Kuhlmann, Ernest Luckenbach, and Fritz Heyer; (third row) August Schaefer, August Klinksiek, Wm. Gellermann, Henry Klinksiek, Henry Cowan, Louis Ebers, and Gus Weirich; (fourth row) John Rausch, Fritz Kirchhoff, Henry Filter Sr., Carl Rausch, Willie Tatsch, and Robert Hohenberger. (Courtesy of Kilman Collection.)

Six

Agriculture and Commerce

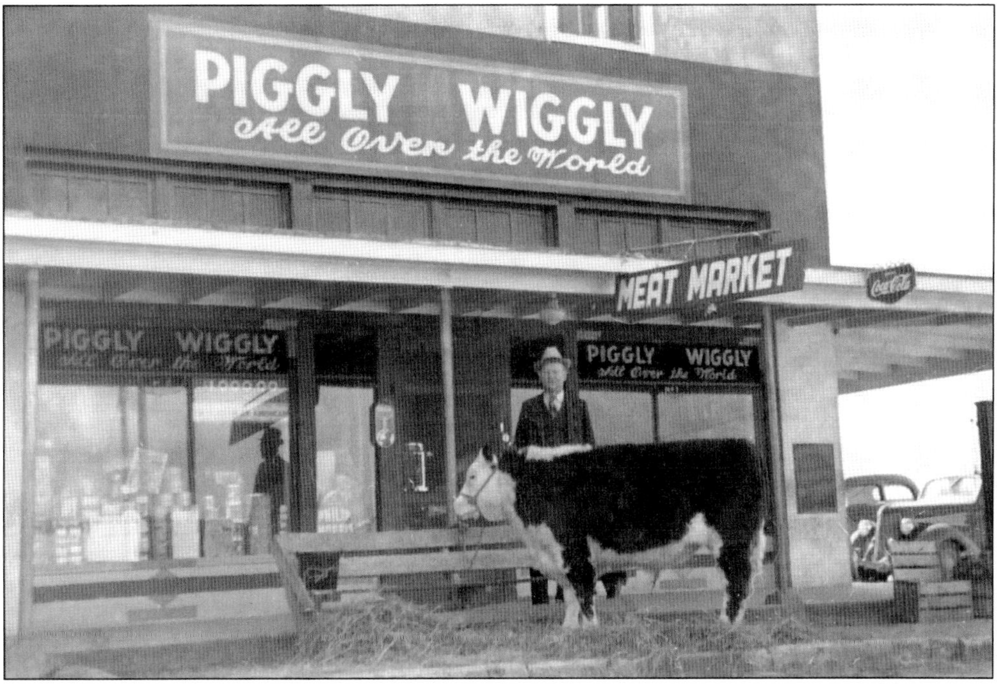

Gillespie County merchants have long supported annual Youth Livestock Shows, held annually in January, paying $477,000 in 2012 to support Gillespie County 4-Hers and Fredericksburg and Harper FFA members. In 1940, Henry Maier poses in front of the Piggly Wiggly store and meat market with the champion calf he had purchased. Piggly Wiggly was located on the southeast corner of Main and Adams Streets. (Courtesy of Bill Teague.)

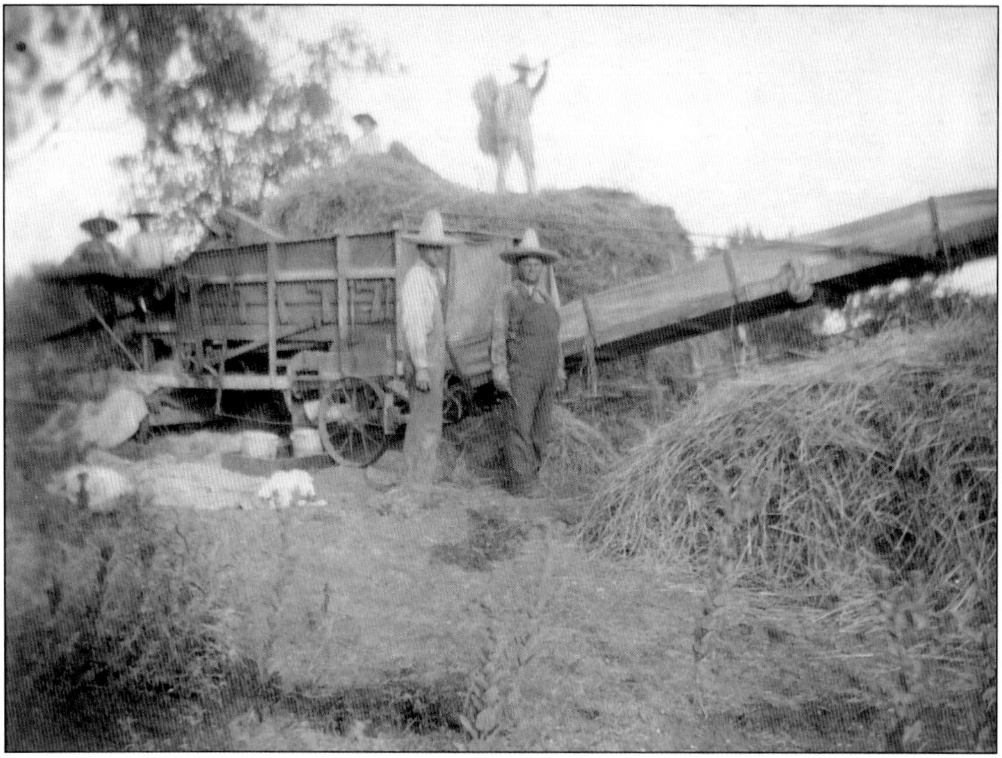

From the late 1800s into the 1930s, farm families worked together to harvest grain using a steam engine–operated threshing machine. Willie and Emil Eckert worked farms throughout the Bear Creek Community using this thresher. Tractor-drawn combined reaper-threshers, later called combines, began replacing the threshers in the 1920s. Threshing required a huge amount of labor, including for women who prepared meals for the workers. (Courtesy of John D. Eckert family.)

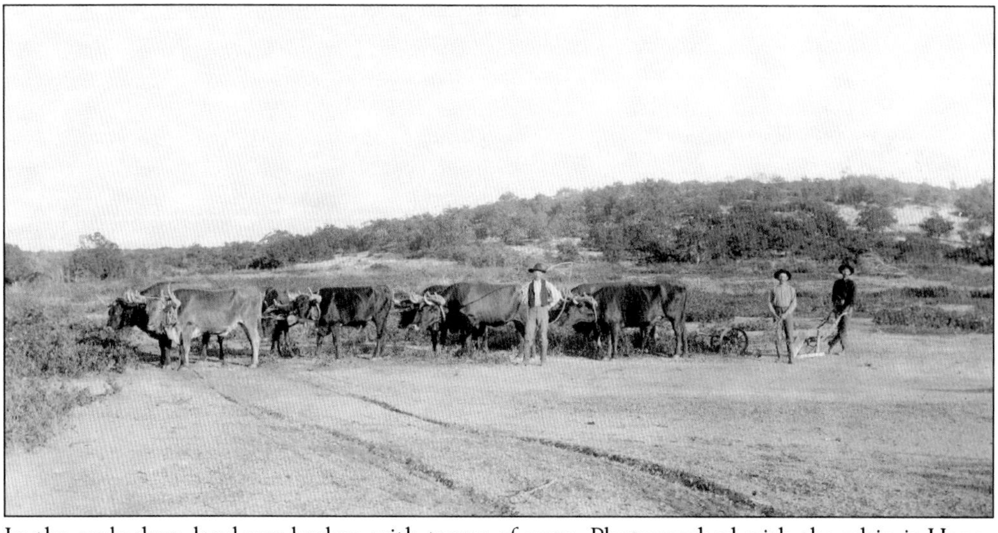

In the early days, land was broken with teams of oxen. Photographed with the whip is Henry Herman Ahrens; he lived in the Cherry Spring Community making a living as a farmer and teamster. Later, draft horses and mules replaced most of the oxen, and of course, tractors later replaced all draft animals. (Courtesy of Weinheimer Collection.)

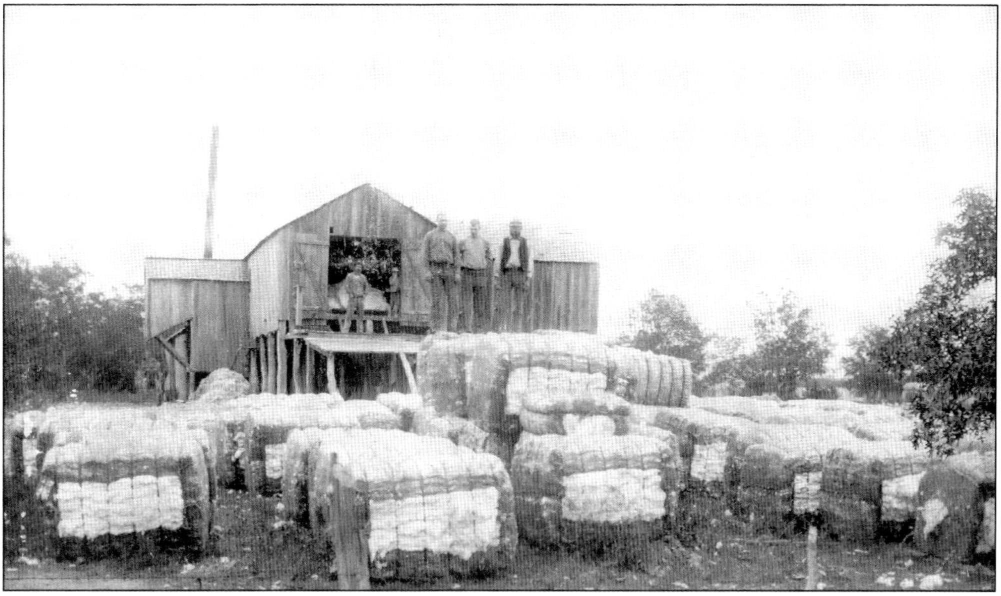

Before the first gin in Doss was built, cotton farmers had to haul their cotton to Morris Ranch. Around 1917, the Doss gin was owned by Willie Rosenbusch. He bought out his brother, Robert, who had bought the gin from the MacDonald brothers, the owners of the second gin in Doss. In 1924, two thousand bales were ginned, loaded, and shipped to market from this gin. (Courtesy of Gertrude and Harvey Land.)

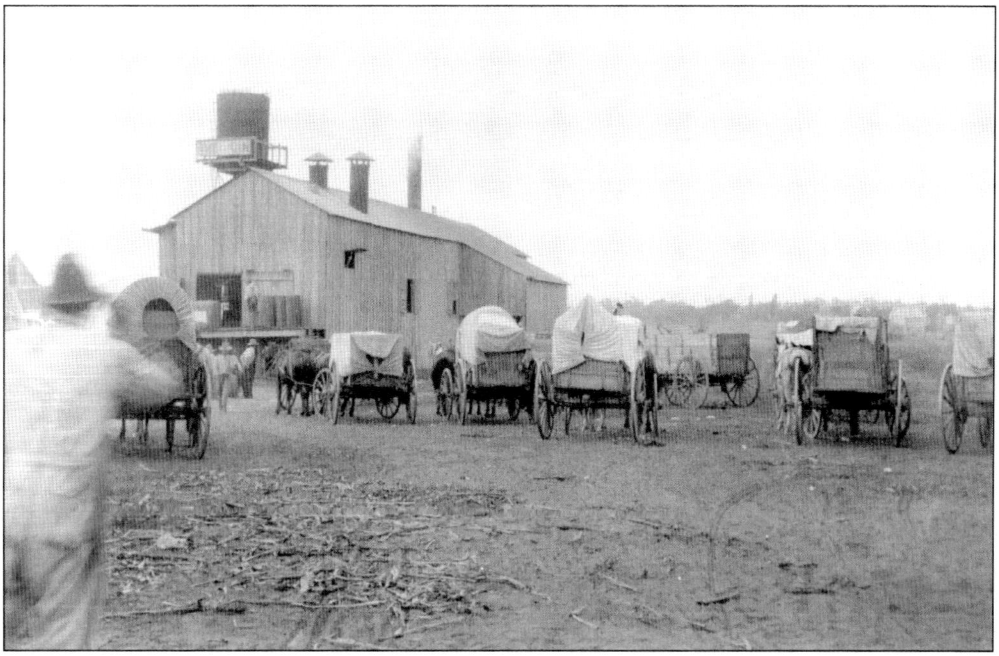

Cotton was an important cash crop for Gillespie County from its beginning until the boll weevils could not be controlled in 1920s. Pfeil Brothers Gin, whose trademark was an arrow (*pfeil* means "arrow" in German) was one of 17 gins in Gillespie County. Built by G.A. Pfeil on "Orphans Land" he had bought, it was called the G.A. Pfeil Addition. When his sons Otto and Felix became the owners, they retained the name. (Courtesy of GCHS.)

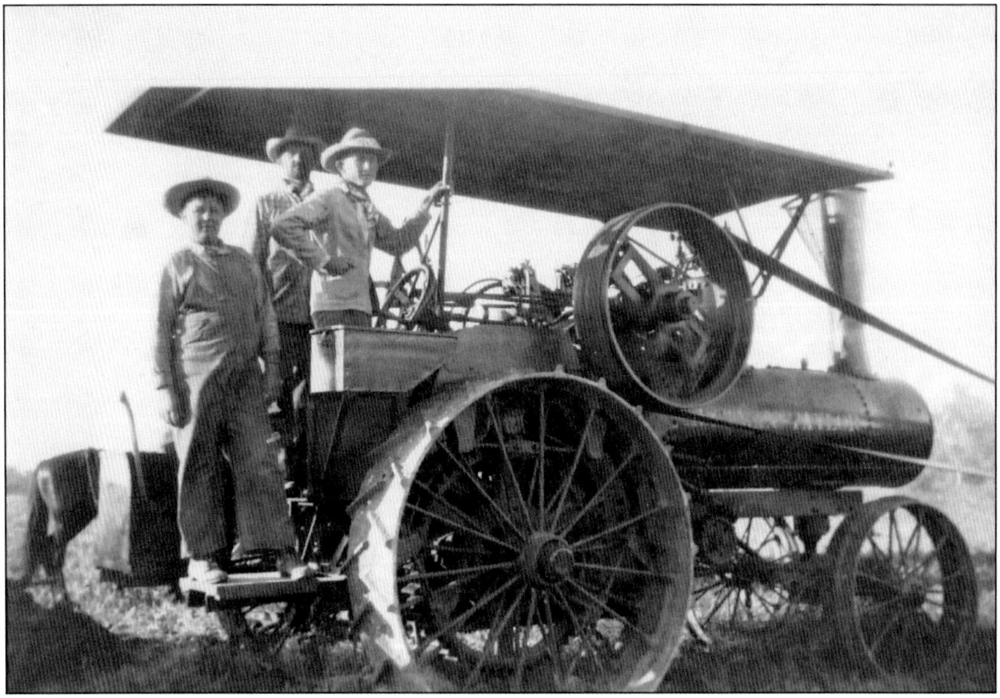

Three men pose on a large steam-driven tractor powering a threshing machine with a flat-belt drive in the Bear Creek Community. Those identified are William Eckert and Walter Heimann. This type of tractor was considered very large and very modern. (Courtesy of Gertrude and Harvey Land.)

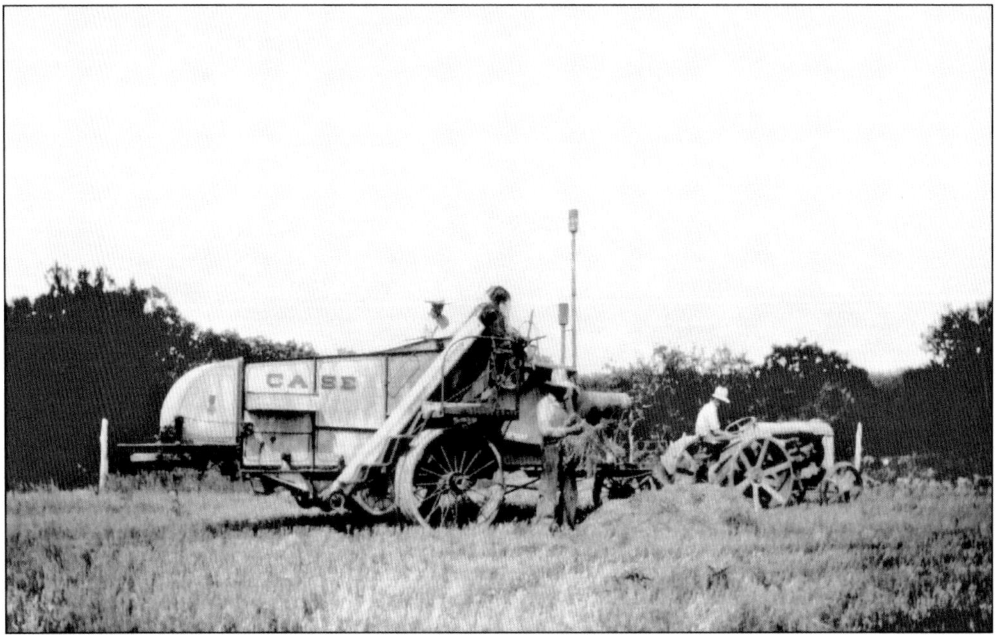

By the 1920s, combines began replacing trashing machines. A Case combine is being pulled by a tractor operated by Albert Kleck. By the 1950s, modern farmers began using self-propelled combines. (Courtesy of Bill Teague.)

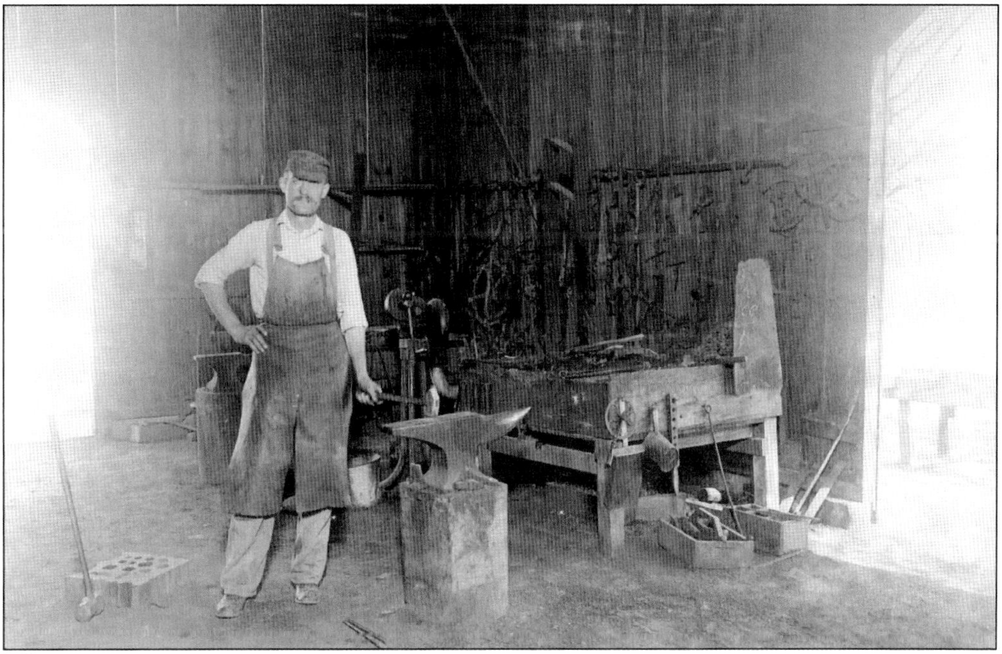

Early farm machinery was commonly repaired by a blacksmith. Arthur Fischer stands by a large anvil at a shop owned by Henry Franz, which was located on the corner of North Adams and East Austin Streets where Wesley Franz continued operations as a blacksmith, welder, and general auto repair until the 1970s. The old longleaf pine building still stands today. (Courtesy of GCHS.)

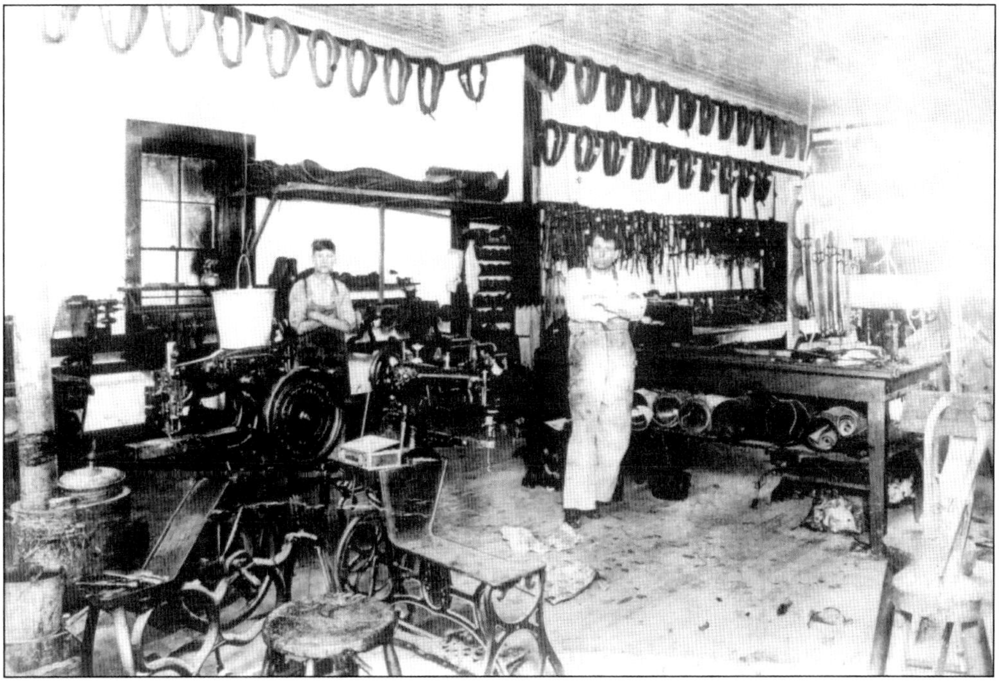

An important business in a city the size of Fredericksburg was a saddle shop. Arthur Schaetter (left), a 14-year-old employee, stands in the Alex Maier Saddle Shop. The saddle shop remained open for many years, operated by Alex Maier's son-in-law, "Joe" Duderstadt. (Courtesy of Bill Teague.)

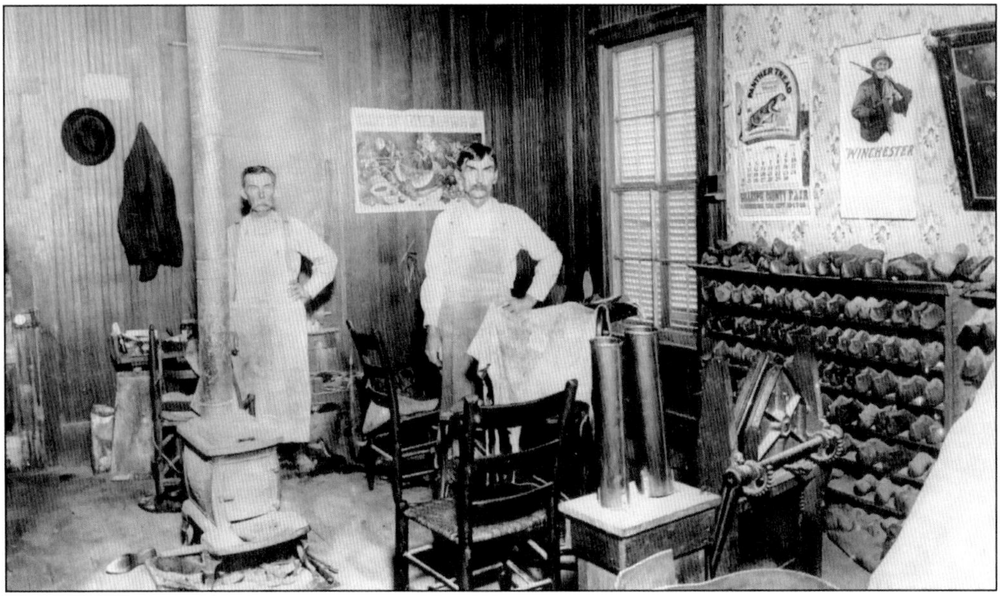

Early citizens considered shoes an investment needing maintenance and repair. Friedrich is photographed standing next to chimney of a wood stove with Richard Ludwig, who is standing in the midst of their trade inside Ludwig Shoe Shop located at 414 East Main Street in Fredericksburg. The calendar on the wall tells that the year is 1915. The bottom of the calendar advertises the Gillespie County Fair being held September 16 to 18. (Courtesy of Wehmeyer, Johnson Collection.)

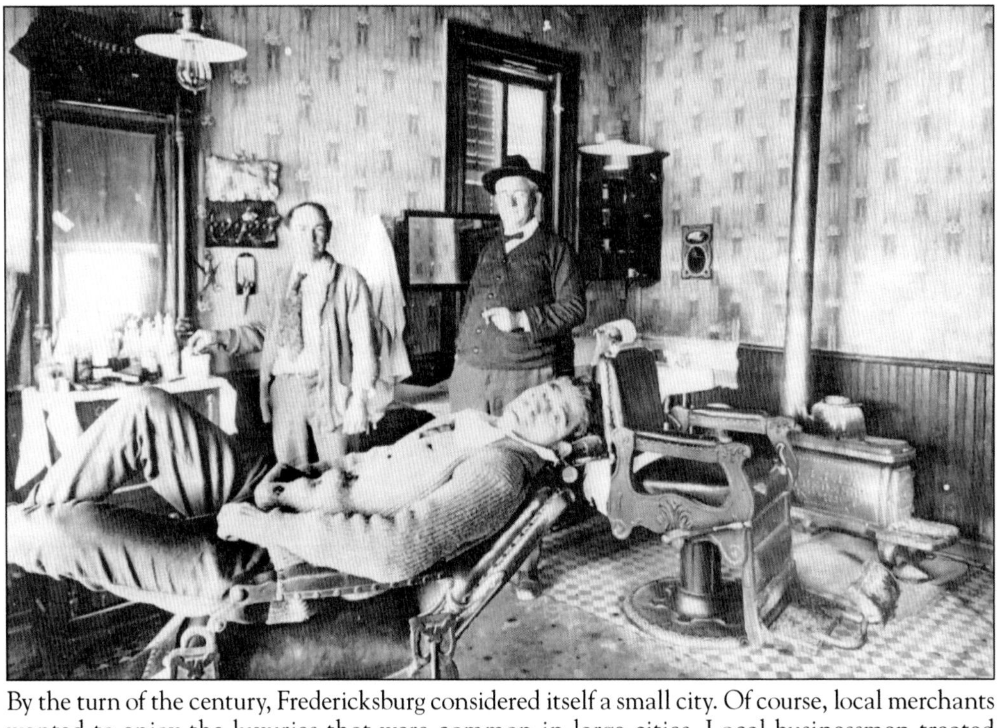

By the turn of the century, Fredericksburg considered itself a small city. Of course, local merchants wanted to enjoy the luxuries that were common in large cities. Local businessmen treated themselves to a shave at Grobe's Barber Shop. Seated is a Mr. Metzger, while a Mr. Gold enjoys a cigar. (Courtesy of Bill Teague.)

Lena Neffendorf (right) and Olga Frantzen are stirring the syrup from sugarcane, which is being cooked in a big vat, holding 60 gallons, and forming fine molasses at the Neffendorf Molasses Press. The cooking process was being fired by a new and modern propane gas burner, having eliminated the cumbersome wood-burning process. An average of 106 to 108 gallons of molasses was cooked daily. (Courtesy of Dietel Collection.)

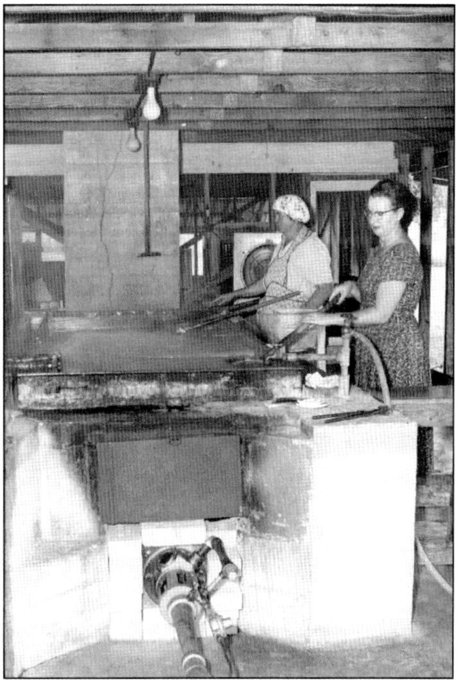

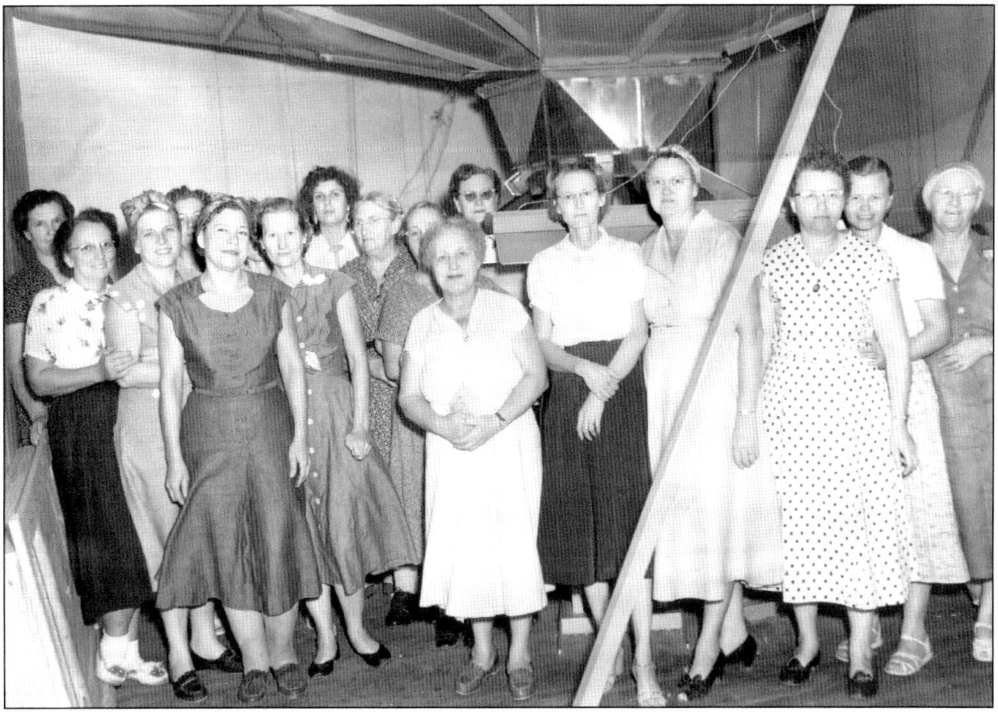

Peanuts were graded by ladies sitting at vibrating tables. As peanuts moved across the table, ladies would remove the bad ones. Quality Peanut Company celebrated completion of its remodeled plant with an open house on October 7, 1955. The company had in its employ 55 people, of whom 35, all women, worked on the picking table, with 18 on one shift and 17 on the other, this group being one shift. (Courtesy of Dietel Collection.)

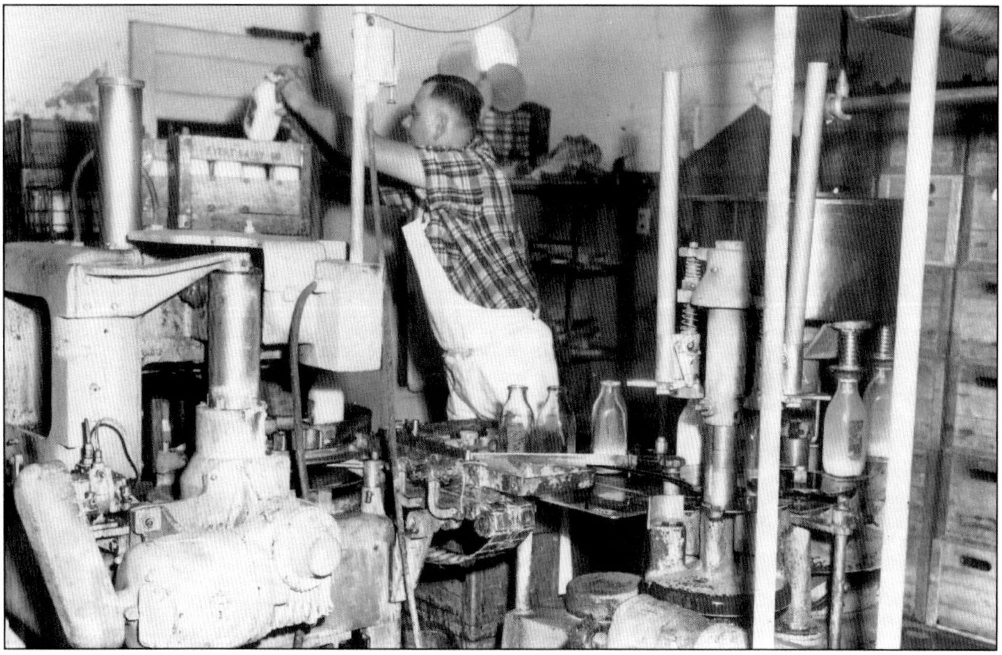

Johnny Sagebiel is busy bottling fresh pasteurized Gillespie County milk at Evers Dairy, owned by Alonzo and John Evers. The business located at 116 South Crockett Street used milk from local graded dairies and delivered milk house to house in sanitized glass bottles. (Courtesy of Dietel Collection.)

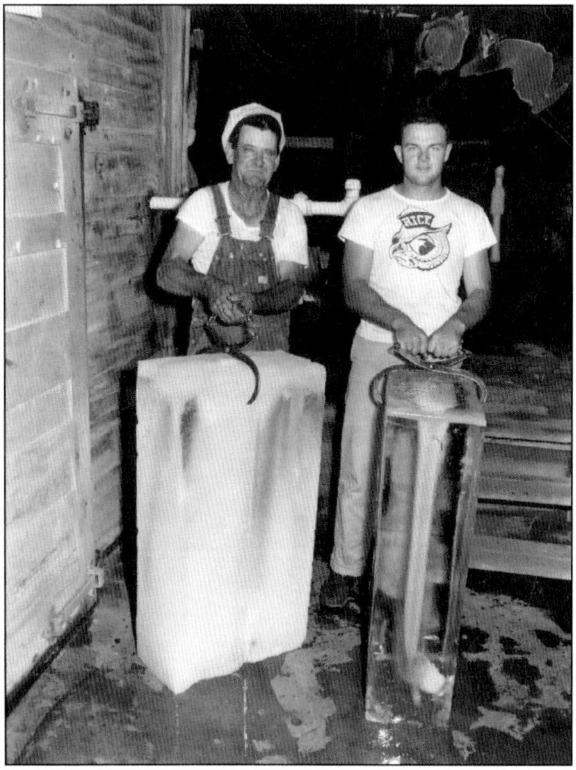

Otto Klaerner (left) and A.J. Loth of Stein Ice Factory stand with a 1950s graphic comparison of ice to show customers the cause of cloudy ice. The bar at the left, made from city water, had been chemically treated and therefore was not clear, transparent ice such as the one on right made from ordinary rainwater caught from an unfiltered roof. Before refrigerators became common, bought factory ice was the only way to preserve perishables in the county. (Courtesy of Dietel Collection.)

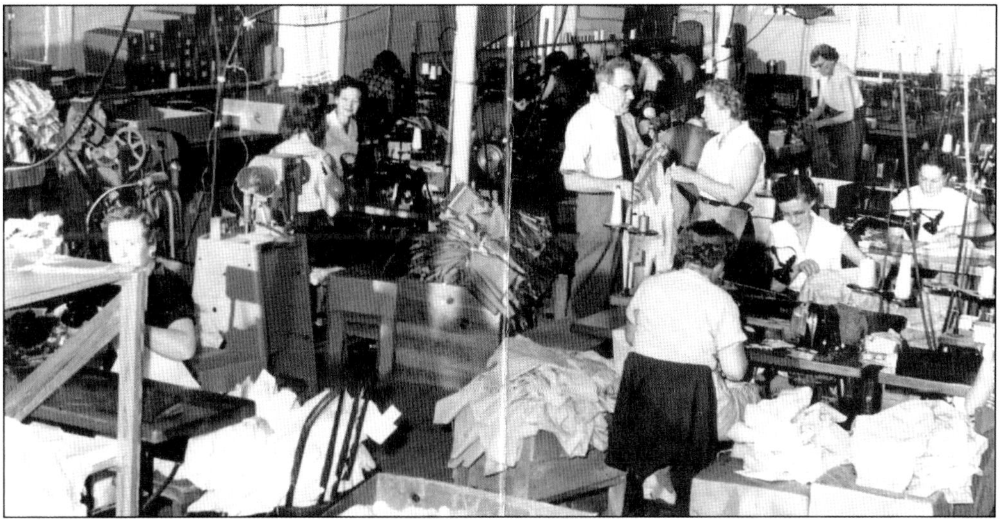

A branch of a San Antonio garment manufacturer, Westway Manufacturing Company, provided jobs for ladies of Gillespie County during the 1940s until the 1960s. The sewing factory, a name used by local people, was located on the second floor of the Schwarz Building in the 200 block of West Main Street. The building later housed a tire dealer and an insurance agency and is now an art gallery. (Courtesy of Dietel Collection.)

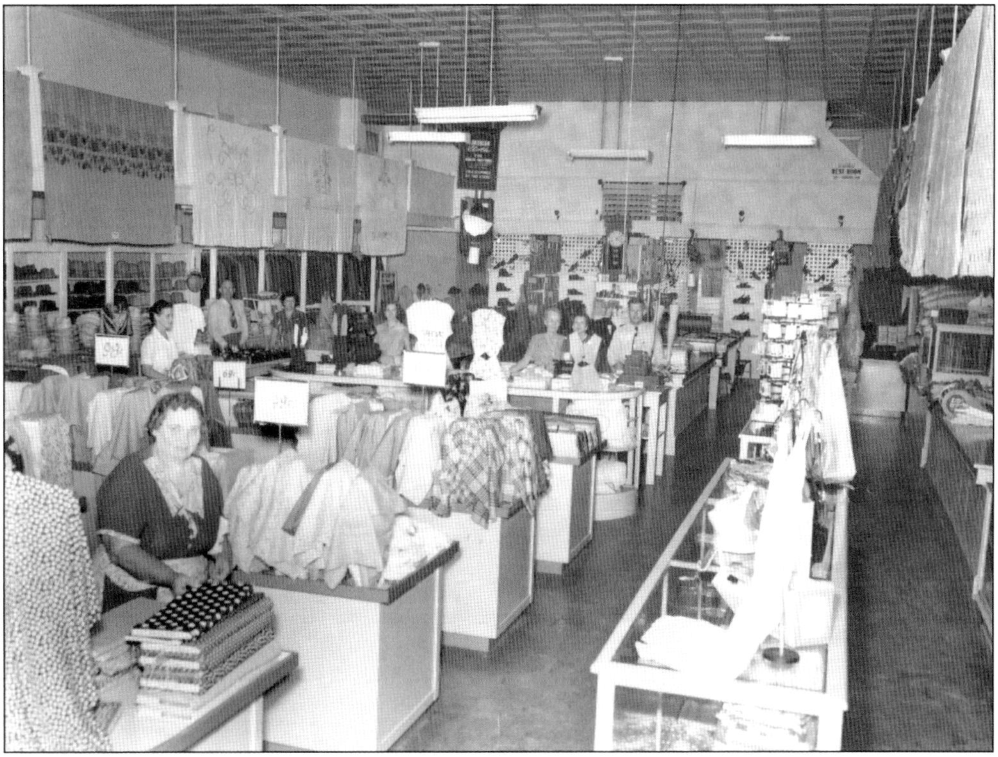

Schroeder Dry Goods did a brisk business as is evidenced by the store's interior. Red Schroeder is at the cash register, while Clarence Schroeder stands in back. Fabric is for sale for 49¢ to 98¢ a yard. Clarence later became the sole owner of the store until his retirement around 1970. (Courtesy of Dietel Collection.)

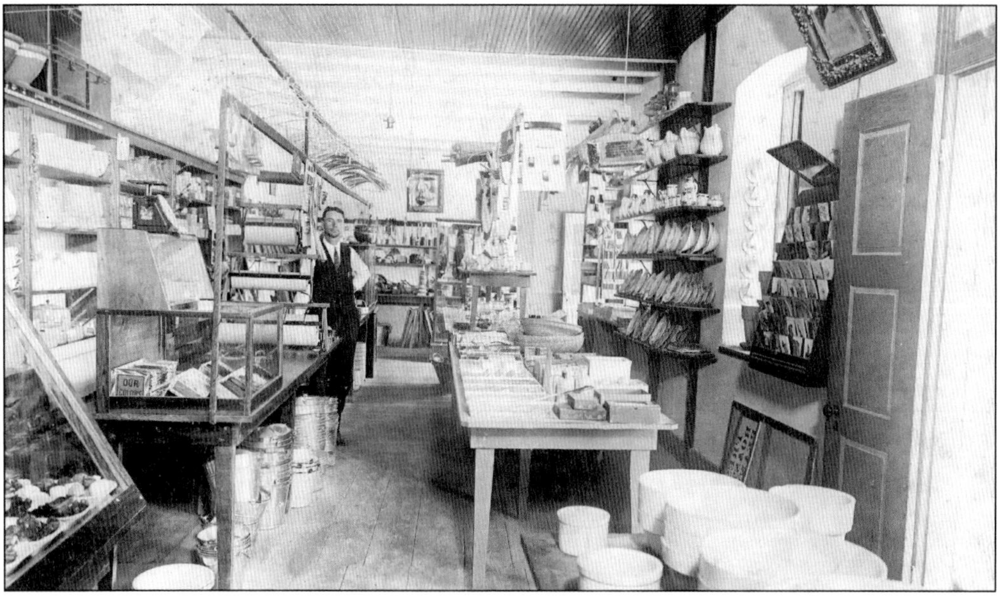

Otto Kiehne operated a variety store for over 55 years in the 200 block of West Main Street. The store opened in 1913. He sold everything from toys to school supplies to cookware. Up until the early 1970s, he carried almost everything needed for the simple lifestyle of the times. (Courtesy of Richard Klein.)

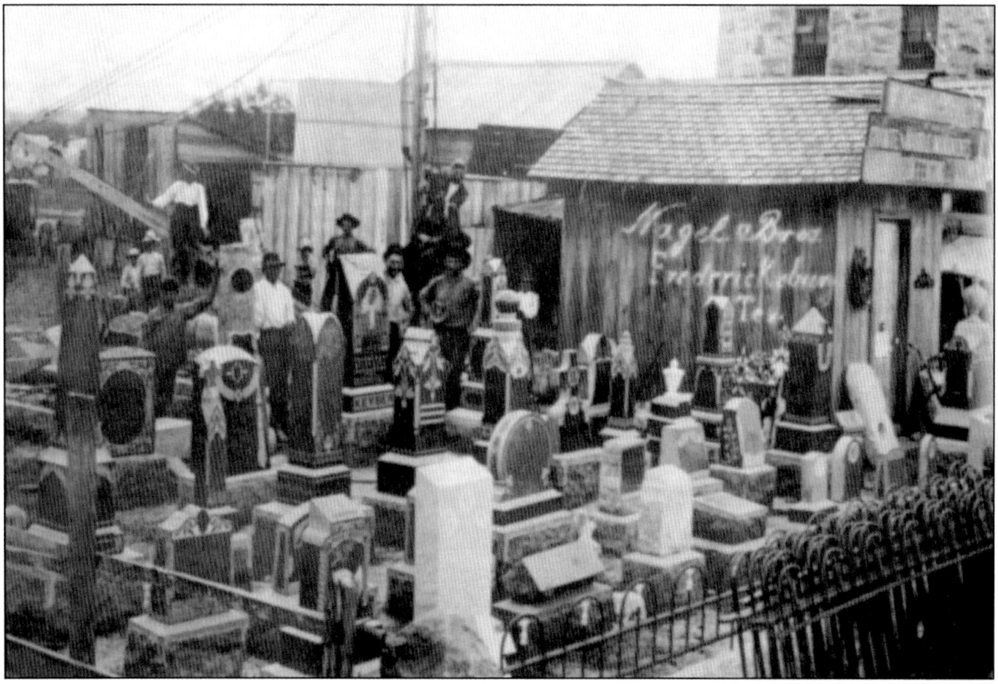

Nagel Brothers Monumental Works had moved to their current location on West San Antonio Street, next to the old jail, by 1910. The monuments were popular around the turn of the century. Most of the stones were quarried at Bear Mountain, which is a few miles north of the city. Nagel had salesmen who sold the red granite monuments throughout central Texas, especially in German-speaking communities. (Courtesy of Nagel Collection.)

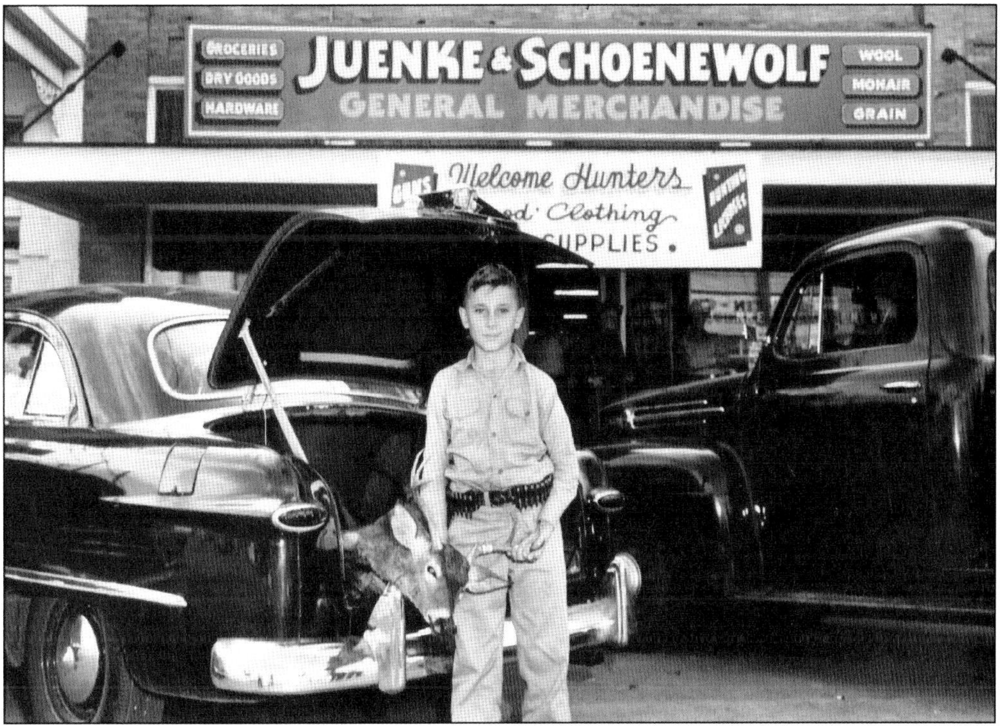

Deer hunting has brought money into Gillespie County in the form of hunting leases and selling supplies to hunters for generations. Around November 28, 1953, a young man shows off a trophy buck in front of Juenke & Schoenewolf General Merchandise Store. The building is now part of Dooley's on East Main Street. (Courtesy of Dietel Collection.)

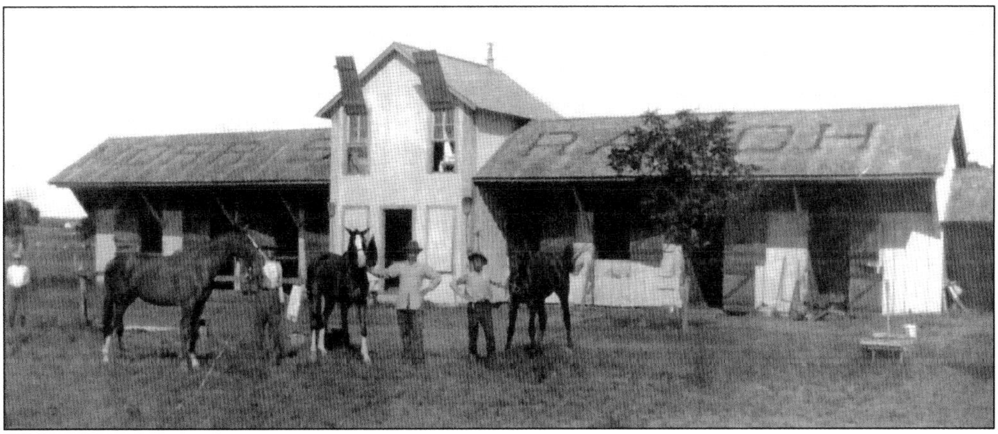

Morris Ranch began in 1856 when Francis Morris purchased 23,000 acres for breeding and training thoroughbred racehorses. Max Hirsch, who trained a Kentucky Derby winner, got his start training horses at Morris Ranch. A small town grew around the ranch headquarters. (Courtesy of Bill Teague Collection.)

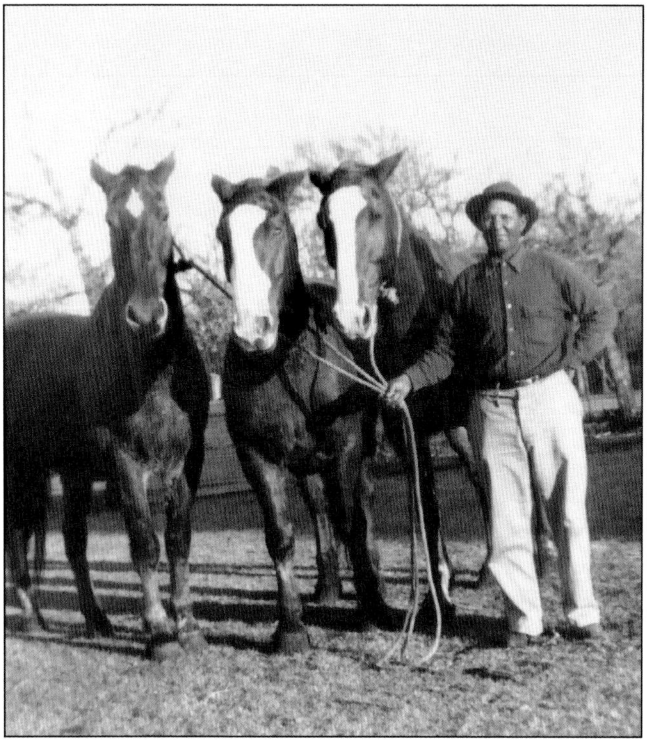

Because Gillespie County was heavily engaged in stock farming and ranching, services of a veterinarian were often needed. For many years, a self-educated man who spoke German fluently, Paul Phillips Sr., was the only veterinarian in the county. Farmers and ranchers needing a veterinarian never hesitated to seek this man's advice. Dr. Phillips proudly stands with his team of draft horses used on his farm east of Fredericksburg. (Courtesy of Dietel Collection.)

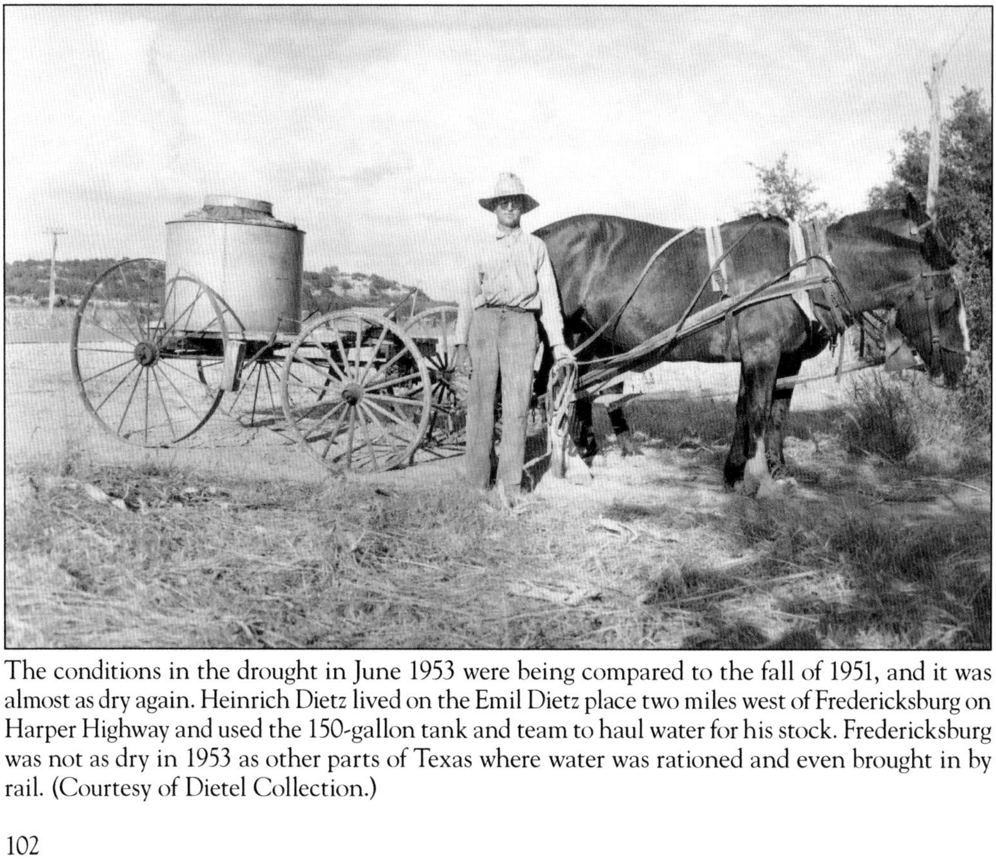

The conditions in the drought in June 1953 were being compared to the fall of 1951, and it was almost as dry again. Heinrich Dietz lived on the Emil Dietz place two miles west of Fredericksburg on Harper Highway and used the 150-gallon tank and team to haul water for his stock. Fredericksburg was not as dry in 1953 as other parts of Texas where water was rationed and even brought in by rail. (Courtesy of Dietel Collection.)

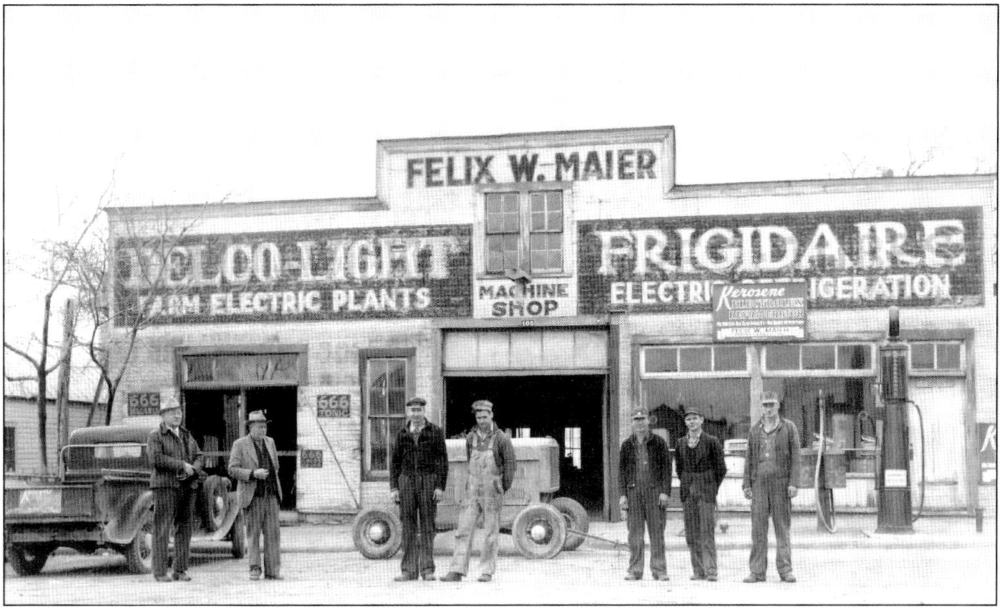

Before the Rural Electrification Administration, created in 1935, brought electricity to rural Gillespie County, farmers and ranchers depended on light plants for electric power. Felix Maier sold not only light plants, but also electric appliances during the 1920 and 1930s. The firm evolved into a machine shop and appliance dealership after rural electrification around 1937. (Courtesy of Bill Teague.)

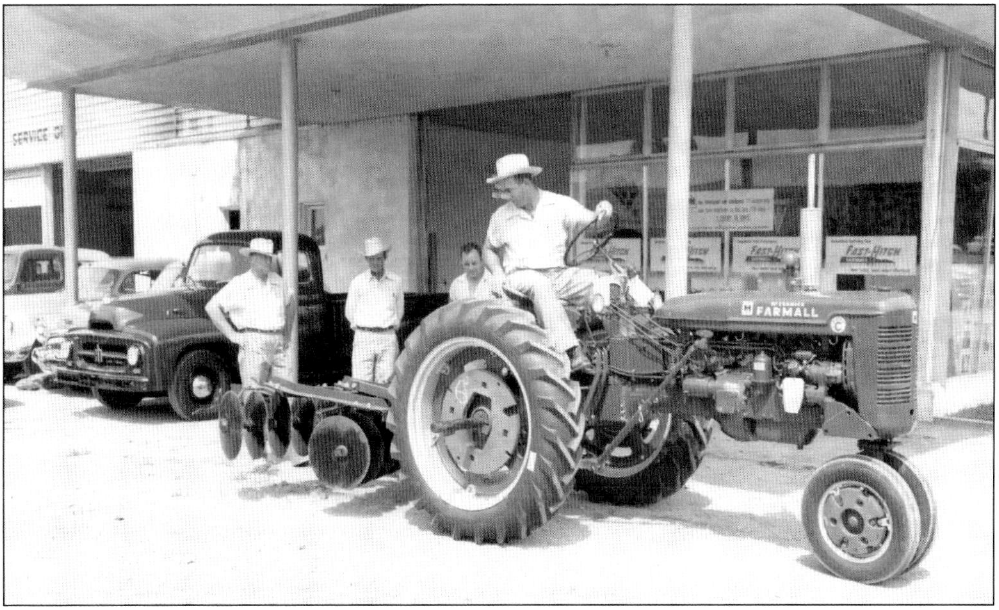

Hill Country Implement, in the 200 block of East Main Street, was organized in the late 1940s as an International Harvester distributor. Here, Gilbert Eckhardt demonstrates a new hitch on a Farmall Super C tractor with a disc plow. Eckhardt, an employee, was quoted as saying the new hitch makes attaching and disengaging implements on the new tractor mere child's play. The men observing are, from left to right, Ben Faubion, Theo Arlitt, and Leroy Habenicht of Comfort. (Courtesy of Dietel Collection.)

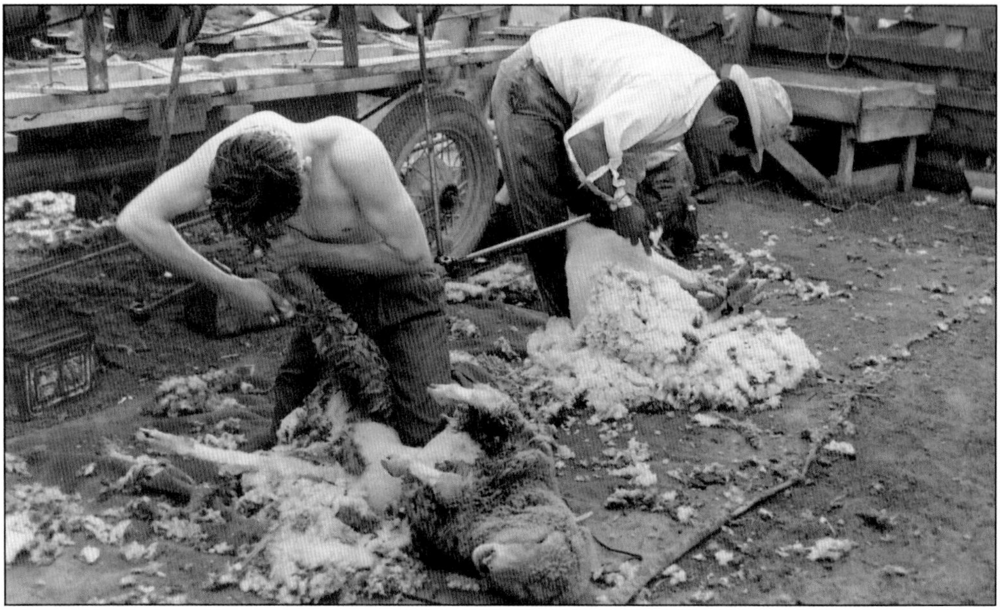

Wool and mohair has long been an important cash crop in Gillespie County. Sheep grow heavy wool for warmth in the winter. The wool must then be shorn before the summer heat sets in. Here, two men using a portable rig mounted on a trailer are shearing sheep. Shearing has always been very hard labor. (Courtesy of Sam Whitten.)

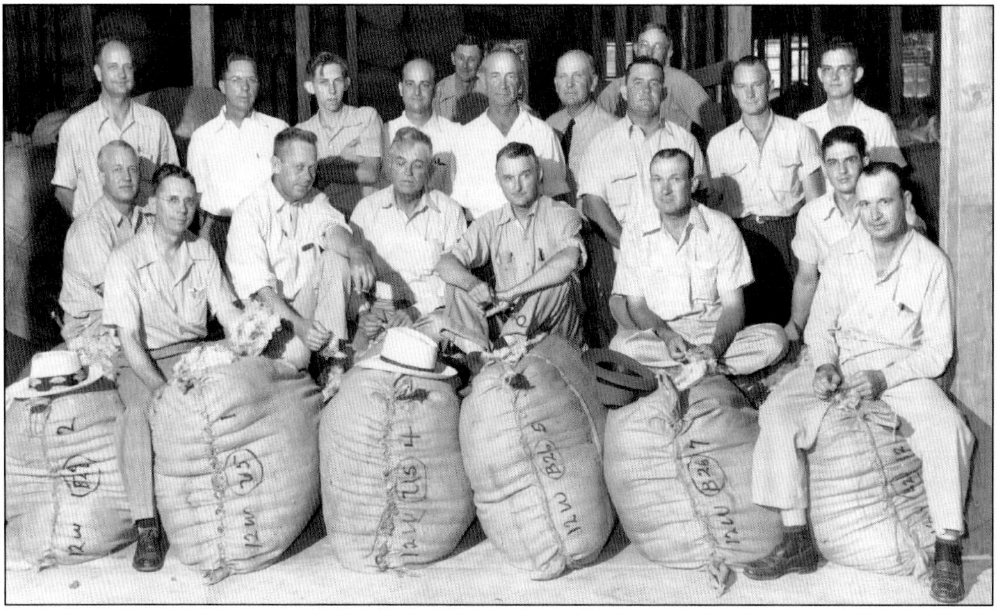

Wool production is a large cash crop for Gillespie County. Here, local wool producers pose with wool ready to be shown to buyers in 1953. At that time, wool buyers came from all parts of the United States for this Woerner Warehouse wool sale. Most wool was processed at the Wool Center in Boston, Massachusetts. Erwin Woerner is at far left in the front row, Lee Roy Woerner at far right on the second row, and Elwood Woerner standing at far right. Standing in back are employees Edgar Treibs and Theo Lange. The rest are wool buyers from around the United States. (Courtesy of Dietel Collection.)

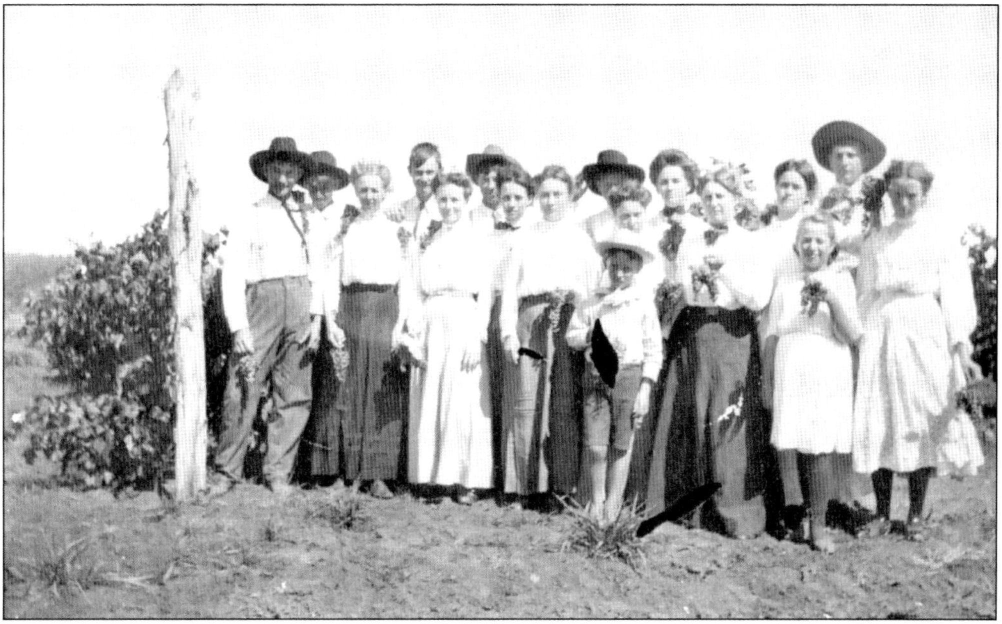

Viticulture and wine-making was well established in Gillespie County until Prohibition only allowed communion wine. Here, each family member is holding a bunch of grapes in the August Lorenz vineyard. Viticulture is again becoming an important industry in Gillespie County, which now has many vineyards and wineries. (Courtesy of Wahl Collection.)

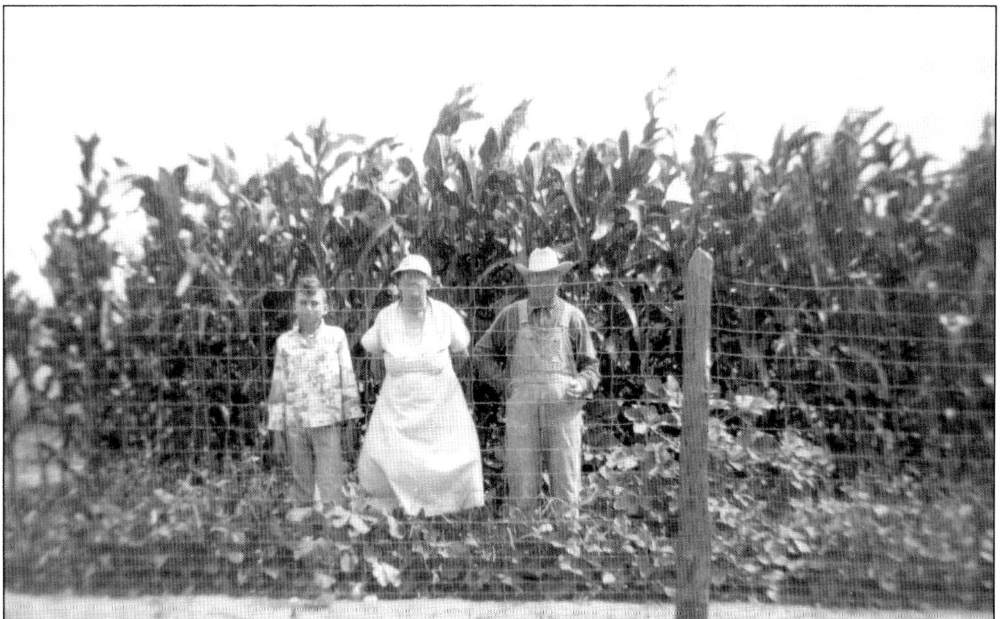

Before Luckenbach became famous for its music, the community depended on agriculture. Walter and Meta Barsch, posing with their son, ArLee, stand in a patch of black-eyed peas with some very tall corn in the background. This photograph, taken during the mid-1950s, demonstrates how the deep, dark soil of fields in the Luckenbach area held moisture during the mid-1950s severe drought. (Courtesy of Dietel Collection.)

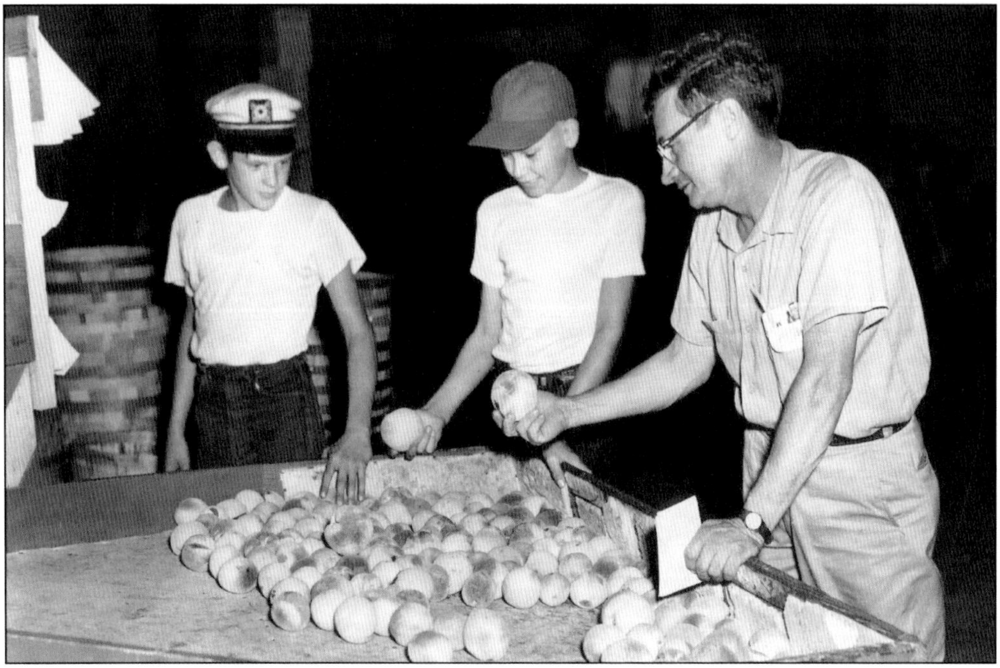

Gillespie County has become famous for its peaches. The Gillespie County Fruit Growers Association is a co-op organized to grade, pack, and market Gillespie County fruit. The association operated a packing shed for peaches as well as apples in Stonewall. Victor Doebbler is demonstrating peach grading for Stonewall youth at summer jobs in 1958. (Courtesy of Dietel Collection.)

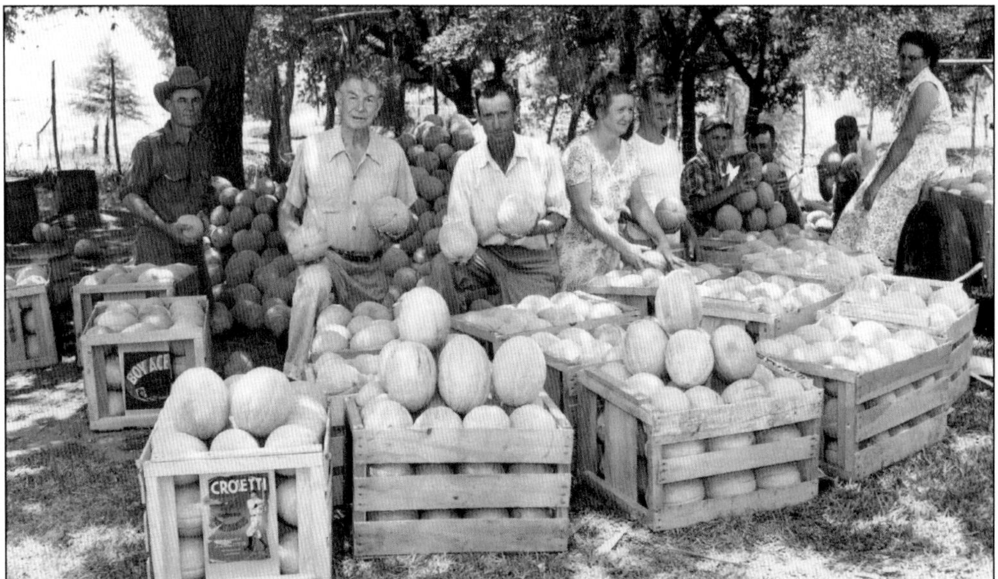

The Achtzehn ranch was heavily involved in truck farming. Lugs (crates) of cantaloupes are being displayed by Fred Achtzehn, Adolph, and Christine Schneider. Neighbors and schoolboys helped during the 1956 summer harvest. Pictured are, from left to right, Clarence Feller, Fred Achtzehn, Adolph Schneider, Christina Schneider, Gerald Schneider, Belton Feller, Stephen Reeh, Gene Reeh, Daniel Schneider, and Evelyn Reeh. (Courtesy of Dietel Collection.)

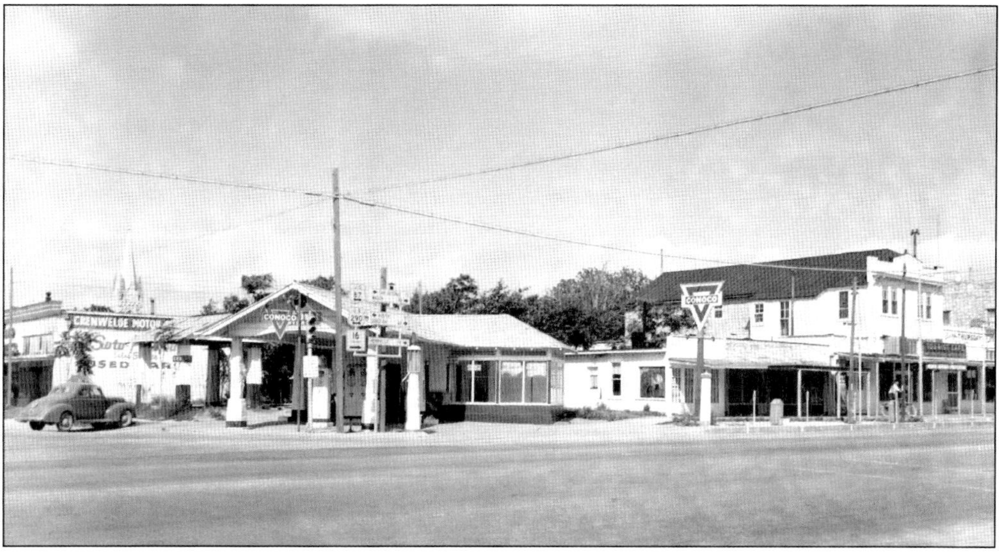

By the 1940s, the first gas station in Fredericksburg located at East Main and South Llano Streets had been expanded with a larger canopy, a wash rack, and a grease pit. Ruben Crenwelge operated the gas station as well as the old Reinbach Drug Store and sold DeSoto and Plymouth automobiles. He operated here until he built his own building in the 400 block of West Main Street in 1948. (Courtesy of Dietel Collection.)

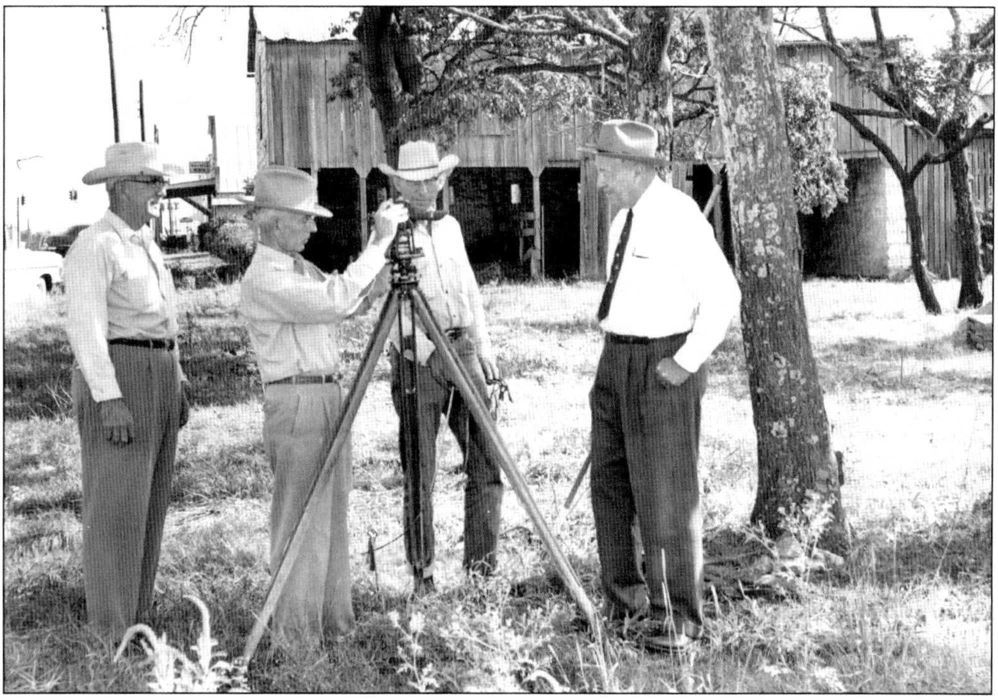

B.L. Enderle had a long career as schoolteacher, peach grower, civil engineer, and surveyor. Here, county surveyor B.L. Enderle adjusts his transit on the old Moellering property at the corner of East San Antonio and South Llano Streets. This was to become the site of the new Southwest State Telephone Company building. During the 1950s and 1960s, many 1800s buildings were razed because Fredericksburg wanted to become a modern city. (Courtesy of Dietel Collection.)

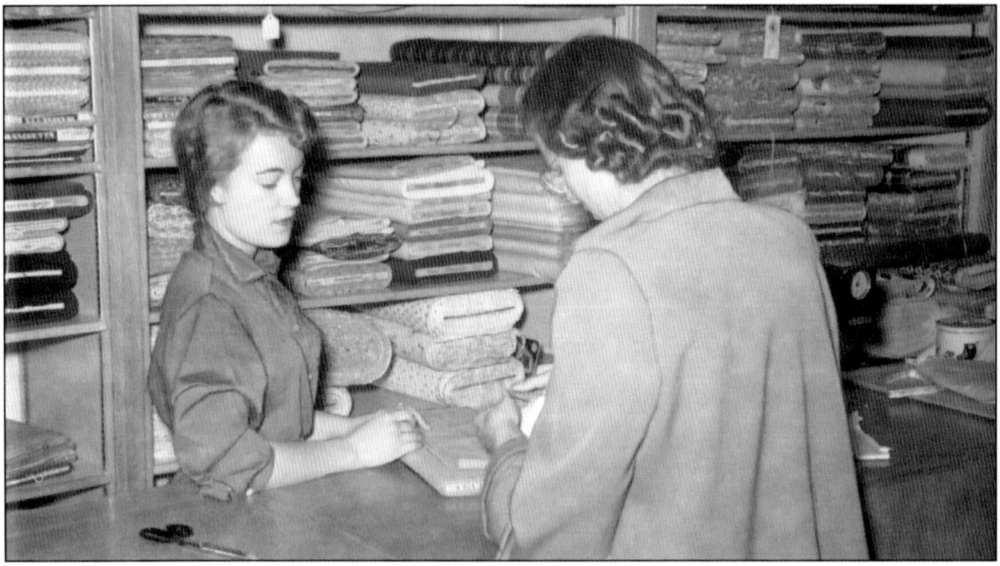

In the 1950s, Fredericksburg Independent School District taught distributive education, where students received hands-on training by working at local businesses. Katherine Moellering is helping a customer select fabric in the Knopp & Metzger Dry Goods Department. The photograph was used in a newspaper advertisement for Public School Week in 1955. (Courtesy of Dietel Collection.)

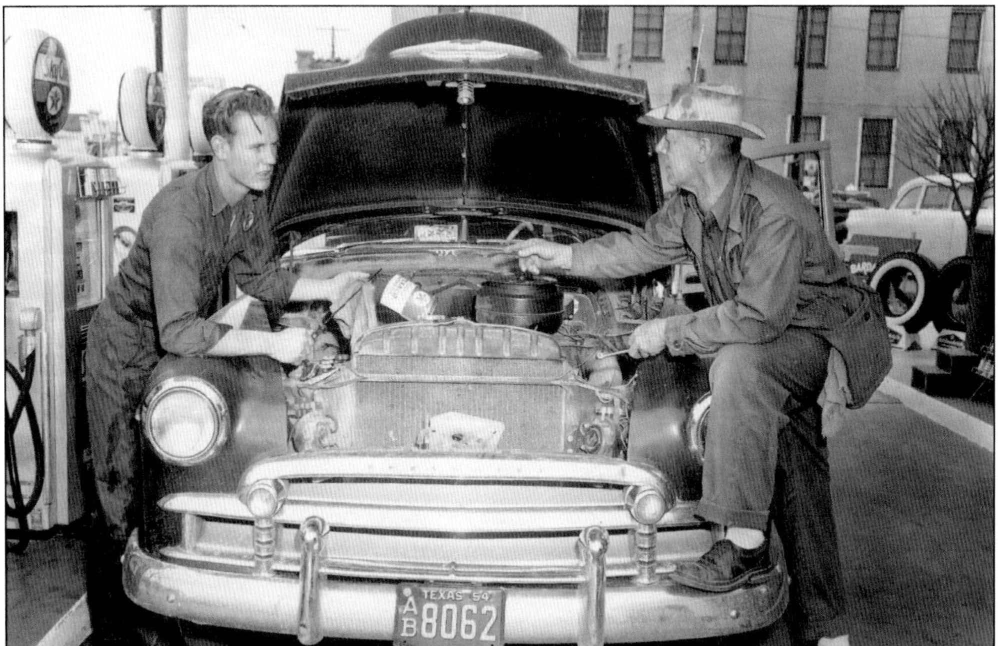

Many local businesses demonstrated their support for high school students through the distributive education program. In the 1950s, Gerry Gunnels (DE teacher) assisted Jerry Gold (left) in finding a job at the Texaco gasoline station owned by Herman Fischer (right). Classroom time as well as time on the job provided a pathway to entering the workforce after high school or college. (Courtesy of Dietel Collection.)

Seven

County at Play

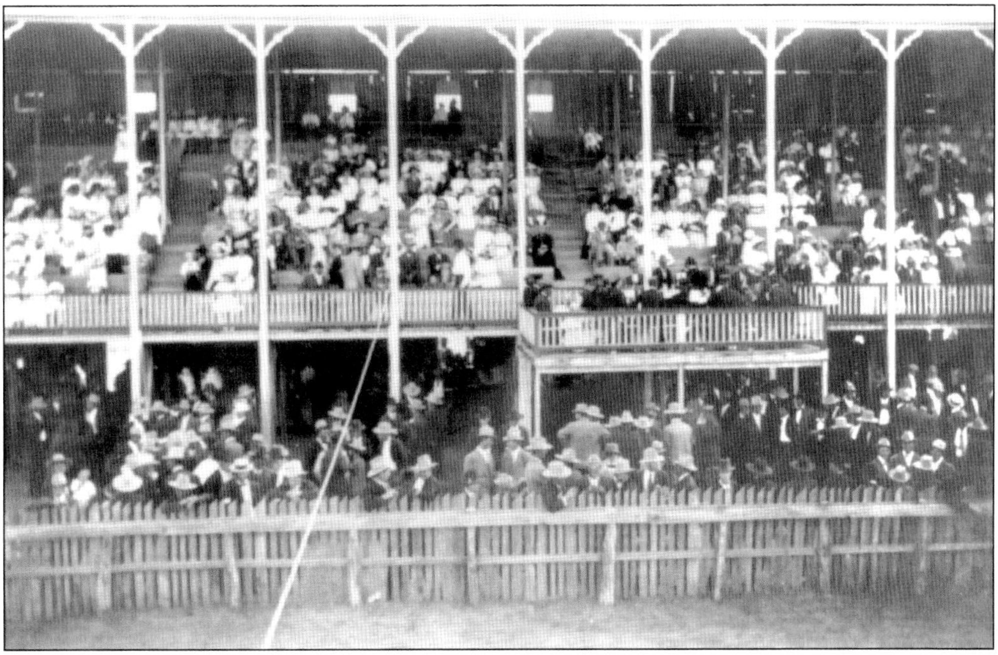

Gillespie County has the oldest racetrack in Texas. Bands in the balcony frequently entertained between races. This grandstand, part of the third Gillespie County Fairgrounds located at Ufer Street and Highway 16 South, was built in 1926 by Stein Lumber Company at a cost of $7,960. The first fair was held on the grounds of the former Fort Martin Scott and in 1889, the fair was moved to the second location, Central Park, site of the present Fredericksburg Turner Hall. (Courtesy of GCHS.)

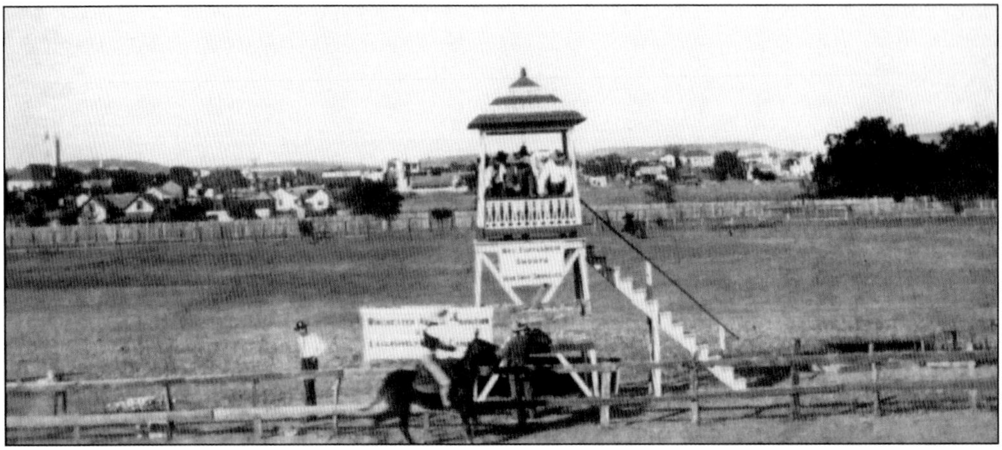

The judges watch from their stand at the Gillespie County Fairgrounds' third location in Fredericksburg as the winning mule crosses the finish line. Signs promote other entertainment such as "Mrs. Topperwein Shoots, Dead Shot Smokeless," and "Winchester Army Ammunition Exhibition." Elizabeth "Plinky" Topperwein was the wife of Ad Topperwein, a legendary marksman. Both were employed by Winchester. (Courtesy of Bill Teague.)

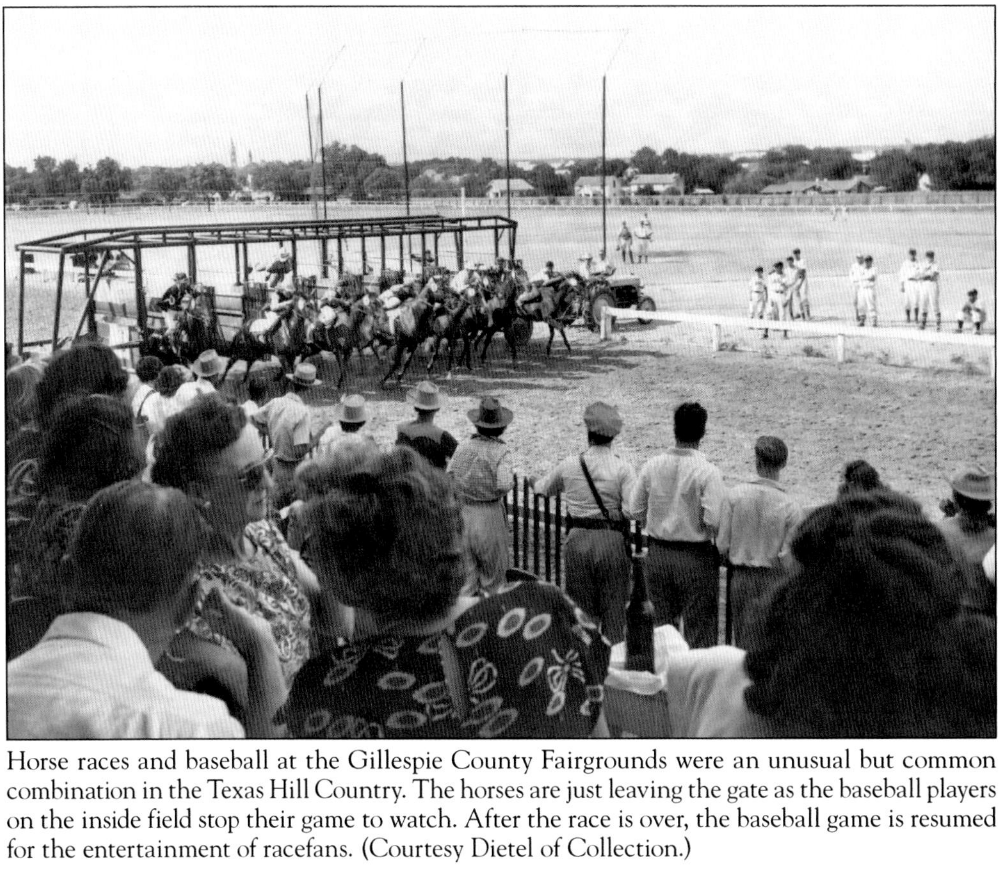

Horse races and baseball at the Gillespie County Fairgrounds were an unusual but common combination in the Texas Hill Country. The horses are just leaving the gate as the baseball players on the inside field stop their game to watch. After the race is over, the baseball game is resumed for the entertainment of racefans. (Courtesy Dietel of Collection.)

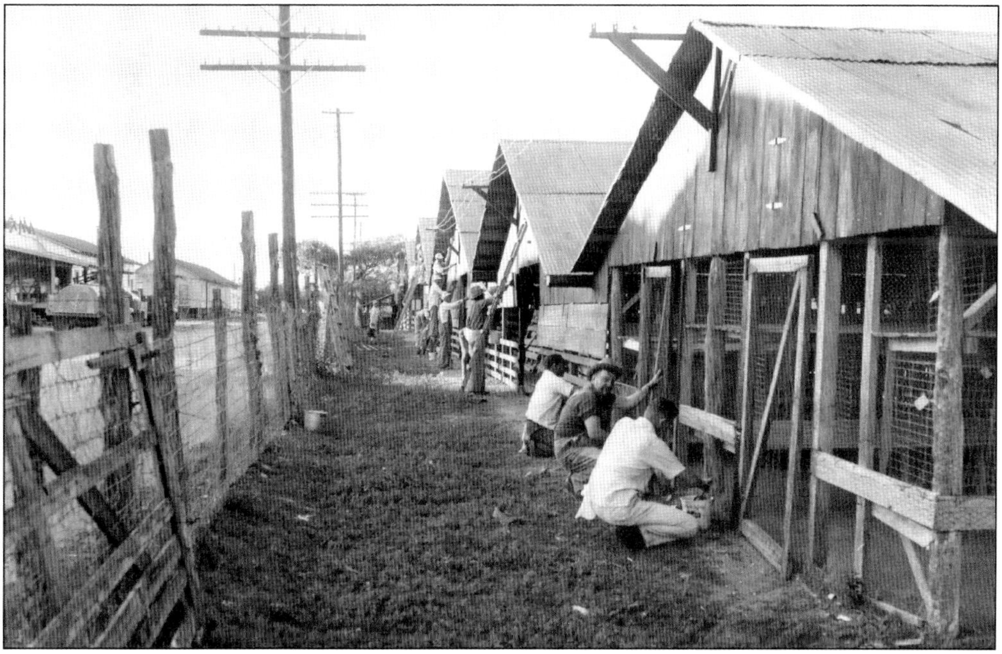

In October following the 1954 fair, there was work to be done to repair poultry barns. About 30 Gillespie County Fair Association members and other volunteers put 26 gallons of paint on the outside of the entire barns at the old Gillespie County Fairgrounds on the Park Street side. Afterward, the group consumed huge amounts of barbecue chicken prepared by chefs Werner Lindenberg, Elgin Heimann, and Gilbert Eckhardt. (Courtesy of Dietel Collection.)

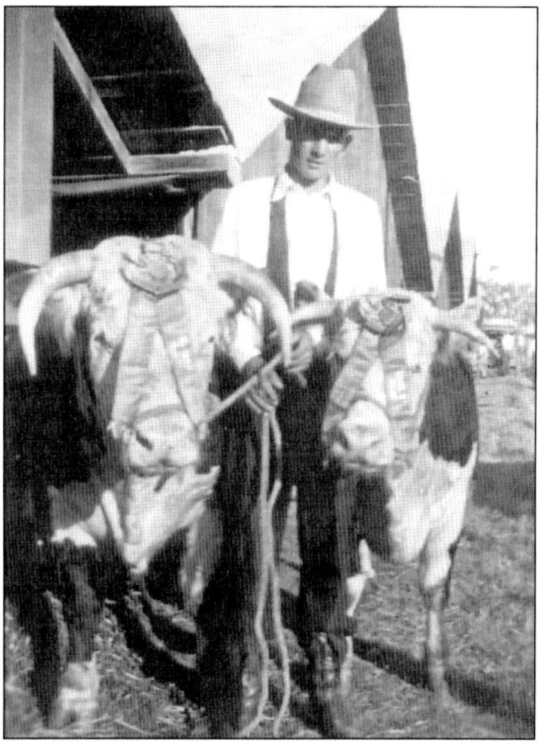

Norbert Roeder stands near the livestock barns with his Grand Champion Hereford bull and cow at the 1931 Gillespie County Fairgrounds in Fredericksburg, Texas. These grounds were the third site for the county fair, founded in 1881 and the oldest continuously operated county fair in Texas. The barns were built and a fence was placed around the racetrack in 1924. Livestock and agricultural exhibits have always been a part of the fair. (Courtesy of Elmond J. Roeder.)

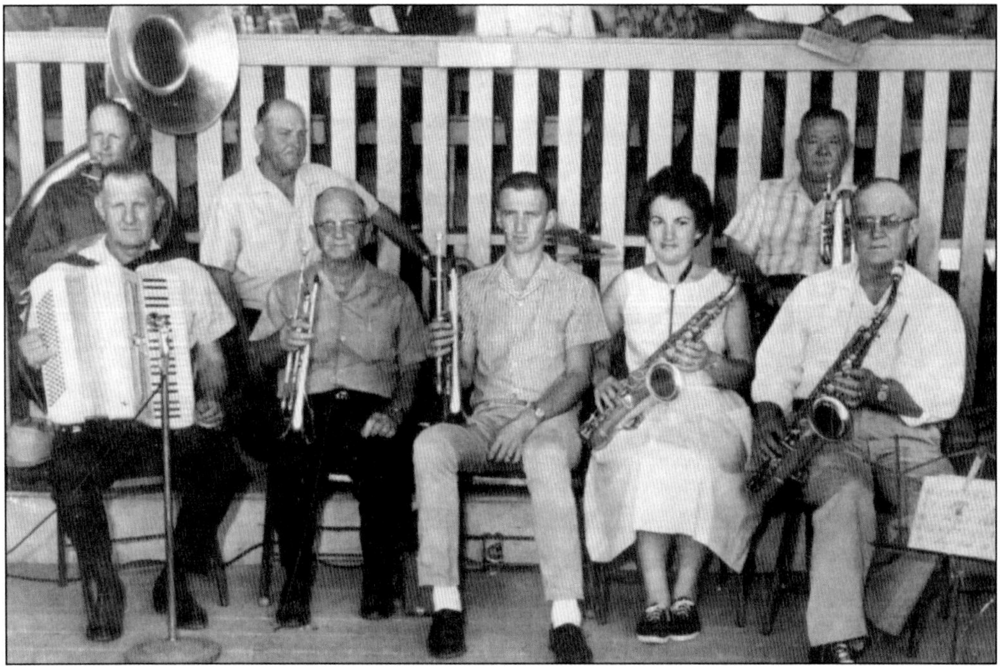

Felix Pehl's Oompah Band was one band that played between horse races for many years. The members of the Gillespie County Fair band in the late 1950s and early 1960s are, from left to right, (first row) Arthur Klein, Felix Pehl, Charles Schandua, Karen Schandua, and Chester Schuch; (second row) Albert Meier, Frank Wehmeyer, and Hugo Klaerner. (Courtesy of Doris Eckert.)

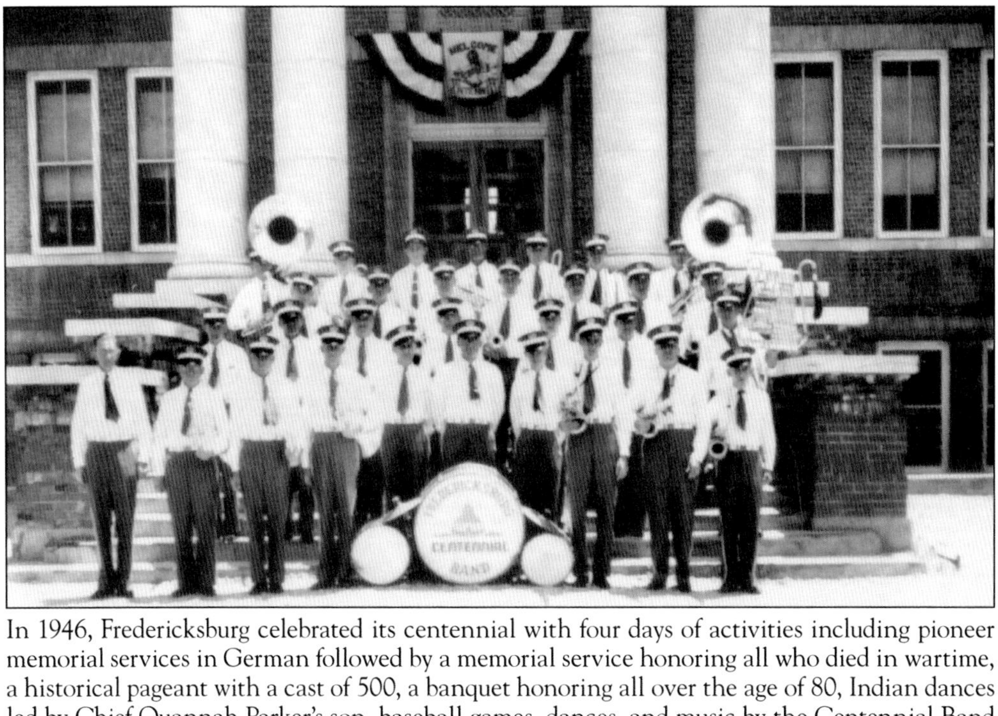

In 1946, Fredericksburg celebrated its centennial with four days of activities including pioneer memorial services in German followed by a memorial service honoring all who died in wartime, a historical pageant with a cast of 500, a banquet honoring all over the age of 80, Indian dances led by Chief Quannah Parker's son, baseball games, dances, and music by the Centennial Band of Fredericksburg, directed by Alfred Pehl. (Courtesy of John H. Kothmann.)

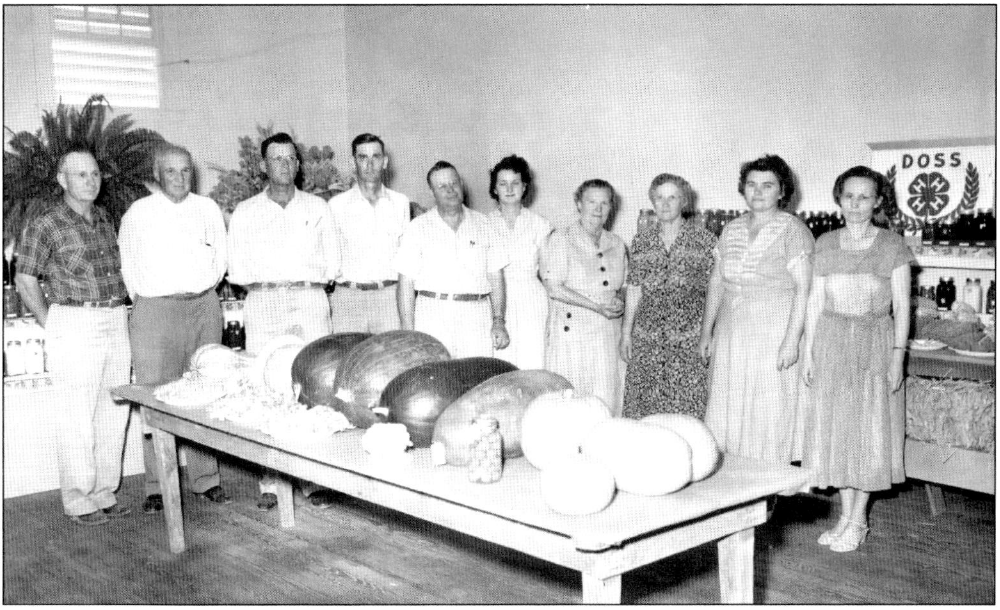

The committee members had a big part in the exhibition and arrangement of the agricultural, garden, fruit, and canned goods display at 1952 Doss Fair. Pictured are, from left to right, Arnold Rode (community club chairman), Albert Wendel, Paul Sauer, Otto Spaeth, Ed Hyman (Mason County county agent and judge), Lucille Conrads (Gillespie County home demonstration agent and judge); Olga Dittmar (judge), Selma Wendel, Alice Sauer, and Martha Spaeth. (Courtesy of Dietel Collection.)

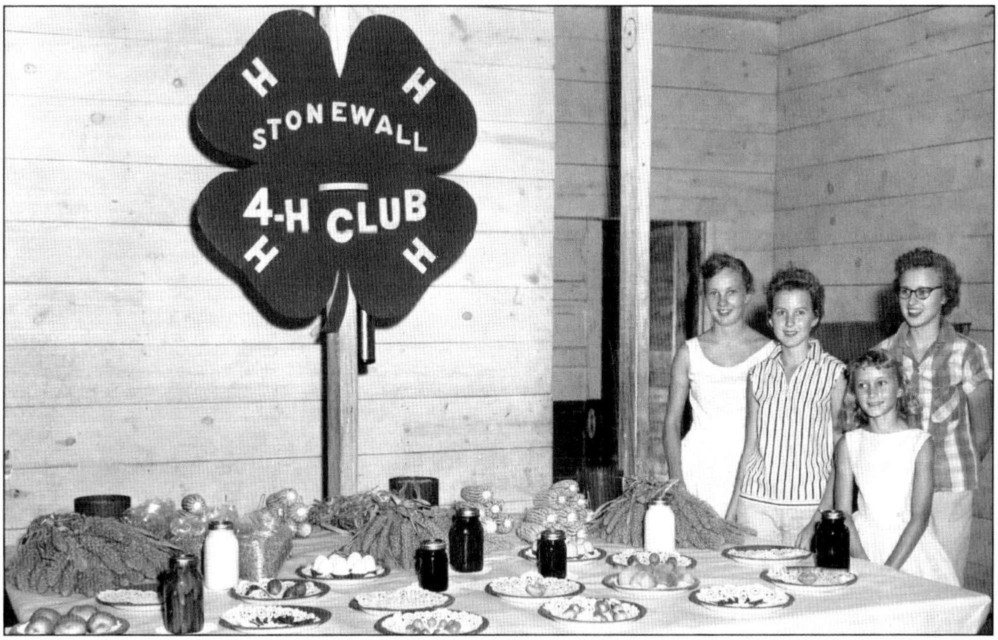

Stonewall Community Fair was held in early August before the Gillespie County Fair. The 4-H Club exhibit included agricultural crops of maize, corn, eggs, peaches, figs, potatoes, peppers, and canned goods. Girls pictured are Alice Klein, Kathy Burg, Joan Burg, and Loretta Klein. The exhibits were displayed in the Stonewall School gym. (Courtesy of Dietel Collection.)

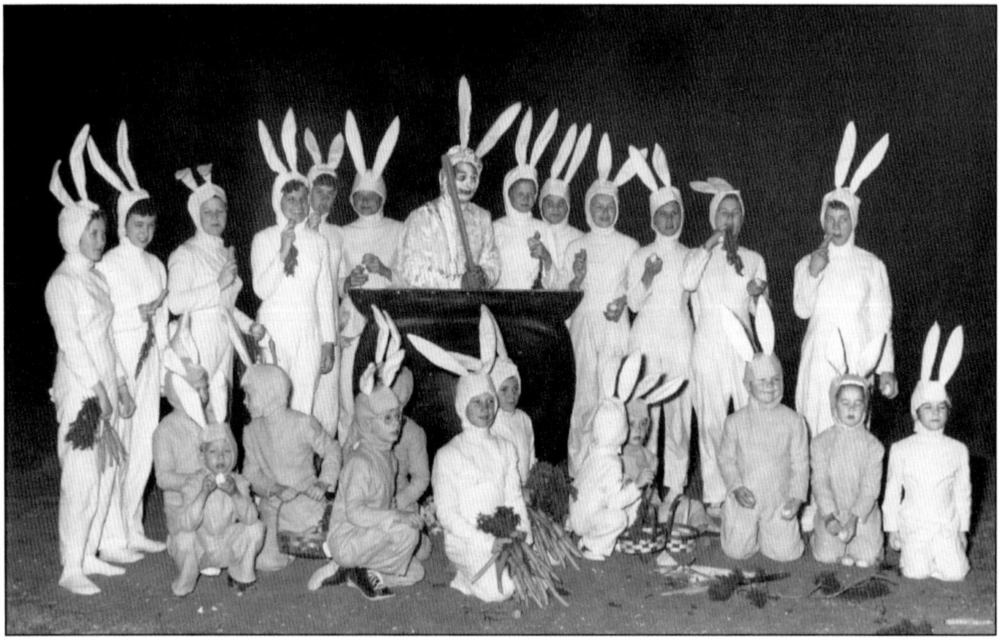

Each year beginning around 1948, the Gillespie County Fair Association's Easter Fires Pageant occurred on the Saturday night before Easter. The cast of hundreds included bunnies of all ages. This Easter rabbit on April 21, 1949, was played with enthusiasm and vigor by Alex Frantzen, helping bunnies stir up a batch of dye in the big kettle. The pageant was discontinued in 2004. (Courtesy of Dietel Collection.)

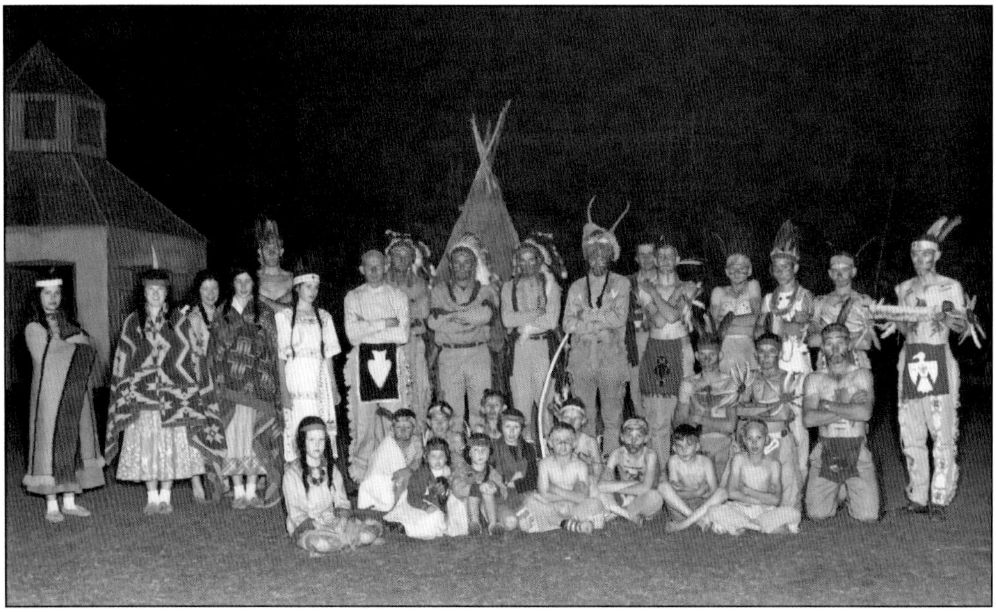

The Easter Fires Pageant told the story of the founding of Fredericksburg on May 8, 1846. For this performance, the parts of the Indians were taken by the members of the Order of the Arrow, honorary Boy Scout fraternity, of Austin, whose dances and tribal presentations were well-known across the United States. The women and children and the betrothed Indian bride (Princess White Fawn) and brave are Gillespie County residents. (Courtesy of Dietel Collection.)

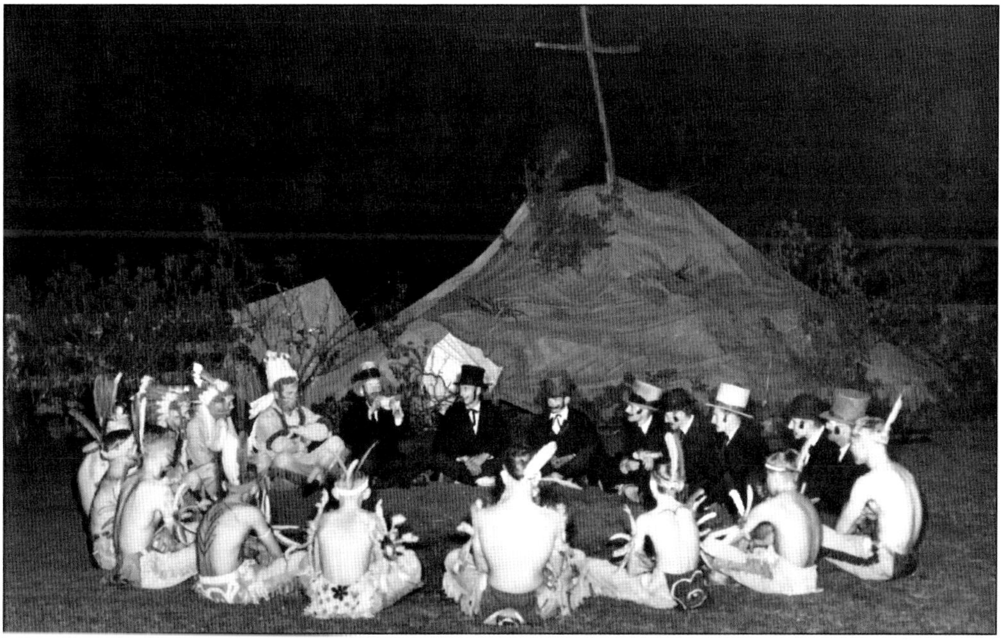

The pageant cast members portray the peace treaty signing between the Comanche Indians and John O. Meusebach. The Easter fires legend is based upon fires on the hills around Fredericksburg as seen by families of the colony while Meusebach and his men were gone for the treaty signing. The fires frightened the children and the mother consoled them with the story told in the pageant. (Courtesy of Dietel Collection.)

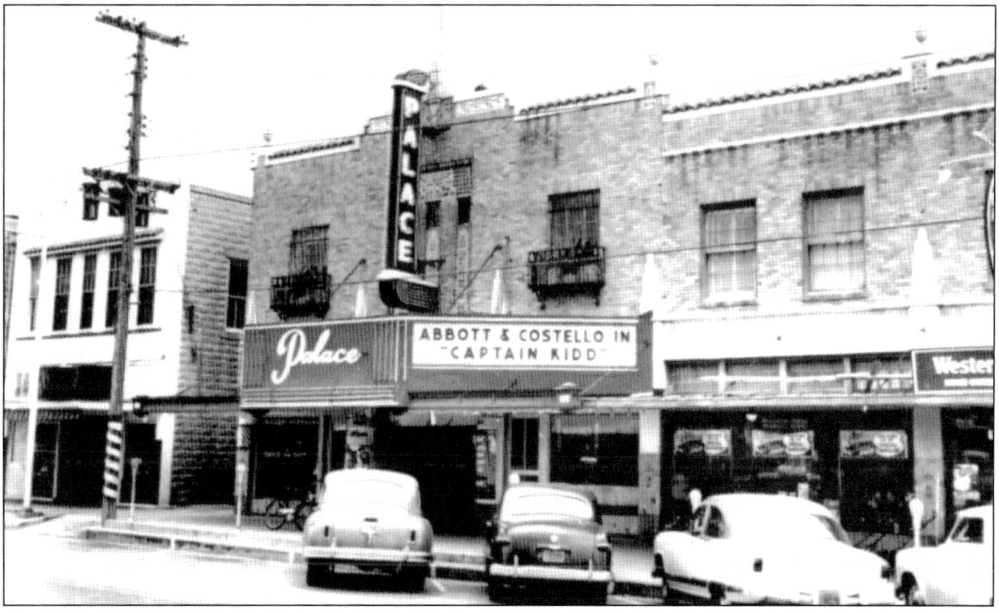

The Palace Theater was run by Walter Knoche in the 1940s when someone could watch a double feature and have popcorn all for less than 25¢. Herbert and Karl Durst opened the 87 Drive-in Theater in 1950 and about three years later became the owners of both theaters. The Durst brothers also sponsored Easter egg hunts for children at the drive-in around the 1950s. (Courtesy of Dietal Collection.)

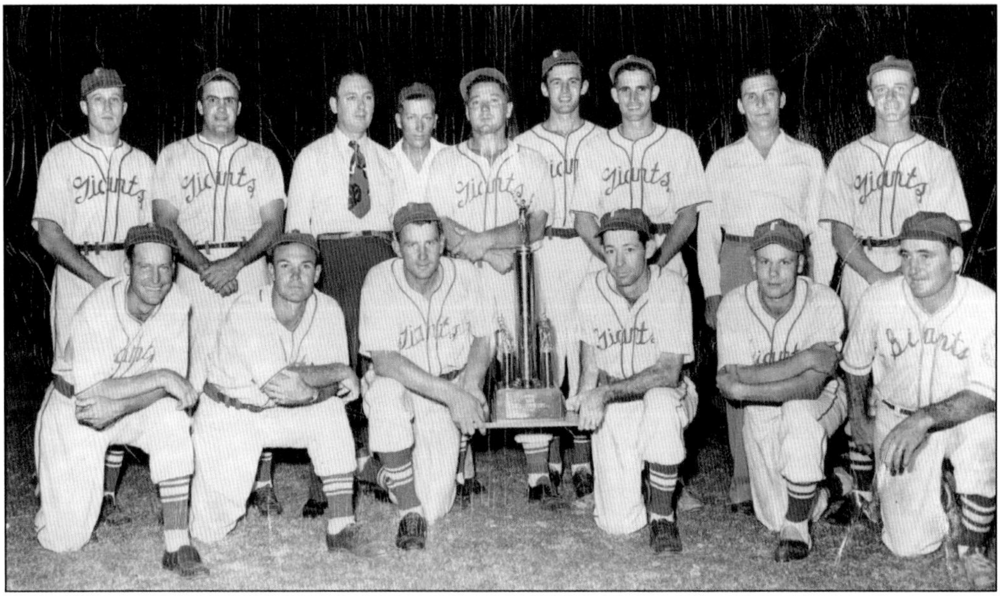

The Fredericksburg Giants, the Hill Country Baseball League champions, defeated Comfort in the final of their three game series 5–2. Members of the 1949 team are clustered around the trophy displayed in show windows throughout the city during the weeks following. Pictured are, (kneeling) Lee Moldenhauer, Roy Langerhans, Roland Bonn (captain), Otto "Britton" Schneider Jr. (manager), Max Ahrens, and Alfons Klaerner; (standing) Lee Itz, Tony Knopp, Dr. Lorence Feller (Fair Association Sports Committee chairman), Max Enderlin Jr., Hugo Klaerner, Ferdinand Jenschke, Johnny Hartmann, Elton Jordan (Hill Country League president), and Monroe Klinksiek. (Courtesy of Otto Schneider.)

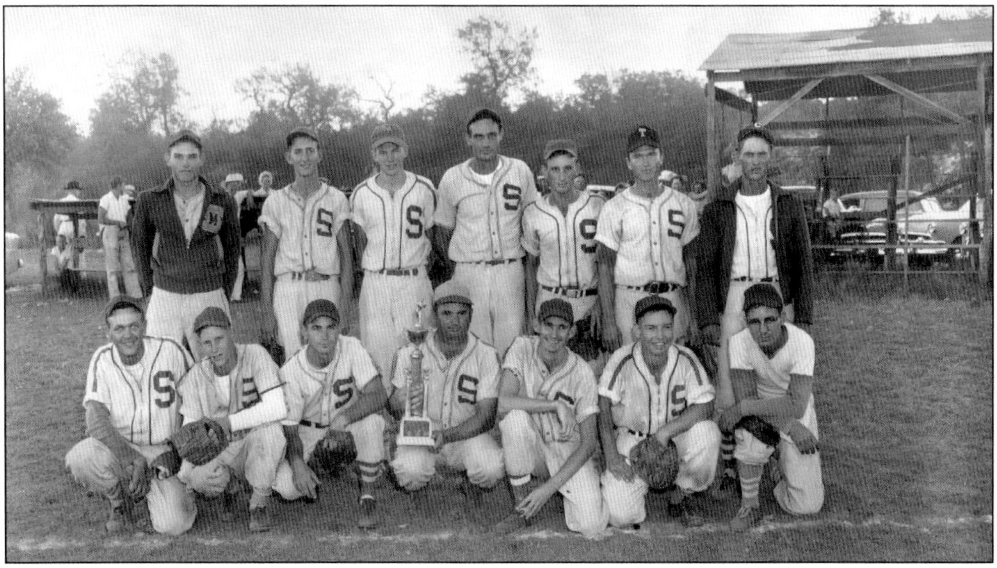

A championship team from Stonewall played in the 1955 Farmer Boys league. The team members pictured are, from left to right, (kneeling) Buddy Grobe, Stanley Deike, Kurt Weinheimer, Jerome Jenschke (manager), Andrew Nebgen, John Staudt, and Delton Behrens; (standing) Joe Kaiser, James Schumann, Erhard Eberle, John Thurmann, James Nebgen, Harvey Eckert, and Kenneth "Wimpy" Eckert. (Courtesy of Dietel Collection.)

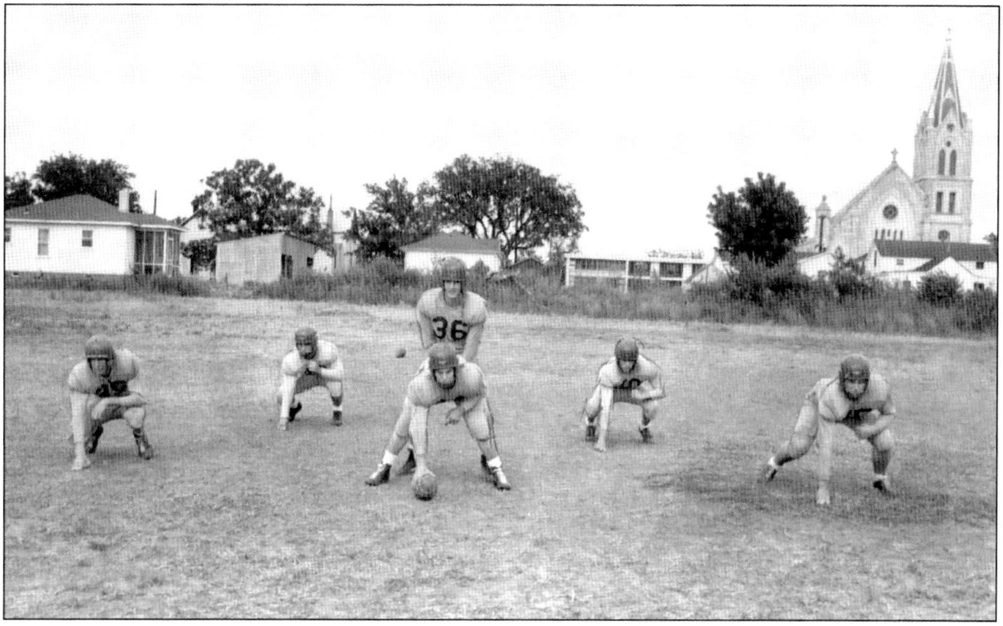

Six-man football was played by the St. Mary's High School Indians and Harper High School Longhorns. St. Mary's played six-man until the 1957 season with no senior boys on the teams, and the coaches agreed to start the juniors in 11-man football. In 1955, St. Mary's football team is seen practicing on the field still used today by St. Mary's Apaches sixth, seventh, and eighth grades for practice and regular games. (Courtesy of Dietel Collection.)

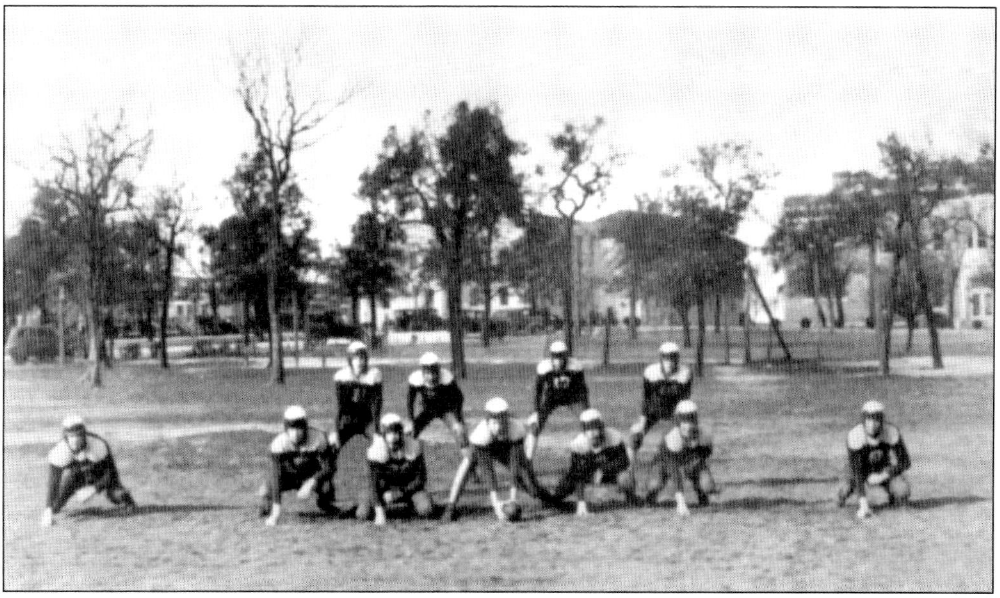

Fredericksburg High School football players in 1937 are posing in their first lineup. The names and position as listed in the yearbook are, from left to right, (first row) Chester Langerhans (end), Walter Fiedler (tackle), Dan Anderegg (guard), Franz Pressler (center), Roy Langerhans (guard), Arthur Pressler (tackle), and William Hahn (end); (second row) Jack Nixon (quarterback), Sipriano Cancino (halfback) Clemens Fiedler (fullback) and E.W. Hahn Jr. (halfback). (Courtesy of Fredericksburg High School *Mesa*.)

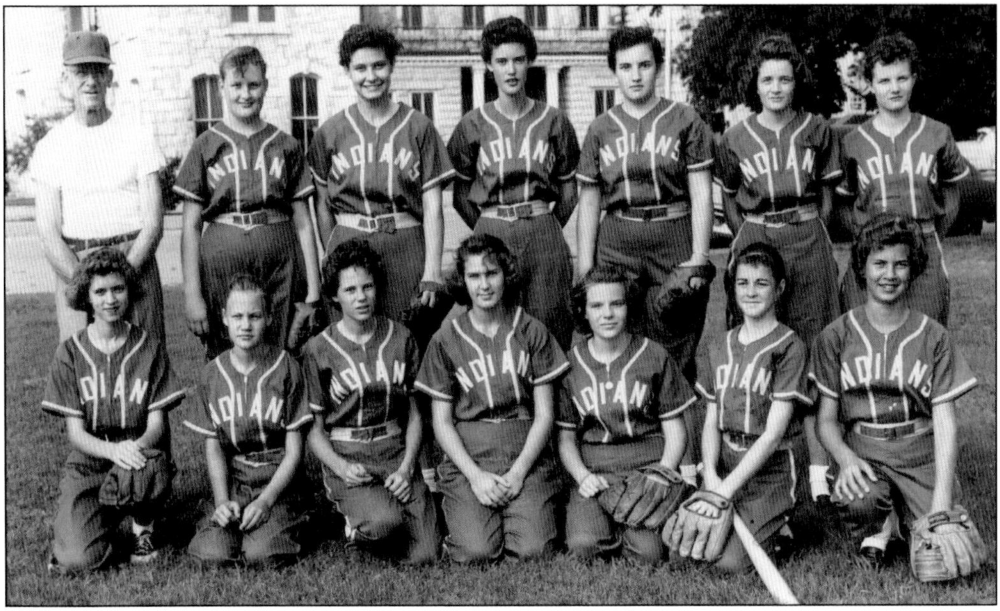

The girls liked to get into the action also. This photograph of the St. Mary's Indians softball team and coach includes, from left to right, (kneeling) Genevieve Behrends, Ann Jenschke, Lynette Pfeiffer, Carol Zenner, Virginia Stehling, Barbara Jung, and Judy Heinemann; (standing) Joseph Paulsen (St. Mary's coach and band director), Gladys Jung, Geraldine Klein, Antoinette Grona, Karen Schandua, Karen Wehmeyer, and Mary Koch. (Courtesy of Dietel Collection.)

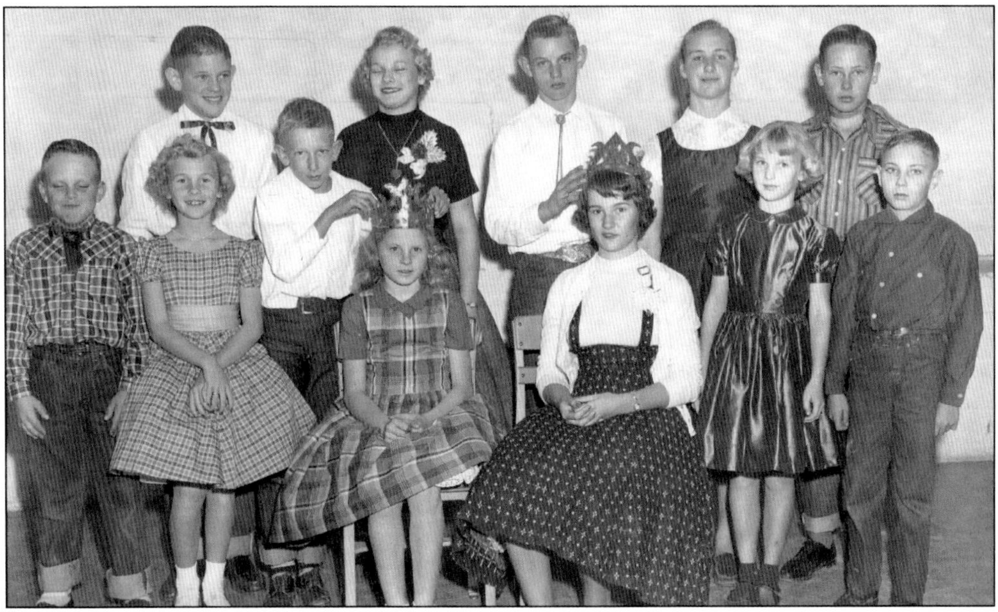

Dances were not just for adults as seen in this image of youngsters at the 1957 Stonewall Chili Dinner and Barn Dance. The Stonewall School event held each November honored young royalty. Pictured are, from left to right, (first row) Curtis Deike, Cheryl Maenius, Kenneth Ray Jenschke, Annie Lou Moldenhauer, Josie Novian, JoNell Nielsen, and Jimmy Duecker; (second row) John Mark Bohls, LaVerne Duecker, J.W. Ottmers, Barbara Jacoby, and Larry Klein. (Courtesy of Dietel Collection.)

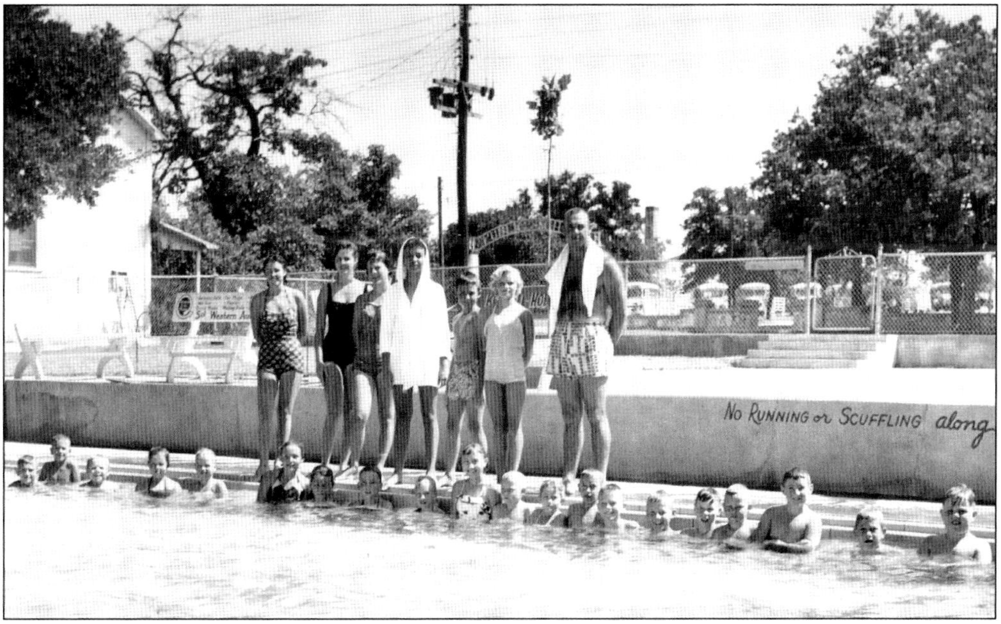

Swimming helped to endure the hot summers. Each summer, junior Red Cross classes were held at the beginners' level. In July 1958, these teenage girls and coach Dale Johanson taught the classes to the young swimmers. Pictured are, from left to right, (standing) Delia Davidson, Sandra Dietz, Ruthie Nettle, Dorothy Behrend, John Davidson, Carole Lee Moldenhauer, and Dale Johanson. Those in the water are unidentified. (Courtesy of Dietel Collection.)

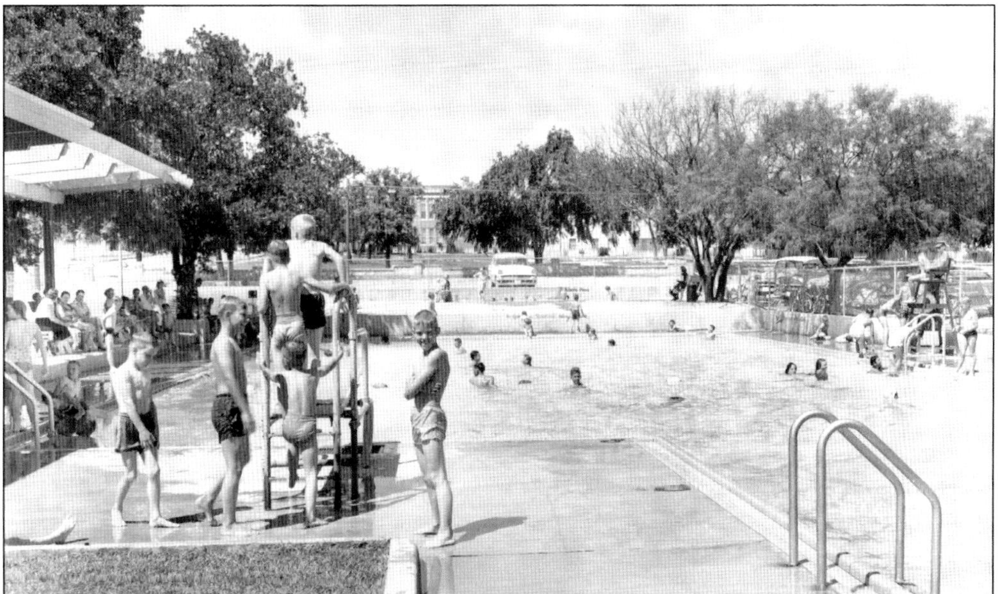

After morning lessons, the youth of Fredericksburg spent many afternoons swimming at the town pool on Travis Street. On a June afternoon in 1957, the young children are swimming and mothers are socializing with friends on the benches in the shade. In 1957, the entire Fredericksburg Independent School Campus was located across the street from the swimming pool. (Courtesy of Dietel Collection.)

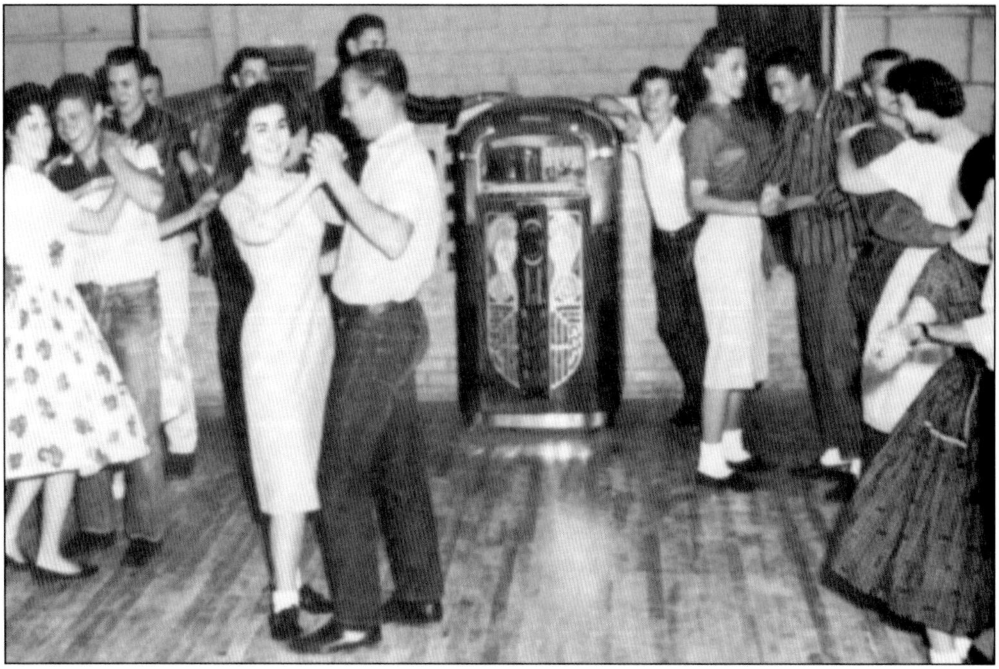

Pat's Hall was known throughout the Hill Country as a place to have fun on Saturday night. The slogan for this popular nightspot was "Where Friends Meet, In the Summertime, Join Us Under the Stars, In Our Outdoor Pavilion." "Pat" and Pauline Patranella operated the hall from 1953 to 1979. (Courtesy of Fredericksburg High School *Mesa*.)

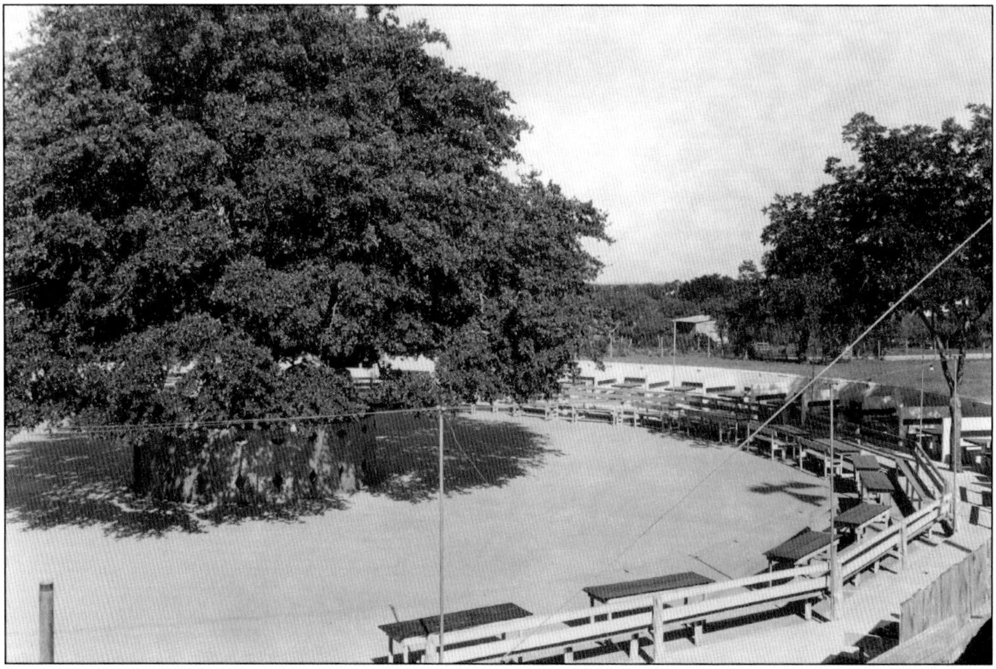

In the spring and summer, the bands at Pat's Hall would move outside and people would dance around the big live oak tree seen here. The hall was known as Seipp's Hall before it became Pat's Hall. The hall, which closed in 1985, has reopened for dancing. (Courtesy of Dietel Collection.)

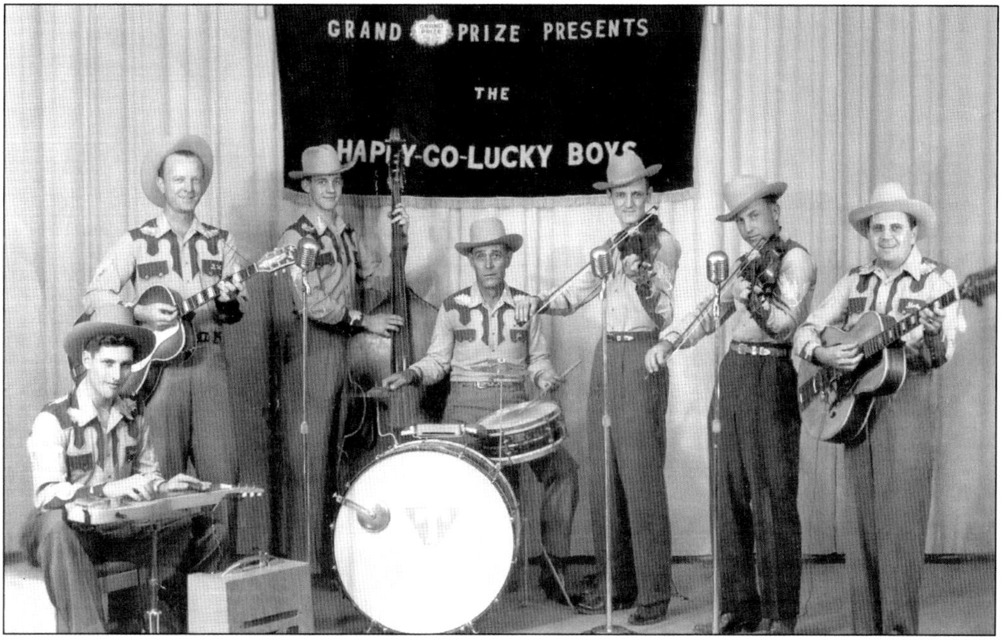

Pictured here are, from left to right, Vernon Schwartz (steel guitar), G.W. Hale (guitar and vocalist), Larkin Robertson (bass), Joe Pruneda Sr. from Kerrville (drums), August "Augie" Voight (violin), Alvin Behrends (violin), Elbert Hahne (guitar and manager). The band was sponsored by Gulf Brewing Company of Houston, brewers of Grand Prize beer, sold locally. Hahne organized the band in 1948 and purchased the custom-made shirts from a Fort Worth company. Shirts ran $35 each. (Courtesy of Elbert Hahne.)

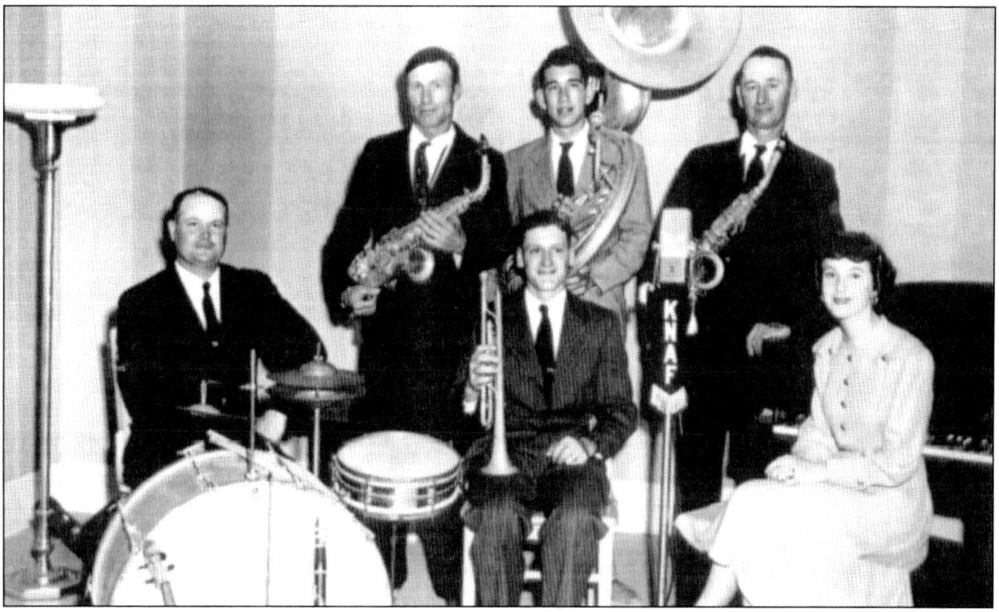

Bands like this one composed of, from left to right, Alex Tatsch (drums), Gilbert Langehennig (saxophone), Ralph Weiershausen (trumpet), Jay M. Ebert (tuba), Henry Frantzen (saxophone), and Jannibelle Kuebel (piano) played for dances at the dance halls throughout Gillespie County. Here, the band poses at radio station KNAF around 1947. (Courtesy of Marcella Weiershausen.)

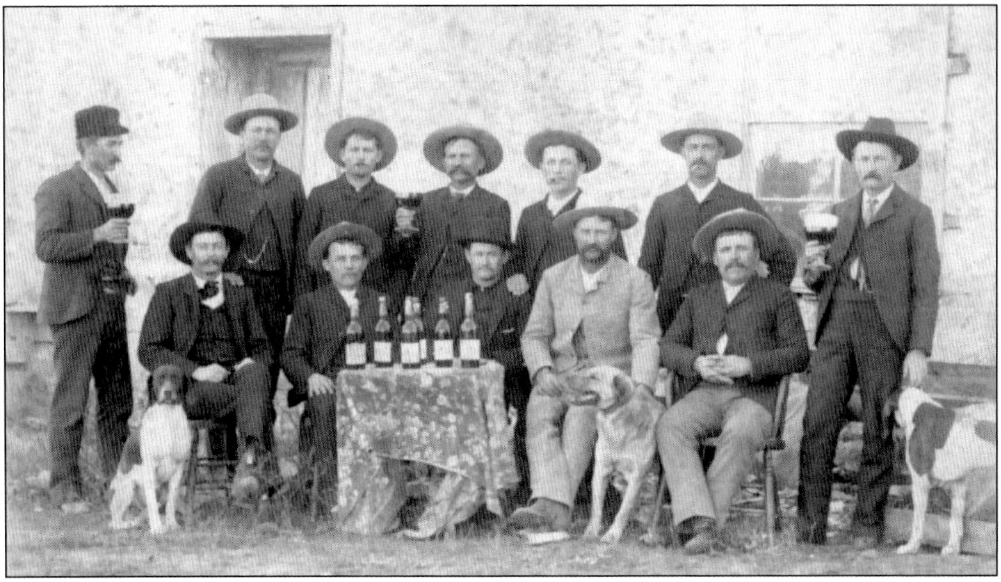

Before his marriage to Maria Theresa Schandua on October 15, 1894, J. Ferdinand Meckel gathered with his friends at Rudolph Itz' Saloon at 316 West Main Street. Pictured are, from left to right, (seated) unidentified, Adolph Meckel, Jacob Kraus, Charles Hotopp, and Anton Knopp; (standing) Oscar Krauskopf, Rudolph Itz, two unidentified men, Ferdinand Meckel, unidentified, and Hermann Ochs. (Courtesy of GCHS.)

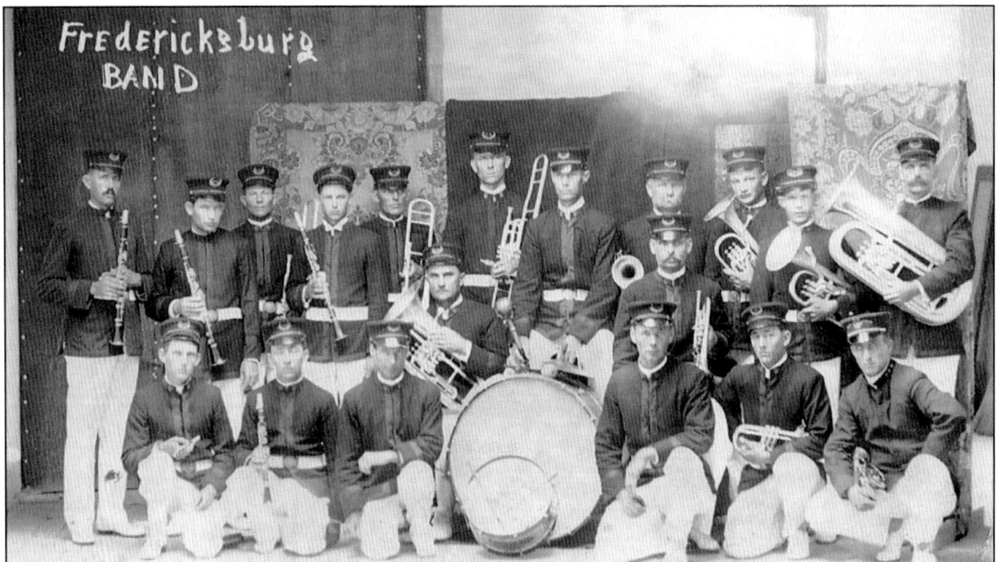

The Hoeltzer Band played in Fredericksburg during the early days and won fame throughout the state for both its music and marching. This band was created when the Blumenthal Band merged with the William Hoeltzer Cain City Band in 1905. Pictured are, from left to right, (first row) Arthur Brodbeck, Clemens Pahl, Hubert Tatsch, Ad Hopf, Alfred Schlueter, Robert Wehmeyer, Willie Petermann, and Felix Keller; (second row) Reinhard Frantzen, Alfred Schaefer, Edward Tatsch, Oswald Behrends, Henry Petermann, Richard Brehmer, director William Hoeltzer, Willie Schlueter, Hugo Schaefer, Ernst Meier, and Louis Wehmeyer. August Schlueter was missing from the photograph. (Courtesy of Douglas and Joreen Wehmeyer.)

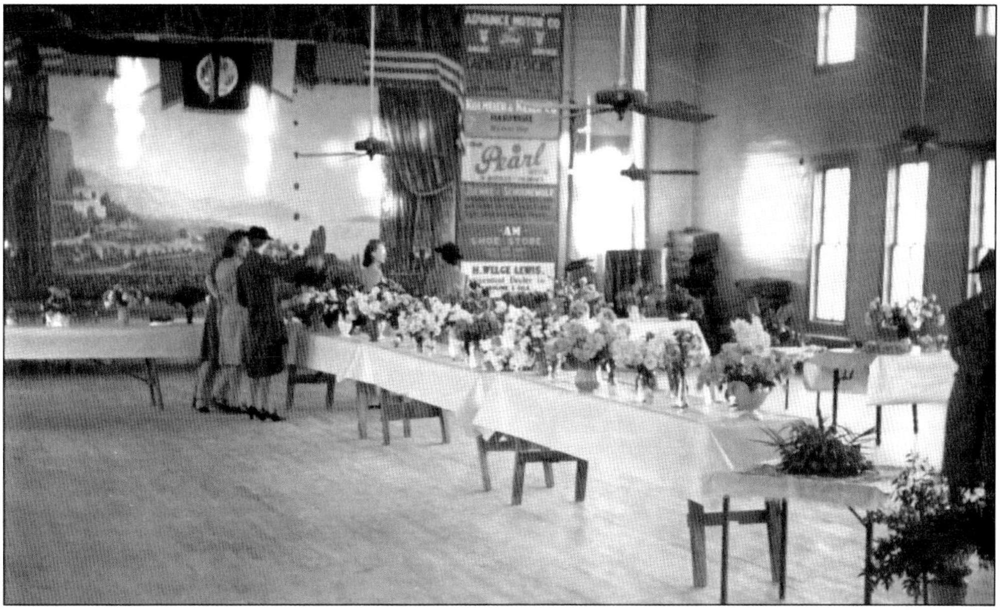

Peter's Hall and Opera House was a famous bar, opera house, and dance hall on Main Street at the Orange Street intersection. The hall also doubled as a place to hold programs and exhibits like the Fredericksburg Garden Club's Flower Show. The building is no longer standing. (Courtesy of Bill Teague.)

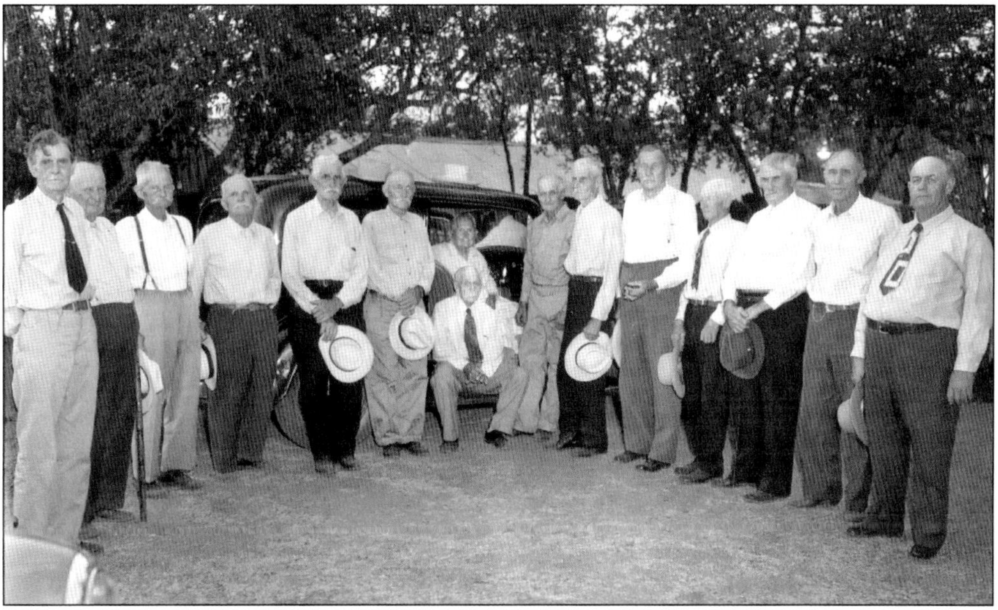

Eighteen older Gillespie County citizens who attended the annual "old teamsters" reunion at Klaerner's new park on the Harper highway in 1951 are grouped around Ad Heimann, age 90 (oldest member), Albert Kott, and John Stehling. Kott and Stehling were the only two surviving men of the old teamsters who at one time drove ox wagons from Fredericksburg across the Texas Plains country to the Panhandle and to Fort Stockton in West Texas. At this meeting, a motion was made to disband the association, but it failed due to the lack of a second and the reunions continue today. (Courtesy of Dietel Collection.)

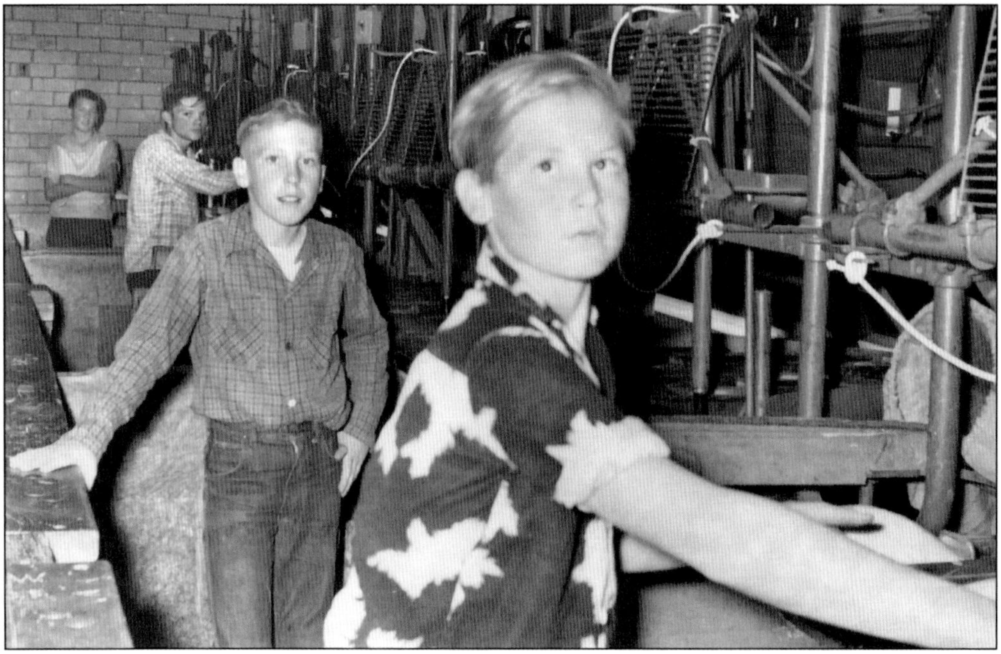

Bowling was not always automated as it is today. These pinsetters in March 1957 worked for 25¢ a night at the Turner Hall and Hermann Sons Bowling Alleys. School-age boys reset the pins to make their spending money. The Hermann Sons Hall was located on the corner of Crockett and Austin Streets and installed automatic pinsetters in 1962. (Courtesy of Dietel Collection.)

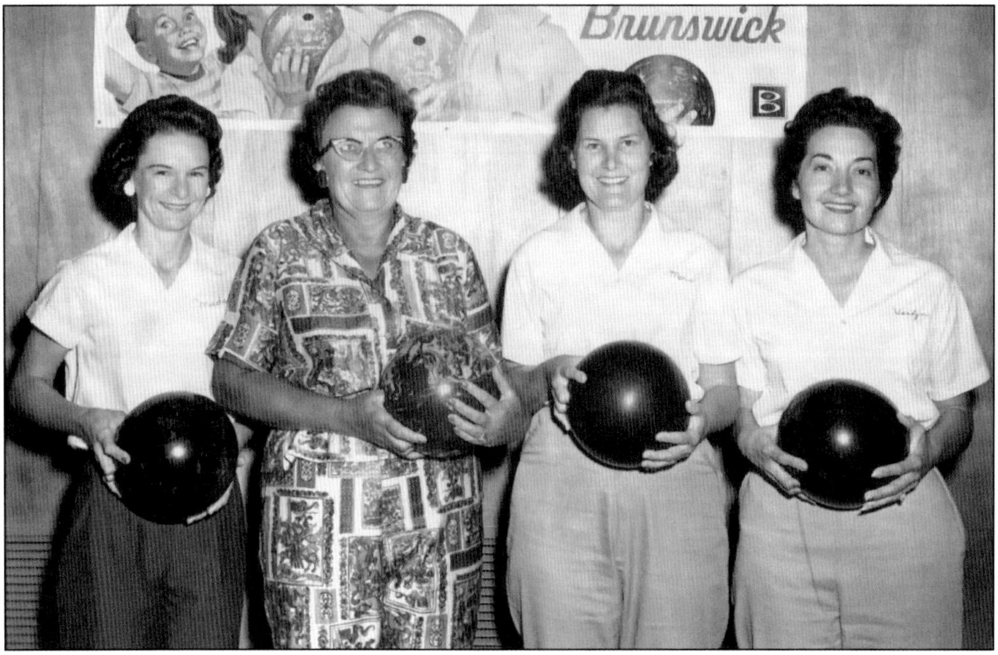

In playoffs on June 13, 1961, the Tower Drive-In team defeated a strong Comfort team for championship of the Ladies Morning League of Kegel Lanes, winning two out of three. The members of the bowling team are, from left to right, Madelyn Hoffmann, Margaret Kordzik, Mary Pyka, and Verlyn Turrentine. (Courtesy of Dietel Collection.)

Dr. Felix Tybor's bowling quintet won the men's commercial league championship at Turner Hall on December 4, 1958, when they defeated the Knopp Insurance team. The quintet includes, from left to right, (kneeling) Mike Schmidt and Al Givigliano; (standing) Hubert Molberg, Spike Zatopek, and Dr. Tybor, who had been sponsoring teams for 10 years, but this was the first year his team came out on top. (Courtesy of Dietel Collection.)

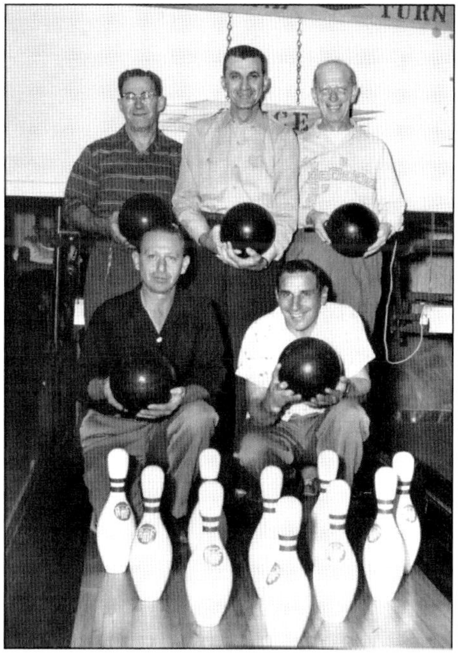

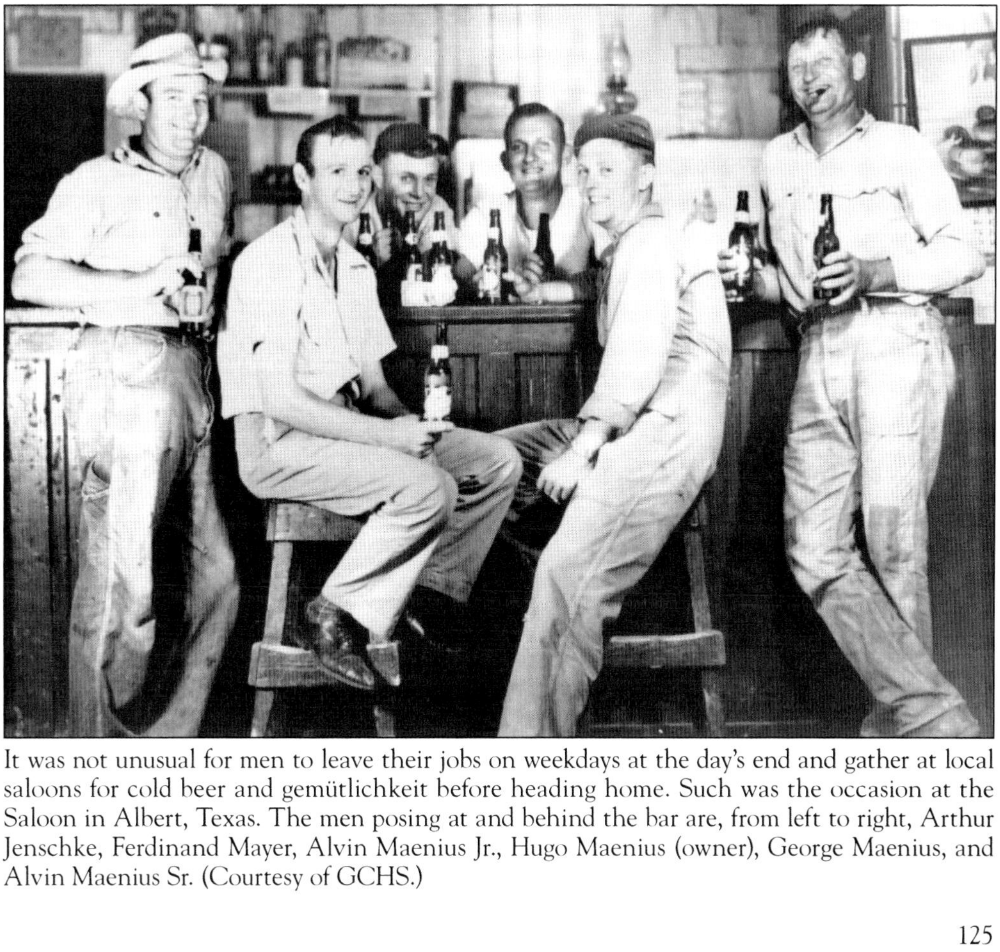

It was not unusual for men to leave their jobs on weekdays at the day's end and gather at local saloons for cold beer and gemütlichkeit before heading home. Such was the occasion at the Saloon in Albert, Texas. The men posing at and behind the bar are, from left to right, Arthur Jenschke, Ferdinand Mayer, Alvin Maenius Jr., Hugo Maenius (owner), George Maenius, and Alvin Maenius Sr. (Courtesy of GCHS.)

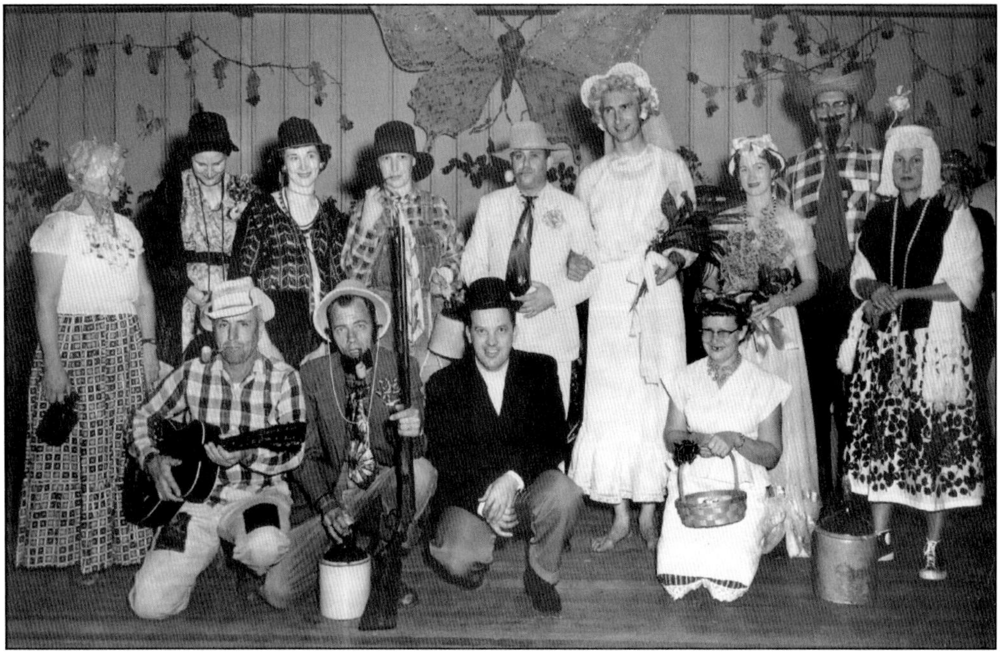

A mock hillbilly wedding is the motif of this group at the Gillespie County Historical Society annual Masquerade Ball in 1961. Pictured are, from left to right, (kneeling) Jim Burgess, "Papa" Felix Hahne Jr., Matthew Pyka Jr. (preacher), and Beatrice Kaiser (flower girl); (standing) Mrs. Jim Burgess, Mary Pyka, Genevieve Rech, Kay Hahne (best man), Henry Itri (groom), Norman Rech (bride), Marie Itri (bridesmaid), and Mr. and Mrs. Norman Mayer. Grandpa Fred and Grandma Cellie Dietel were also in the group. (Courtesy of Dietel Collection.)

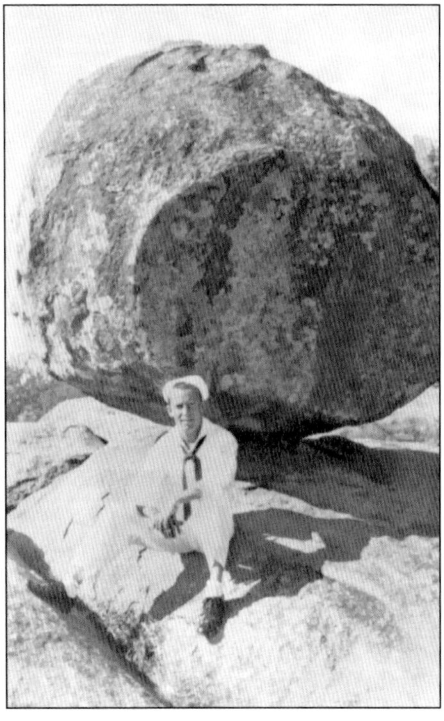

Balanced Rock attracted visitors for over a century. The large balanced boulder is no more but earlier attracted local families as well as visitors to the community, guys and their gals, and hometown boys on military leave—all for photo opportunities. Erwin F. Kammlah, son of Louis and Amalia Kammlah, served in the US Navy from 1943 to 1945. (Courtesy of Erwin and Helen Kammlah.)

BIBLIOGRAPHY

Biggers, Don H. *German Pioneers in Texas*. Fredericksburg, TX: Fredericksburg Publishing Company, 1983.

Gillespie County Historical Society. *Pioneers in God's Hills, Volume II*. Fredericksburg, TX: Gillespie County Historical Society, 1974.

King, Irene Marschall. *John O. Meusebach*. Austin: University of Texas Press, 1967.

Kowert, Elise. *Historical Homes in and Around Fredericksburg*. Fredericksburg, TX: Fredericksburg Publishing Company, 1980.

———. *Old Homes and Buildings of Fredericksburg*. Fredericksburg, TX: Fredericksburg Publishing Company, 1977.

Penniger, Robert. *Fredericksburg, Texas . . . The First Fifty Years: A Translation of Penniger's 50th Anniversary Festival Edition*. Fredericksburg, TX: Fredericksburg Publishing Company, 1971.

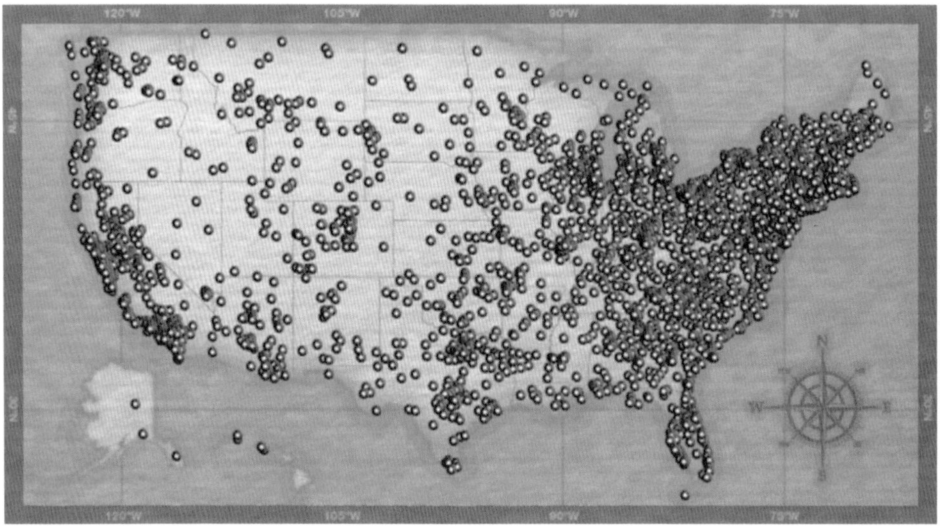